# THE PHOTOGRAPHY LAW HANDBOOK

# THE PHOTOGRAPHY LAW HANDBOOK

Steven M. Richman

Cover design by Anthony Nuccio.



Printed in the United States of America.

18 17 16 15 14 5 4 3 2 1

**Library of Congress Cataloging-in-Publication Data**

Richman, Steven M. (lawyer) author

The photography law handbook / Steven M. Richman.

p. cm.

ISBN 978-1-62722-668-4 (alk. paper)

1. Photography—Law and legislation—United States. I. Title.

KF2042.P45R53 2014

343.7307'877--dc23

2014018651

Discounts are available for books ordered in bulk. Special consideration is given to state bars, CLE programs, and other bar-related organizations. Inquire at Book Publishing, ABA Publishing, American Bar Association, 321 N. Clark Street, Chicago, Illinois 60654-7598.

www.ShopABA.org

# Dedication

To the late Jacob F. Raskin, lawyer to authors and publishers.

# Contents

# Preface

The law as it relates to photographers is constantly evolving as technology continues to change, and the diversity of means and ends of photography also changes. From its generally acknowledged birth in 1839, photography has lived a passive-aggressive existence. Passive in the sense that the photographer is engaged in the making of art or utilitarian functions, and aggressive in that the subject matter of photography often impacts directly on the rights, both personal and institutional, of others. Both professional and amateur photographers wrestle on a daily basis with the parameters of this passive-aggressive status and, in more cases than not, cannot be absolutely sure of the outcome of their work. Will an image lead to acclaim or a lawsuit? Or both?

Photography also entails two critical acts: the taking of the photograph and the use of the photograph. Each step implicates particular legal rights as well as potential liabilities, and in some cases the taking or use of an image might have criminal repercussions. Some commentators have added a third act: the subsequent application of the photograph by others, but I consider this part of the "use" act.

Unfortunately, no matter how clearly certain legal principles are stated, in most cases the resolution will be fact-sensitive and, worse, the same set of facts might not even yield the same result if decided by different judges or because the law might differ somewhat from jurisdiction to jurisdiction, even within the United States.

Nonetheless, there are baselines. Statutes, rules, and precedent do exist, and we do well to note them, even if sometimes they are ambiguous or incomplete. As Supreme Court Justice Oliver Wendell Holmes famously observed in his book *The Common Law*, "The life of the law has not been logic; it has been experience." As a lawyer, I am able to read and comprehend cases, understand precedent, read and extrapolate from statutes, and do the other things that lawyers do to ascertain as much certainty as possible. As a photographer, I am often in doubt and governed by a different set of concerns. If the lawyer is conservative in advice, the artist is often radical in application, seeking to expand the contours of aesthetic application.

The purpose of this book is to provide a pragmatic and personal perspective on photographers' rights and obligations. As both photographer and lawyer, I have listened to many people comment on what photographers can and cannot do, much of it not necessarily legally tenable one way or another. I wanted to fill in the cracks and address certain issues relating to travel photography—such as, for example, the implications of foreign law and what happens when you take photographs overseas and then publish them online. Among other things, I wanted to pursue an understanding of the increasingly precarious contours of privacy law. As a practicing lawyer and photographer, I wanted to provide what should be a working guide—the kind of book I wanted to read. Photographers want short answers: Can I photograph that? If so, can I sell it? On the other hand, there are many nuances, and often easily stated principles lead to page upon page of analysis by the courts in their application to the particular facts before them. I have attempted to cite a variety of cases for those who want to probe more deeply or gain a broader understanding.

I have organized this book around eight basic topic areas, by chapter; there remains some unavoidable overlap. Sometimes a case is based on several different theories and appears in two different sections. I have attempted to write in plain language and set out basic "rules" or, more correctly, general principles and how they have been applied in the real world. I provide actual case discussion to show the tensions and resolution and have often quoted from the cases themselves so the principles can be seen and understood in their "legal" language. In this way, you can see exactly how the rules and principles are stated, rather than relying on secondhand rephrasing. This is not a form book and not a book on running a photography business. It is not meant to be, nor can it be, a comprehensive treatise addressing all manner of intellectual property law. It is meant to be illustrative. One of the first things you learn as a lawyer is that, in many cases, law is unpredictable at worst and ambiguous at best. There are few black-and-white rules that really are black-and-white.

To give an example: Suppose you are standing across the street from Fort Whatever, a military base in your state. You are not trespassing; you are on a public street. Across the street is the gated entranceway into the fort. A bored soldier sits in the small kiosk in the entrance; a movable bar rests across the driveway. A 10-foot-high brick wall extends on either side of the base, with no windows, for quite some ways in each direction. A billboard-like sign over the driveway tells us this is "Fort Whatever" in three-foot-high letters.

What catches your eye is the sky—it is a moment of luminescent light, particularly just over the sign and below an extraordinarily emotive cloudscape. You lift your camera and photograph the sky, clouds, light—and the sign that says Fort Whatever, to anchor the image to the earth. That sign accounts for less than 10 percent of the space in the picture. The subject matter is the sky, the clouds, and the light. The sign helps identify the place and, you feel, adds an aesthetic touch.

How would a lawyer figure this out?

We start with the statute that covers photography of a military base. It is 18 U.S.C. § 795(a), and it states:

> Whenever, in the interests of national defense, the President defines certain vital military and naval installations or equipment as requiring protection against the general dissemination of information relative thereto, it shall be unlawful to make any photograph, sketch, picture, drawing, map, or graphical representation of such vital military and naval installations or equipment without first obtaining permission of the commanding officer of the military or naval post, camp, or station, or naval vessels, military and naval aircraft, and any separate military or naval command concerned, or higher authority, and promptly submitting the product obtained to such commanding officer or higher authority for censorship or such other action as he may deem necessary.

Assume that Fort Whatever has been so designated, and you have not asked permission of anyone to take your image. Have you violated the statute? Is the sign, which is certainly a part of the military installation, *the* military installation? How much of the base do you need to photograph to meet the definition? Similarly, suppose (and still from across the street), you zoom in to the brick wall and photograph just a section of bricks. You like the color and texture. Anyone looking at the image will have no clue where it is, or even what it is—a wall? A building? Once again, you have photographed "the military base," but have you violated the statute? There is no magic to the law; it is a question of reading statutes and cases, and understanding and applying principles. The ambiguities arise when we are forced to apply literal language to, perhaps, nonliteral situations.

What would a court say? Run a search on this statute or on photographing military bases, or planes at an air show, and not surprisingly, you turn up a host of free advice on the Internet. Be careful of this; often there are no citations, and you are not always able to check it out. So you decide to talk to a lawyer, and she turns up a case in which the statute, and photography of a military base, is at issue. Does this give you guidance? Let's see.

In *Genovese v. Town of Southampton*,[1] Nancy Genovese stopped her car at the side of County Road 31 in Suffolk, New York, on Long Island. According to the decision, she wanted to take pictures of a restored helicopter she saw outside Francis S. Gabreski Airport. She also had a semiautomatic assault rifle in a gun case in her car. An off-duty police officer saw her photographing the airport fence line. Because he observed Genovese then driving in a stop-and-go fashion, he followed her to the airport entrance, watched her take more photographs, and then questioned her as to whether she was aware of the signs that prohibited photography of the airport. Such signs constituted the "designation" called for under the statute, so the statute applied to this base. She said she was photographing the helicopter, but the photographs nonetheless did contain "barbed wire areas and other security features of the fence."[2]

The off-duty officer contacted the local police, and when one of the airport guards finally joined her, they noticed the gun case. Genovese said she had been to a shooting range. Ultimately, Genovese was arrested and charged with criminal trespass, which was subsequently dismissed. She was

1. 921 F. Supp. 2d 8 (E.D.N.Y. 2013).
2. *Id.* at 15.

not charged with violating the federal statute or for possession of the gun. Genovese, feeling aggrieved, then sued under 42 U.S.C. § 1983, a civil rights statute pursuant to which you can sue a governmental entity for violation of your rights by someone acting under color of authority.

Genovese, in her deposition, said she "pulled over on the side of the road and take [*sic*] pictures of the display helicopter that is sitting on the road." Her purpose: "I was making a web page to support our troops, and they're the rescue for the space shuttle. There is a sign joining the two. I wanted to make a web page [for the troops] for Christmas." It was not a planned expedition and she used her daughter's camera. Genovese said she was an amateur and testified: "I tried to put on my glasses, they were broken. The leg was broken, so I couldn't see very well trying to take the photographs. So, I kind of got my thumb, pictures of my thumb, my leg, the sky, the fence, it's a mess. Pictures of everything. I have pictures of everything. In other words, I was snapping. I didn't know how to use the camera. My glasses were falling off." She shot the pictures from her car; she then got out of the car and managed to take one or two photographs of the helicopter from outside the car and without telephone wires.[3]

The defendants' (Southampton and the off duty officer, Lieutenant Iberger) brief, available on PACER, summarized Genovese's activity in this way:

> While approaching the Gabreski Airport, the plaintiff noticed a restored helicopter that she desired to photograph, thinking it might be a worthy addition to a planned website that she was going to build for the purpose of demonstrating support for our troops overseas. . . . At the time that the plaintiff was taking these pictures in July of 2009, there were warning signs on the fence at Gabreski Airport indicating that it was a military facility, as well as signs warning that photographing the facility was in violation of federal law. . . . Either unaware of the signs, or in knowing violation of them, the plaintiff nonetheless began snapping photographs from different positions

3. References to documents available through PACER.

> along the roadway, allegedly trying to obtain a useful one of the helicopter in question." The photographs showed: "the signs indicating the name of the airport, of the fence, of the barbed wire areas and security features on the fence, consisting of a cable that ran along the fence."

In a footnote to its brief, defendants noted that "While the plaintiff may in fact have been lawfully coming from a shooting range, and further truthfully attempting to obtain a photograph of the helicopter, in light of the illegality of this activity, Lt. Iberger's investigatory stop was not only reasonable, but justified."

There was no question that the photographs contained pictures of the helicopter and that the helicopter was outside the fenced-in portion of the airport.

Of relevance to us was her motion for summary judgment on the issue of false arrest. The officer claimed there was probable cause to detain her for violating 18 U.S.C. § 795—that is, "for photographing a vital military installation."[4] In discussing what she was doing, there was no distinction between her just photographing the helicopter. The officer saw her photographing the base. The court dismissed her suit against the Southampton police officers.

Was she really photographing the military base, though?

There was no discussion on a photograph-by-photograph basis; as noted, she was not charged with violating the federal statute. Had she been, perhaps there would have been a discussion as to just how much of the installation needed to be in the image, or whether any portion was sufficient. There was the picture of the fence, as an apparent result of shooting the helicopter with the fence as backdrop.

Interestingly enough, I was able to go to google.com/maps in satellite version and pull up the helicopter just off County Road 31, outside the fence. You can see inside the base and, using the street-view icon, you have a clear view of the helicopter and the fence—including signs that have, in capital red letters, the word "WARNING." I was unable to read the rest of

4. *Genovese*, 921 F. Supp. 2d at 18.

the wording on the sign, but I assume those contained the prohibitions. A sign near the helicopter identifies this as a base.

So, if anyone can view the photographic image of the base on Google, including from street level, despite the warning signs, what does that say with regard to probable cause for stopping someone from making the same photograph from the public street? What does that say for enforcement of § 795? Did Google have permission? On the other hand—and here is the point—who wants to be the test case? Again, as photographers and artists, we may want to take the chance, but as lawyers, we may well be counseling a far more cautious approach. Understanding photographers' rights and potential liabilities, like any other decision, is an assessment of costs and benefits, risks and advantages.

For our purposes, though, we see an example of what can happen when a photographer decides to go up against the line. Can you take a picture of a helicopter as your main subject if it is in front of a military installation that has signs prohibiting photography? In the *Genovese* case, even if ultimately she was not charged with violating the statute, it is a case study in what can happen if you are observed making the image. You need to understand that being right is not always enough; as a photographer, do you want to spend an afternoon in a police station?

The bottom line is there is a statute, and there is a real world of practical experience of photographers being stopped or prohibited or arrested.

It is therefore difficult to write with any authority about what is or is not "acceptable" behavior in every situation. And as *Genovese* demonstrates, there are practical considerations we will discuss. The American Civil Liberties Union (ACLU) website tells us that as long as you are standing in a public place, you can photograph a public building and, further, that no one can make you delete your image once taken.[5]

I also was once stopped from photographing the Uhlerstown-Frenchtown Bridge, which crosses the Delaware River in its upper reaches along the Pennsylvania–New Jersey border. A police officer stopped me and told me he would permit it, but his partner (across the bridge at the moment)

5. www.aclu.org/free-speech/know-your-rights-photographers [accessed June 4,2014].

would not. Why? I asked. Security, I was told. This was sometime after the first Gulf War, but before the second; Saddam Hussein was still in power. I recall asking whether he was seriously suggesting that Uhlerstown and Frenchtown were key strategic points regarding any invasion of Washington. He seemed to agree and enlightened me as to the ability at that time to use Google satellite features to see online what I was not being permitted to photograph. We will discuss security concerns later, but we also have to recognize a certain amount of "cosmetic" security concerns. Stopping someone from taking a picture of the George Washington Bridge, when so much of its visual and engineering detail is clearly viewable on Google Maps, and has been available for decades, seems difficult to rationalize.

A colleague from a photography club who photographed the changing colors of the lights on top of the Empire State Building some years ago told me a police officer stopped him. I told him he had the right to make those images. He replied, essentially: "You're a lawyer and you know these things. I am not a lawyer, and a cop with a gun at his side told me to stop." The happy ending to the story was that the photographer ended up licensing his photos for sale. On a more personal level, I have heard stories of photographers being stopped from taking pictures of bridges that are under the jurisdiction of the Port Authority of New York and New Jersey, and yet my book, *The Bridges of New Jersey*, which features (among others) the George Washington Bridge, is on the Port Authority website for its informational value.

Not everything is a function of national security. Once, in Toronto, I was stopped by an individual who wanted to make sure I had not photographed him (I had not, and I showed him). In Frankfurt, Germany, a museum guard made the same inquiry of me (again, I had not photographed him). The laws in Canada (and in this case, Ontario) and in Germany are not the same as the laws in the United States. The photographer needs to understand concepts of territoriality and the vast difference in laws across jurisdictions.

So we see that there is the law, and there is the way things are.

At the other end of things, of course, photographers have to deal with perceptions. The photographer is an artist, and the question of how important "art" is does arise. I have had people ask how important is it, really, for photographers or artists to make images, when there are life-and-death issues at stake. I would suggest it is a false dichotomy, but paparazzi invading people's lives and, in some cases, causing physical injury colors the issue in a negative way.

How important is it? As we shall see, photographers have rights under the First Amendment. But beyond, or at least before, all that, I note a short story written by Ray Bradbury called "The Pedestrian," published in 1951.[6] In that story, a man was taking a walk on a crisp winter night while everyone else was watching television. The police stopped him and asked what he was doing. He said he was walking. The police asked why. The man said just walking. For air. To see. The police pressed him:

> "But you haven't explained for what purpose."
>
> "I explained; for air, and to see, and just to walk."

They arrested him.

In his book *Why Photography Matters*, the photographer and critic Jerry L. Thompson writes:

> Photography matters now for two interrelated reasons: One, because of how it works, not only as an artistic but also as an epistemological medium; and Two, because it presents an instructive example of what might be called *present-day understanding*. How we now—today—understand what photography is and how it works tells us something about how we understand *anything*. And it may appear that how we understand anything is not unrelated to how photography works.[7]

We look at iconic photographs, such as Dorothea Lange's *Migrant Mother*, and never forget them. We are moved by them. They inform our existence. They resonate. We go to the Museum of Modern Art in New York, look at Vincent van Gogh's *Starry Night*, and are thrilled by the original, by

6. Originally published in THE REPORTER, Aug. 7, 1951, and reprinted in the collection THE GOLDEN APPLES OF THE SUN (1953).

7. JERRY L. THOMPSON, WHY PHOTOGRAPHY MATTERS (MIT Press 2013) (emphasis in original).

the insight, by what it does to us. We react. Our ancestors must have felt the same: cave drawings from 40,000 years ago attest to the compelling nature of us to record our surroundings in interpretative ways. To those who ask what is so important about the ability of someone to take a picture, the answer is that it is essential to our humanity and our being. And that needs to be protected.

## Chapter One

# The Legal Terrain

## Getting Started

Let's take that image of Dorothea Lange, just mentioned in the preface. This is one of the most famous and iconic American photographs, or at least one version of it. Made by American photographer Dorothea Lange for the Farm Security Administration during the Depression, this particular image is now in the public domain and available on a variety of websites, including that of the Library of Congress. The Farm Security Administration title is *Destitute pea pickers in California. Mother of seven children*. Other public domain copies of this image around the Web show some differences in contrast and cropping. The more well-known "final" image, also on the Library of Congress website, does not have the thumb visible, as here it is in the bottom right corner. The Library of Congress site also notes that in the 1930s the negative was retouched to eliminate the mother's thumb. The photograph is generally known as *Migrant Mother*. The woman's name was Florence Thompson.

The photograph raises a host of issues that we will cover in this book, among others. First, there are issues involving copyright. Who owned this copyright, Lange or the Farm Security Administration? Can you use the image as an example in a book such as this? What rights do others have when they use it? For example, can someone download this, process it, and offer it for sale on a website, with proper attribution to Dorothea Lange?

Beyond copyright, there are tort issues. There are issues relating to the use of the image and its impact—was it used with permission and for the

Dorothea Lange's *Migrant Mother*.

purposes represented? Did it defame or humiliate the mother? The children? Did it invade her privacy or that of her family?

A third set of issues relates to the difference between the taking of an image and the use of the image once taken. When we dig into the background of this image, we find contradictory accounts by Lange—who stated she had implicit, if not explicit permission—and by Thompson's grandson—who contended that Lange misrepresented the ultimate use of the images (she apparently took six such photos). Another set of legal issues involve the government. The Farm Security Administration directed photographers to document the Depression in an effort to explain the current administration's programs.

Moving beyond these legal issues, there are also ethical issues. The image was "manipulated"—that is, the removal of the thumb from the negative. This sort of thing did not originate with the digital age. What issues as to authenticity are raised by such an act?

How claims are categorized determines legal rights and obligations. There are a variety of different legal issues affecting photographers. They include intellectual property, which broadly encompasses four main areas: copyright, trademark, patents, and trade secrets. Privacy rights may be implicated by virtue of either statute or common (judge-made) law. Photographers also need to be concerned about the law of defamation. Governmental restrictions may also preclude certain photographic activity, particularly in the post-9/11 world. Licensing rights and other contractual rights may limit photographers. Celebrities have certain rights over the use of their images, and at the other extreme, obscenity is governed by criminal statutes. A variation on copyright is plagiarism. Sometimes the distinctions are blurred or conflated—and sometimes understood differently (or simply misunderstood) by various courts and lawyers alike. Not every case is appealed, and sometimes appellate courts in different jurisdictions themselves disagree.

Not every photograph implicates every legal issue, and there are areas of the law that will not be covered by this book, even though photography touches on them. For example, for the most part, we are not involved with patent issues or photography used by law enforcement agencies or issues of surveillance or Fourth Amendment searches. We are mainly concerned here with the photographer as artist, whether for commercial or editorial use. While many photographers are professional journalists or photojournalists, and issues raised here will be relevant, the main focus of this book is to explore the terrain facing those who take pictures for sale, for their websites, for museum display, and for the occasional book or article. We are not concerned with the business aspects of running a photography studio.

Most photographers want simple answers: Can I take that picture and, if so, can I use it? Lest there be any misapprehension that these are narrow issues affecting only a small group of people, we should consider the magnitude of photography and its omnipresence in contemporary life.

## The Prevalence of Image

Although movable type first made its appearance in the 11th century in China, it was Johannes Gutenberg whose printing press and use of movable type revolutionized the written word in the mid-15th century. Four hundred years later, in 1839, the invention of the photographic negative by William Henry Fox Talbot marked the birth of photography. However, photographic images preceded the publication of that process. In 1826 or 1827, Joseph Nicephore Niepce made *View from the Window at Le Gras*. In 1828, Louis-Jacques-Mande Daguerre made *Boulevard du Temple, Paris* and displayed it in 1839; it is considered the first photograph image to feature people. As a daguerreotype, it was one of a kind, not capable of reproduction in the same manner of Talbot's negative process.

In 1975, Steven Sasson of Eastman Kodak invented the prototype for the digital camera. Understand the magnitude of this invention: the Consumer Electronics Association reported in 2012 that 84 percent of United States households own a digital camera.[1] Images are not made simply on cameras; they are made from cell phones, tablet computers, and portable MP3 players. Of the total devices used to make photographs, 55 percent are made by point and shoot cameras, and 11 percent are made by digital single-lens reflex (SLR) cameras. The mean number of photographs per month taken by digital SLR cameras is 61.8, and those by digital point and shoot cameras is 32.5. Interestingly, most photographs, according to the study, are taken on the spur of the moment: roughly 61 percent to 39 percent. Less than a third of all photographers are advanced or professional/expert users

1. PHOTO MKTG. ASS'N, DIGITAL CAMERA MARKET OVERVIEW (2012), http://www.pmai.org/WorkArea/DownloadAsset.aspx?id=23245 (last visited April 14, 2014).

*Boulevadr du Temple* by Daguerre.

(29 percent). The *Herald Sun* reported in 2011 that 380 billion photographs were taken a year, with over 140 billion of them appearing on Facebook.[2]

I read somewhere that the camera is to the 20th century what the printing press was to the 15th century. If the past 500 years were the age of the written word, the 20th century, and certainly the 21st, are the age of the visual image. What Gutenberg was to the written word, Talbot was to the visual image, and perhaps Sasson is even more so. The digital technology dwarfs the prior chemical processes in prevalence as preferred media. Regardless, we are not merely in the digital age, but unquestionably in the visual age. We communicate by image and, more often than not, by photograph. Even prose has moved toward anime and graphic novels. In some way, we have come full circle, to the 40,000-year-old paintings in the cave of El Castillo. As John Berger observed in his critical set of visual and text essays titled

2. Brendan Casey, *Number of Photos Taken Has Quadrupled to 380 Billion a Year*, HERALD SUN (Sept. 27, 2011), http://www.heraldsun.com.au/news/victoria/smile-youre-probably-on-facebook/story-fn7x8me2-1226147301935.

*Ways of Seeing*: "Seeing comes before words. The child looks and recognizes before it can speak."[3]

We are obsessed with taking pictures. Go to the Louvre, and the *Mona Lisa* is like a rock star. No one seems to view the painting for its intrinsic value. All that seems to matter is that the viewer takes a picture of the picture.

Photographing the *Mona Lisa.*

Observing the painting is like being at a concert or press conference. People pose in front of the painting or seem to view it only through a camera.

In the chapter on photography and ethics, we shall have occasion to think about those who whip out their cell phone to photograph people in distress, or dying, as they walk past.

It is not just visualization that marks the age but an instant ability to satisfy primal needs to communicate. Glance at YouTube to understand

3. John Berger, *Ways of Seeing*, British Broadcasting Corporation & Penguin Books, 1972 (Penguin USA 1977) at page 7.

this. People aim cell phone cameras at everything; crimes are videotaped. Some have suggested that there is no longer any such thing as privacy. Others may be able to explain the self-exhibiting nature of the apparently millions of nude portraits posted by people of themselves. The behavior of the American president taking a picture of himself and two other national leaders with a cell phone speaks for itself.

It is also an age of increased security and uneasiness. Not only has government taken steps to prevent imaging of certain buildings and structures on the alleged basis of national security, but various jurisdictions have enacted laws devoted to protecting the privacy of individuals. In one of the great paradoxes of our time, governments (and in common-law jurisdictions, courts) simultaneously have expanded rights of privacy and data protection while on the other hand have required more and more disclosure of confidential individual information. We can go on Google and utilize its maps feature; I was able to see the basketball hoop next to my driveway on one such image. (See the discussion of Google Maps in Chapter 3.)

On a fundamental level, we are witnessing a confrontation between the rights of individuals "to pursue happiness" (as our own Declaration of Independence notes) and the needs of society for collective security. We are also witnessing a clash between individual rights as embodied in the United States' First Amendment and artistic freedom and expression, including constitutionally protected creative activity, with those asserting privacy and even commercial rights to their personal and property images. Further to this, of course, are the differences in laws of defamation and the sliding scale of free speech versus individual rights of not being defamed. In addition, courts and legislatures are struggling to keep up with rapid changes in technology in these areas, as well as traditional intellectual property areas, trying to apply age-old principles and the specific words of legislation to the impact of such technology. Finally, we are increasingly confronted with the impact of different laws in the supposedly "borderless" world; despite the clichés, law remains territorial within political boundaries.

For some time after photography—primarily the negative—was brought forward in 1839, there was no unity of opinion as to its artistic as opposed to scientific or utilitarian value. This is important for its later implications in terms of copyright issues, as well as artistic expression. Some legal history is relevant to establish context.

## Photography as Art

We may speak of "taking pictures" or "making images" and distinguish between the casual snapshot and the intentional artwork. A series of snapshots, regardless of their original intent, may well be considered "art," and I have seen such exhibits in creditable museums. The issue of whether the photograph lacks originality because the mechanism of its creation is a machine was decided by the Supreme Court on the side of creativity. The photographer makes art, not simply automatic and purely utilitarian reproductions.

That decision occurred in 1884, when the U.S. Supreme Court, in *Burrow-Giles Lithographic Co. v. Sarony*,[4] held that photography was a form of art, with appropriate creativity to qualify for copyright protection. Napoleon Sarony, a lithographer, sued a lithographic company, claiming the defendant infringed Sarony's copyright in a photograph of Oscar Wilde. The defense was that a photograph was nothing more than "a reproduction on paper of the exact features of some natural object or of some person, is not a writing of which the producer is the author," and therefore not entitled to copyright protection. Finding photographs indistinguishable from maps, charts, engravings, etchings, and prints known to the writers of the Constitution and subsequent copyright statutes, the Court noted that the only reason photographs had not been mentioned was because photography, as we have come to know it, had not then existed. Notably, the Court also rejected the idea that a photograph lacked novelty, invention, or originality. The Court was persuaded by a finding of fact that the photograph before it was a

> useful, new, harmonious, characteristic, and graceful picture, and that said plaintiff made the same . . . entirely from his own original mental conception, to which he gave visible form by posing the said Oscar

4. 111 U.S. 53 (1884).

> Wilde in front of the camera, selecting and arranging the costume, draperies, and other various accessories in said photograph, arranging the subject so as to present graceful outlines, arranging and disposing the light and shade, suggesting and evoking the desired expression, and from such disposition, arrangement, or representation, made entirely by plaintiff, he produced the picture in suit.[5]

It came to the same conclusion as in a comparable British case from the preceding year, *Nottage v. Jackson*.[6] In *Nottage*, Lord Justice Cotton compared the photograph to a painting or drawing, and Lord Justice Bowen claimed it should be treated as art.

In 1903, the Supreme Court made clear that commercial use of a picture was also appropriate for copyright. In *Bleistein v. Donaldson Lithographing Co.*,[7] the Court held that "[a] picture is none the less a picture and none the less a subject of copyright that is used for an advertisement." A century later, another court applied this rationale to photographs of models, finding them not merely factual and with creativity established through on poses, lighting, and other factors.[8]

Writing in 1857 in *London Quarterly Review*, author, art critic, and art historian Lady Elizabeth Eastlake addressed the potential of the photograph and dismissed claims that lacked aesthetic considerations:

> The broader the ground which the machine may occupy, the higher will that of the intelligent agent be found to stand. If, therefore, the time should ever come when art is sought, as it ought to be, mainly for its own sake, our artists and our patrons will be of a far more elevated order than now: and if anything can bring about so desirable a climax, it will be the introduction of Photography.[9]

5. *Id.* at 54–55.
6. 11 Q.B.D. 627 (1883).
7. 188 U.S. 239, 251 (1903).
8. Nunez v. Caribbean Int'l News Corp., 235 F.3d 18, 22–23 (1st Cir. 2000).
9. Lady Elizabeth Eastlake, *Photography*, LONDON Q. REV. 442–68 (April 1857), *available at* http://www.photokaboom.com/photography/pdfs/Lady_Eastlake.pdf (last visited April 14, 2014).

Not all were so enthralled. Poet and critic Charles Baudelaire offered a contrary view:

> If photography is allowed to supplement art in some of its functions, it will soon have supplanted or corrupted it altogether, thanks to the stupidity of the multitude which is its natural ally. . . . [I]f it be allowed to encroach upon the domain of the impalpable and the imaginary, upon anything whose value depends solely upon the addition of something of a man's soul, then it will be so much the worse for us![10]

The contrasting views have significance. As we will find in contemporary case law attempting to resolve conflicting rights of privacy and free expression, as well as transformation issues under copyright law, courts now essentially take for granted the artistic basis of photography.

For example, in *Ets-Hokin v. Skyy Spirits, Inc.*,[11] the court stated that "it is well recognized that photography is a form of artistic expression, requiring numerous artistic judgments." In *Ets-Hokin*, the Ninth Circuit noted the majority view that photographic originality starts from the premise that the photographer engages in a personal influence, and "courts have recognized repeatedly that the creative decisions involved in producing a photograph may render it sufficiently original to be copyrightable and have carefully delineated selection of subject, posture, background, lighting, and perhaps even perspective alone as protectable elements of a photographer's work."[12] Noting further a photograph can be a derivative work, the court clarified that "simply because photographs are in this colloquial sense 'derived' from their subject matter, it does not necessarily follow that they are derivative works under copyright law."[13] A photograph will not be derivative unless it is based on a preexisting work, and the preexisting work must be one that is copyrightable. In *Ets-Hokin*, the underlying subject—a Skyy vodka

10. Charles Baudelaire, *On Photography*, from THE SALON OF 1859, http://www.csus.edu/indiv/o/obriene/art109/readings/11%20baudelaire%20photography.htm (last visited April 14, 2014).

11. 225 F.3d 1068, 1073 (9th Cir. 2000).

12. *Id.* at 1077 (citation omitted).

13. *Id.* at 1078.

bottle—was not copyrightable, but a photograph of it could be copyrighted and was not a derisive work.[14]

Even photographs "of common, industrial items" are entitled to protection; the level of creativity is low, and as long as there is more than "slavish copying," copyright protection can attach to the work.[15] Importantly, it is not the amount of work that goes into making the copy; "slavish copying" may be found even when extensive efforts were employed in reproduction if there is no minimal originality.[16] While the copier's innocent intent is not a defense to *liability* for copyright infringement, it is relevant to remedies and determination of statutory damages.[17]

*Burrow-Giles* persists. It continues to be cited as the seminal case that extends copyright protection to photographs and relies on the premise that photography is a form of art and not merely "utilitarian."[18] The *Monge* court was addressing a set of privately taken photographs of a celebrity couple. The images were on a memory card that was stolen. The digital images were then turned over to a magazine, which printed them. The couple registered copyrights in the pictures and then sued the magazine. The main issue in the case was whether the magazine's publication was fair use. In analyzing the factor of the nature of the copyrighted work, in order to evaluate whether there was anything copyrightable that could be deemed infringed, the court addressed the level of creativity necessary in what otherwise appeared to be mere snapshots. Of interest is the court's comment that an otherwise superficially factual photograph can nonetheless achieve "iconic" status.[19] Needless to say, these cases become fact-specific.

14. *See also* Rogers v. Koons, 960 F.2d 301, 307 (2d Cir.), *cert. denied*, 506 U.S. 934 (1992) ("Elements of originality in a photograph may include posing the subjects, lighting, angle, selection of film and camera, evoking the desired expression, and almost any other variant involved." (citations omitted)); Pagano v. Charles Beseler Co., 234 F. 963 (S.D.N.Y. 1916) ("Any one may take a photograph of a public building and of the surrounding scene.").

15. Eastern America Trio Prods. v. Tang Elec., 97 F. Supp. 2d 395, 417 (S.D.N.Y. 2000).

16. *See* Hearn v. Meyer, 663 F. Supp. 832 (S.D.N.Y. 1987).

17. Shropshire v. Canning, 809 F. Supp. 2d 1139, 1147 n.2 (N.D. Cal. 2011); *see also* 17 U.S.C. § 504(c)(2).

18. *See* Monge v. Maya Magazines, Inc., 688 F.2d 1164, 1177 (9th Cir. 2012).

19. *Id.*; *see also* Threadgill v. Orleans Parish Sch. Bd., No. 02-1122, 2013 U.S. Dist. 27598 (E.D. La. Feb. 28, 2013) (citing *Burrow-Giles* for proposition that "[t]he originator of a photograph may claim copyright in his work").

On the other hand, there is no meaningful disagreement today that photography is an art form. While there is some residual bickering among "traditional" film photographers and "digital" photographers, no one can seriously dispute that digital photography is photography in terms of its place in the arts. It would be like objecting to film as not "real" photography because "real" photographers used glass-plate negatives.

As an art form, photography has its own critical theory. Space in this book does not permit an exhaustive study, but as the courts have referred to the critical canon from time to time, we can summarize some of photography's critical underpinnings.

## Critical Photography

Understanding something of photography in terms of critical theory is relevant to understanding legal issues surrounding photography. For example, in *Mendler v. Winterland Production, Ltd.*,[20] a straightforward contract interpretation dispute, the court had to resolve whether the use of the plaintiff's photograph was authorized by the defendant under the licensing agreement with the defendant. At issue was language in the license agreement that gave the defendant the right to use the image as "guides, models, and examples, for illustrations to be used on screenprinted T-shirts or other sportswear."[21] When the defendant used a different technique on the image based on a digitally scanned version, it was different from the line drawings displayed on the prior apparel. Plaintiff sued, claiming, inter alia, copyright infringement. With regard to the copyright claim, the court found the use to be within the scope of the license. The plaintiff's principal objection had been that the defendant had "transformed the image on the T-shirt from a photograph into an illustration based on a photograph."[22] To this extent, the majority and dissent disagreed over whether the defendant's manipulation

20. 207 F.3d 1119 (9th Cir. 2000).
21. *Id.* at 1120.
22. *Id.* at 1122.

of the image was "significant."[23] Interestingly, the majority described photography as a distinctive art form because "the light does the writing."[24] It then cited one of photography's principal critical writers, Susan Sontag, for the majority's statement: "The photographer can compose the shot, but once he triggers the shutter, anything visible to the eye is captured exactly as an observer would see it."[25] The importance of Sontag to photographic criticism is well recognized.[26] The court went on to note what it called "the two qualities we most associate with photographic images: lifelike appearance and objective accuracy."

> The former is why we like photographs so much—they're the next best thing to seeing something in the flesh . . . . The latter is why we trust photographs—since there's no willful agency intervening between the actual scene and its recording of the film we tend to regard photographs as infallible and unimpeachable witnesses.[27]

In other words, the court, in attempting to decide a legal issue as to the scope of a license agreement, sought to understand something of the nature of the photograph to evaluate the contract issue. The majority did not need to cite a leading photography critic for a relatively basic set of comments or observations. It did so, however, and went on to add its own observations—perhaps not knowing the breadth of photographic criticism that discusses and deconstructs those very concepts. Indeed, the majority's observation that "we like photographs so much" because they are "the next best thing" to the reality calls to mind Walter Benjamin's 1936 *The Work of Art in*

23. *Id.*

24. *Id.*

25. *Id.* (citing *On Photography* for the statement that "[i]n most uses of the camera, the photograph's naive or descriptive function is paramount"). The quotation is from Sontag's essay *Photographic Evangels* (On Photography 115–49 [1977]), in which she argued for photography as an art form and not merely a means of mechanical reproduction.

26. *See, e.g.*, Ashley La Grange, Basic Critical Theory for Photographers, at viii (Focal Press 1995) ("This collection of essays is undoubtedly one of the most influential pieces of photographic criticism written.").

27. *Id.*

*the Age of Mechanical Reproduction*[28] in which he discusses the difference between the original and the reproduction, and the loss of the former's aura while at the same time establishing a new connection with the masses who now have accessibility to an image of the original. Robert Adams, one of the most significant American photographers of the 20th century, authored a volume titled *Why People Photograph* and wrote: "At our best and most fortunate we make pictures because of what stands in front of the camera, to honor what is greater and more interesting than we are."[29]

John Szarkowski, former photography curator at the Museum of Modern Art, wrote in *The Photographer's Eye* that "more convincingly than any other kind of picture, a photograph evokes the tangible presence of reality."[30] Stephen Shore, one of America's premier living photographers, in his critical work, *The Nature of Photographs*,[31] also writes that "the photographic image depicts, within certain formal constraints, an aspect of the world." Each has four attributes: flatness, frame, time, and focus.

Renowned essayist and philosopher Roland Barthes developed his personal reactions to the photograph in *Camera Lucida*. Writing in 1981 at the predawn of the digital age, he nonetheless noted the prevalence of photography: "I see photographs everywhere, like everyone else, nowadays; they come from the world to me, without my asking; they are only 'images,' their mode of appearance is heterogeneous."[32] Distinctive and memorable photographs were a function of what he called the "studium" (the general cultural and political and social background we bring to the image) and the "punctum" (the puncturing element in the image that jars us and seems to come from the image itself).

A cornerstone of the photographic canon, and mentioned above, is Susan Sontag's *On Photography*, a series of essays that explores the impact of the photograph. For our purposes, I note her comment in the essay "In Plato's Cave": "Photographs, which cannot themselves explain anything, are

28. Reprinted in *Vicki Goldberg, Photography in Print* (1981).
29. ROBERT ADAMS, *Two Landscapes*, *in* WHY PEOPLE PHOTOGRAPH 179 (1994).
30. *The Thing Itself*, *in* THE PHOTOGRAPHER'S EYE 12 (1966).
31. STEPHEN SHORE, THE NATURE OF PHOTOGRAPHS (2d ed. 2009).
32. ROLAND BARTHES, CAMERA LUCIDA 16 (1981).

inexhaustible invitations to deduction, speculation, and fantasy."[33] To say that and then think about a photograph as a mechanical capture of "reality" cannot be done. More to our point, though, as to the photograph as artistic endeavor and not merely mechanical application, is Sontag's comment in *The Image World* that "a photograph is not only an image (as a painting is an image), an interpretation of the real; it is also a trace, something directly stenciled off the real, like a footprint or a death mask."[34]

The notion of truth in photography, and what is real and what is not, traces back to the beginning of the art. Photography, like painting, covers a variety of media. Photography, like painting and other art forms, has also reflected movements in the history of art. Photographers at one point engaged in "pictorialism," a self-conscious imitation of painting. These were posed, and while the photograph may have been "real," the scene that was shot was re-created. The British photographer Roger Fenton (who was also a lawyer by profession) shot "Eastern" shots featuring exotically costumed models to portray the Orient, even though he had never been.

Others recognized the unique nature and limitations (or challenges) of photography that was rooted in the real, and these "photo secessionists" began to focus on what the photograph itself could do that, really, painting could not. Photographers produced abstract images, surrealist images, even impressionist-style work. Even before the availability of filters in image-processing programs, collages and other types of artificial subjects were the focus of photographers. Photography is taught as a subject unto itself, and a significant body of criticism has grown up around it. Photography has both commercial and editorial purpose, and the line between these is less a line than a blurred area. Similarly, we have an affinity for "street photography" and its ability to capture what the leading photographer Henri Cartier-Bresson dubbed the "decisive moment," but we have little sympathy for the "paparazzi" who harass.

To understand the legal terrain of photography is not simply to know that certain laws and rules exist. We must understand and accept that, on

33. SUSAN SONTAG, *In Plato's Cave*, *in* ON PHOTOGRAPHY 23 (1977).
34. *Id. The Image World*, at 153–154.

a very real level, photography is art and photographs are made by artists. Even photojournalists are making art at the same time they are seeking to document for news value; perhaps one of the most known examples is the work of war photographer Robert Capa.

We need not go further here into either the history of photography or various critical approaches to it. However, as seen in *Mendler*, an understanding not only of the technical nature of photography but its philosophical and critical aspects can assist in fashioning arguments even in the seemingly more mundane cases of contract interpretation. A selection of critical works is included in the bibliography.

## Choice of Law

To understand the legal terrain of photography, you first have to understand choice-of-law principles and whose law applies. We are fond of defending the rule of law, but apart from an argument as to consistency and predictability of law, and integrity to its administration, there are significant philosophical differences among countries that lead to real differences in substantive law. Whose law and whose rule? Consequently, we need to understand certain basic precepts. Another philosophical issue involves determination of whose law will govern a dispute involving photographers' rights (and obligations). Different nations not only have different laws but, in some cases, differences in fundamental concepts.

First and foremost, law is territorial. You are subject to the laws of where you are physically at the time. If you are in France, the laws of France apply to you. If you are in New York, the laws of New York apply. Even within the United States, there are significant differences. New York's law of privacy, for example, is different from the law of adjacent state New Jersey. To some extent, U.S. laws apply across international borders (extraterritorially), but those are generally laws that establish liability, but do not afford rights. Such territoriality is not implied; courts look to explicit congressional intent. For example, the Foreign Corrupt Practices Act applies to Americans wherever they commit prohibited acts. On the other hand, when acts are committed in foreign countries, those acts will not necessarily provide a cause of action in the United States.[35] In *Morrison v. National Australia Bank, Ltd.*, the Court refused to allow a cause of action under the American securities laws to foreign plaintiffs suing foreign and American defendants for acts that occurred relating to securities traded on foreign exchanges. Following *Morrison*, the Supreme Court held in *Kiobel v. Royal Dutch Petroleum Co.* that the Alien Tort Statute, providing tort remedies in the United States for violations of international law, would apply where the violations of the law occurred outside the United States only if they "touch and concern the territory of the United States . . . with sufficient force" to override a presumption of non-extraterritoriality.[36]

In other words, whether or not someone from another country has the right to sue you in the United States for violating a federal or state statute may depend on if all the acts occurred in the foreign country. This can have application if you are being sued under various state civil rights laws based on your photographic activity in a foreign country.

In certain circumstances, nations have agreed by treaty either to a more uniform and harmonized set of laws to cover particular areas or that they agree to treat another nation's laws with deference. It is also the case that on occasion a nation will allow acts occurring beyond its borders to be actionable or even criminal, such that when the nation has *personal jurisdiction* over someone, it can consider those acts as elements of the civil or criminal action. However, the basic premises remains the same: law is territorial. When you are in another country, you are subject to its laws.

What does this mean? It means that Americans accustomed to certain First Amendment "free speech" rights that protect acts in the United States may find themselves prosecuted criminally, if not liable civilly, in another country for engaging in the exact same conduct. Ignorance of the law, generally speaking, is not an excuse.

Different laws also vary within the United States itself, from state to state. Apart from certain federal statutes that are intended to *preempt* the field, such as the copyright law, each state generally establishes by statute or

35. *See, e.g.*, Morrison v. Nat'l Austl. Bank, Ltd., 561 U.S. 247 (2010).
36. 133 S. Ct. 1659, 1664 (2013).

common law its own substantive laws, such as those relating to defamation. (The notable exception to this is the SPEECH (Securing the Protection of [O]ur Enduring and Established Constitutional Heritage) Act, relating to the effect for foreign defamation judgments, discussed in Chapter 6.) The United States is a federal system, with federal statutes applying wherever you are in the United States. Federal statutes that preempt the field mean that there can be no state laws that purport to address the same subject matter in the same way; there are no state copyright laws. Even the interpretation of federal laws may vary from state to state and even within a state that has multiple federal districts. At the appellate level, there may be actual conflicts and, more commonly, shifts in emphasis and analysis among the circuit courts of appeal. State laws are not always uniform. When you are in one state, you are subject to its laws.

What renders this even more problematic from the standpoint of photographers seeking certainty is that even with such a federal statute, the law may differ from place to place in its interpretation. Different federal trial courts, known as district courts, may themselves differ in interpretation of statutes. The next level up is the appellate level, composed of the circuit courts of appeal, which also have geographic composition (except for the federal circuit court of appeals). It is not uncommon for different circuits to have different views, and those competing views get resolved at the level of the U.S. Supreme Court.

Similarly, laws are enforceable within the borders of the jurisdiction, so that American law stops at its borders, and when you are in a foreign country, you are subject to its laws. An exception exists when Congress deliberately imports extraterritorial effect to a law. This means that you can be liable for acts engaged in outside the United States that violate a law made expressly to have extraterritorial application. Of particular relevance to photographers is the copyright law, which does not have general extraterritorial application unless a particular provision so states.[37] Similarly, the Lanham Act relating to trademarks also does not have extraterritorial

37. Quality King Distribs., Inc. v. L'anza Research Int'l, Inc., 523 U.S. 135, 154 (1998) (Ginsburg, J., concurring).

application.[38] To be clear, though, what this means is that the acts committed abroad by themselves are not enough. However, if the defendant is a United States citizen, there is a conflict between the plaintiff's trademark rights in the United States and defendant's trademark rights under foreign law, and the defendant's conduct has a "substantial effect" on U.S. commerce, then jurisdiction within the United States may be found.[39] Other courts have applied other tests: the First Circuit, for example, in a Lanham Act context, holds that there must be substantial effects in the United States.[40]

Let's take a real-world example to demonstrate this. In *Love v. Associated Newspapers, Ltd.*,[41] the court rejected extraterritorial application of the Lanham Act and California's common-law rights of publicity. (We will discuss these substantive issues later.) The British newspaper *The Mail on Sunday*, published the cover of a compact disc featuring Brian Wilson and three other photographs of the Beach Boys, which included the plaintiff Mike Love. Love had previously acquired the right to use the Beach Boys trademark in live performances as part of a settlement of an earlier case. He sued in the United States for infringement based on the acts that occurred in England. The relevant issue for us was whether the acts occurring in England could give rise to a suit in California—that is, whether the federal court in California had subject-matter jurisdiction (authority) to resolve the case. England did not have a cause of action for right of publicity, as did California, which was why he wanted to sue there. The court held against him on the common law right of publicity claim:

38. Gucci Am., Inc. v. Guess?, Inc., 790 F. Supp. 2d 136 (S.D.N.Y. 2011).

39. Steele v. Bulova Watch Co., 344 U.S. 280 (1952); Vanity Fair Mills, Inc. v. TG Eaton Co., 234 F.2d 633 (2d Cir.), *cert. denied*, 352 U.S. 871 (1956).

40. McBee v. Delica Co., 417 F.3d 107, 111 (1st Cir. 2005). *See also* Star-Kist Foods, Inc. v. P.J. Rhodes & Co., 769 F.2d 1393, 1396 (9th Cir. 1985) ("The effect on United States commerce from the alleged illegal use of the trademarks in trade between the Philippines and other foreign countries is relatively insignificant compared to the effect on Philippine commerce. These factors indicate that the significant interest of the Philippines in restricting the extraterritorial application of the Lanham Act should preclude extension of the Act to wholly foreign commerce in this case.")

41. 611 F.3d 601 (9th Cir. 2010).

> California has no interest in applying its law to the conduct in question. None of the parties remaining in this suit is a citizen of California. The misappropriation in this suit occurred almost exclusively in the United Kingdom and Ireland, where millions of copies of the Mail on Sunday and Good Vibrations were distributed. . . . At most, de minimis conduct occurred in California when a handful of copies of the paper were delivered without the CD, and a handful of copies of Good Vibrations were sent to Wilson's attorney in California.

Regarding the trademark claims, this court analyzed extraterritoriality under a slightly different set of factors, holding that

> (1) the alleged violations must create some effect on American foreign commerce; (2) the effect must be sufficiently great to present a cognizable injury to the plaintiffs under the Lanham Act; and (3) the interests of and links to American foreign commerce must be sufficiently strong in relation to those of other nations to justify an assertion of extraterritorial authority.[42]

In this case, "all relevant acts occurred abroad," and the court found no evidence that such acts caused Love damage in the United States for purposes of trademark infringement.

On the other hand, a copyright holder may sue an infringer in the United States even if the only alleged infringement occurred in the other country and that country's copyright law governs.[43]

---

42. *Id.* at 612–13.

43. Armstrong v. Virgin Records, Ltd., 91 F. Supp. 2d 628, 637 (S.D.N.Y. 2000). *Armstrong* quoted Nimmer on Copyright:

> Even if the United State Copyright Act is clearly inoperative with respect to acts occurring outside of its jurisdiction, it does not necessarily follow that American courts are without [subject matter] jurisdiction in such a case. If the plaintiff has a valid cause of action under the copyright laws of a foreign country, and if personal jurisdiction of the defendant can be obtained in an American court, it is arguable that an action may be brought in such court for infringement of a foreign copyright law. This would be on a theory that copyright infringement constitutes a transitory cause of action, and hence, may be adjudicated in the courts of a sovereign other

Similarly, a common-law tort or its equivalent arising under foreign law based on acts committed in the foreign jurisdiction may also provide the basis for a suit in the United States.[44] So, if you take a picture of someone in a foreign country and publish it in the United States, the aggrieved foreign person can sue you in your home state, since there would be jurisdiction over you, and the court could apply the law of that foreign country to determine your liability.

In short, whether a court has authority to decide substantively a particular case will also depend on the claims involved.

If you are an American and take pictures in France that violate a French entity's copyright or trademark rights under French law, that entity could sue you in France under French law. If there is personal jurisdiction over you, you could be found liable. Whether the French entity could then take that French judgment and enforce it against you in the United States is another matter.

Conversely, if the French entity decided to sue you in your home state in the United States, the issues of extraterritoriality would not preclude the court from deciding the matter, since if it had jurisdiction over you, it would apply the applicable law.

In the reverse situation—if you are the aggrieved party and a French person took photographs of you in France and published them in France, and you believed that person violated your privacy, copyright, and trademark rights and sued that French individual in the United States—even assuming you had personal jurisdiction over that individual, the court might entertain your tort claims but probably not the copyright and trademark claims because of the lack of acts occurring in the United States.

It is important to distinguish between notions of personal jurisdiction, subject-matter jurisdiction, and choice of law. The court's power to

than the one in which the cause of action arose. 3 Nimmer § 17.03.
*See also* Rundquist v. Vapiano SE,, 798 F. Supp. 2d 102, 125–31 (D.D.C. 2011) (rejecting subject matter jurisdiction over allegations of contributory or vicarious liability under U.S. Copyright Act for foreign infringement, but asserting subject matter jurisdiction over foreign copyright claims); Carell v. The Shubert Org., Inc. 104 F. Supp. 2d 236, 258 (S.D.N.Y. 2000); Frink Am., Inc. v. Champion Rd. Mach., Ltd., 961 F. Supp. 398, 404–45 (N.D.N.Y. 1997).

44. Intelsat USA Sales Corp. v. Juch-Tech, Inc., 935 F. Supp. 2d 101 (D.D.C. 2013).

adjudicate a dispute that is binding on you depends on its authority to decide the substantive claim in the first instance, and its personal jurisdiction over you in the second. The law it applies is based on the choice-of-law analysis and provides the rules for analyzing the substantive claim, assuming there is jurisdiction.

American civil law generally divides between tort and contract. Torts are civil wrongs and may be afforded by statute or common law. Contracts are agreements between parties that afford rights and liabilities. In other instances, such as copyright, rights and obligations are defined by statute.

Generally speaking, when a tort is claimed, many American states will follow the *Restatement (Second) of Conflict of Laws*, which states in relevant part:

> § 145 The General Principle
> (1) The rights and liabilities of the parties with respect to an issue in tort are determined by the local law of the state which, with respect to that issue, has the most significant relationship to the occurrence and the parties under the principles stated in § 6.
> (2) Contacts to be taken into account in applying the principles of § 6 to determine the law applicable to an issue include:
> (a) the place where the injury occurred,
> (b) the place where the conduct causing the injury occurred,
> (c) the domicil, residence, nationality, place of incorporation and place of business of the parties, and
> (d) the place where the relationship, if any, between the parties is centered.
> These contacts are to be evaluated according to their relative importance with respect to the particular issue.[45]

Section 6 states:

> § 6 Choice of Law Principles

45. Restatement (Second) of Conflict of Laws § 145 (1971).

(1) A court, subject to constitutional restrictions, will follow a statutory directive of its own state on choice of law.
(2) When there is no such directive, the factors relevant to the choice of the applicable rule of law include
(a) the needs of the interstate and international systems,
(b) the relevant policies of the forum,
(c) the relevant policies of other interested states and the relative interests of those states in the determination of the particular issue,
(d) the protection of justified expectations,
(e) the basic policies underlying the particular field of law,
(f) certainty, predictability and uniformity of result, and
(g) ease in the determination and application of the law to be applied.[46]

This is generally known as the "substantial relationship" test. Some jurisdictions look primarily to the jurisdiction in which the acts occurred (known as the lex loci test), and others will put greater emphasis on the governmental interest of the particular jurisdiction.

The point is that whether you know it or not, you will be held accountable to the law of the jurisdiction in which you commit an act that forms the basis of a claim against you.

## Territorial Considerations and Personal Jurisdiction

Suppose someone in another country uses an image of yours. Perhaps they downloaded it from your website on the Internet and posted it on their own website—which is how you stumbled across it, as you were searching for your own image. You want to sue them in your home state. Can you do it?

For a court to be able to enforce a law with regard to an individual, it needs to have personal jurisdiction over that individual. Personal jurisdiction

46. *Id.* § 6.

is related to the territoriality of law. A court located in a state in the United States has two kinds of jurisdiction, referred to above. The first is subject-matter jurisdiction, which is the authority of the court over substantive matters. Federal courts have jurisdiction granted by Congress. Generally speaking, and for our purposes, federal court jurisdiction is based upon diversity of citizenship; that is, two citizens of different states with over $75,000 in dispute can bring an action in federal court as well as in state court. The other principal type of subject-matter jurisdiction is federal-question jurisdiction. This means that regardless of citizenship, if the subject matter of the dispute derives from a federal statute, such as the antitrust laws or, more likely in our context, the copyright law, then the court has subject-matter jurisdiction and authority to hear the case.

Personal jurisdiction is the authority of the court over an individual. Under the classic formulation in the U.S. Supreme Court case of *International Shoe Co. v. Washington*, there must be minimum contacts and "traditional notions of fair play and substantial justice."[47] Courts refer to general jurisdiction where there are systematic and continuous general business contacts with a jurisdiction; such gives personal jurisdiction with regard to a claim that need not be related to those particular contacts.[48] Specific jurisdiction exists with regard to claims arising out of or relates to a party's "purposeful availment" of a jurisdiction and the contacts that establish that.[49]

In *Calder v. Jones*, a suit by actress Shirley Jones against the *National Enquirer* for libel, invasion of privacy and intentional infliction of emotional harm in California, the Supreme Court held that personal jurisdiction was established over a foreign publication with limited subscribers and other activity in California, where the defendants were "primary participants in an alleged wrongdoing directed at a California resident and jurisdiction over them is proper on that basis."[50] The Court also rejected "the suggestion that

47. 326 U.S. 310, 316 (1945).
48. Helicopteros Nacionales de Colombia, S.A. v. Hall, 466 U.S. 408, 415–16 (1984).
49. *Id.* at 427–28.
50. 465 U.S. 783, 790 (1984).

First Amendment concerns enter into the jurisdictional analysis."[51] *Calder v. Jones* established an "effects test" for defamation cases and whether personal jurisdiction exists, requiring proof that defendants (1) aimed an act at the forum state, (2) knew the act would have harmful effect, and (3) knew injury would be felt in the forum state. Note that in *Walden v. Fiore*,[52] the Court held that "mere injury to a forum resident is not a sufficient connection to the forum. Regardless of where a plaintiff lives or works, an injury is jurisdictionally relevant only insofar as it shows that the defendant has formed a contact with the forum State. The proper question is not where the plaintiff experienced a particular injury or effect but whether the defendant's conduct connects him to the forum in a meaningful way." *Calder* was distinguished in that there the effects of the conduct on the aggrieved party were actually connected to the forum state.

For a real-world example involving the fact situation I outlined above, see, for example, *Noonan v. Winston Co.*[53] In that case, the court declined to find personal jurisdiction over French companies that published a photograph of plaintiff in a French publication, since there was no proof of an intent to direct the image to the forum state in the United States, and therefore there was no reasonable anticipation of being haled into court there.

Most courts require more than a mere assertion that the "defendant knew or should have known that his intentional acts would cause harm in the forum state."[54] *Pavlovich* also noted the impact of Internet use and held:

> A defendant's knowledge that his tortious conduct may harm industries centered in California is undoubtedly relevant to any determination of personal jurisdiction and may support a finding of jurisdiction. We merely hold that this knowledge alone is insufficient to establish express aiming at the forum state as required by the effects test. Because the only evidence in the record even suggesting express aiming

51. *Id.*
52. 134 S. Ct. 1115, 1125 (2014).
53. 135 F.3d 85, 90 (1st Cir. 1998).
54. Pavlovich v. Superior Court, 127 Cal. Rptr. 2d 329, 337 (2002) (summarizing circuit opinions).

> is Pavlovich's knowledge that his conduct may harm industries centered in California, due process requires us to decline jurisdiction over his person.[55]

The fact that a website is accessible everywhere in the world is generally not sufficient by itself to establish personal jurisdiction.[56] *Zippo* became the leading case, and its summary of the implications of a website are the standard employed still by many courts:

> [O]ur review of the available cases and materials reveals that the likelihood that personal jurisdiction can be constitutionally exercised is directly proportionate to the nature and quality of commercial activity that an entity conducts over the Internet. This sliding scale is consistent with well developed personal jurisdiction principles. At one end of the spectrum are situations where a defendant clearly does business over the Internet. If the defendant enters into contracts with residents of a foreign jurisdiction that involve the knowing and repeated transmission of computer files over the Internet, personal jurisdiction is proper. . . . At the opposite end are situations where a defendant has simply posted information on an Internet Web site which is accessible to users in foreign jurisdictions. A passive Web site that does little more than make information available to those who are interested in it is not grounds for the exercise personal jurisdiction. . . . The middle ground is occupied by interactive Web sites where a user can exchange information with the host computer. In these cases, the exercise of jurisdiction is determined by examining the level of interactivity and commercial nature of the exchange of information that occurs on the Web site.[57]

The same is true for you. If you maintain a photography website and someone sues you, whether they have personal jurisdiction over you based on

55. *Id.* at 343.
56. *See, e.g.*, Zippo Mfg. Co. v. Zippo Dot Com, Inc., 952 F. Supp. 1119 (W.D. Pa. 1997).
57. *Id.* at 1124 (citations omitted).

your website, alone or as one of other factors, may well be subject to this type of test. Of course, if you have other relevant contacts with the jurisdiction, that is also part of the analysis.

## Criminal versus Civil Law

There is also a difference between criminal laws and civil laws. As a general proposition, private citizens do not prosecute other citizens for violation of the criminal laws. In some cases, in addition to having the right to sue for civil (noncriminal) wrongs, private citizens in some cases can act as "private attorneys general" and sue for relief under federal regulatory statutes, such as the antitrust laws. People do not, as a rule, go to jail as the result of a civil suit, but imprisonment is certainly an option for more serious criminal violations, varying from state to state. Some claims may yield both criminal and civil responses. A photographer who goes onto private property to take a picture might be prosecuted criminally for trespass, and as a civil matter if the photographer has defamed the subject of the photograph taken while on private property.

Criminal laws are those that carry criminal penalties, such as fine and incarceration. In the United States, there are federal criminal statutes (including some portions of the Copyright Act) and state criminal statutes, many with different definitions, procedures, and penalties. Many people probably do not understand that the same act may be interpreted differently under a state's constitution than the Supreme Court interprets the same conduct under the federal Constitution. Generally, a private citizen does not prosecute criminal proceedings. Some criminal statutes nonetheless entail civil remedies, brought by private litigants. Civil law in the United States involves noncriminal causes of action, either provided by statute or at common law as a matter of either tort (a civil wrong) or contract (a claim based on breach of an agreement).

Sometimes, even when there is a colorable violation of a criminal law, you may find that prosecutors—both federal and state—decline to interest themselves in your case, if they view it more as a collection matter for money or the fraud is relatively small and isolated. In some instances, you may be able to press charges yourself, but the standards in criminal cases are generally higher, and you will not necessarily get the financial result you are seeking.

## Civil Law versus Common Law Jurisdictions

Finally, though not exhaustively in this summary, photographers operating in foreign countries should be aware of the fundamental difference in approach between common-law and civil-law countries. Most of the world's legal systems are "civil law" systems. In the American (excluding Louisiana), British, Australian, and Canadian (except for Quebec) systems, the common-law model is employed. A civil-law system essentially is a code-based system, with no binding precedent, and heavy reliance on treatises. In regimes such as the European Union, the photographer need not only be concerned with national laws but transnational law set in place pursuant to treaties.

## Taking versus Using

I noted above that there are three aspects to the image: its taking, its use by the photographer, and its subsequent applications by others. One of the concepts that runs throughout this book is the distinction between the first two elements—namely, the manner in which the image is taken ("shot") and the use of the image once taken. If you trespass, or violate the legitimate restrictions on photography (in, say, a museum that tells you not to photograph a special exhibit that is on loan), then you have violated the rules with regard to the taking of the image. On the other hand, if you have taken an image legitimately, either by permission or from a public area where you have a right to be, but what you photograph has copyright protection or you have violated the terms of a license, then your subsequent use of the image may violate rights.

## Legal System in a Nutshell

Too many people form too many impressions of the legal system from television, movies, and legal thrillers. Rarely, if ever, does the surprise witness pop up in the courtroom and scream she did it. For photographers, most of your issues will be matters of contract and licensing, potential tort exposure, and intellectual property issues. For the most part, these are technical issues and you should seek out competent legal advice when in doubt. No lawyer is conversant in all areas of the law; any lawyer who tells you that he or she is, is suspect. As you will see in this book, principles are easily stated but difficult in their application, and a lawsuit may take, if you are lucky, two or three years to resolve and can easily cost you, in terms relevant as of this writing, hundreds of thousands of dollars in legal fees and costs. Often, when areas of specialized expertise are involved, you will need to retain experts. Some people will lie, but more frequently, there is a good-faith difference in memory or interpretation. Judges will rely on rules of evidence to parse through information that is, or should not be, properly before them. Do not harbor any illusions about "justice"; the legal system functions on the principle of certainty. Some things are relatively clear, but others are not, and the less clear your factual situation is vis-à-vis legal principles, the less certainty you have and the greater chance you will have for extended litigation—either as plaintiff or defendant. The main point is to understand and assess risk, and make an informed decision.

## Putting It in Perspective

This chapter has emphasized the fundamental point that law is territorial, and your acts as a photographer are determined by where you not only take but where and how you use those images. Whose law applies, where you can sue or be sued, and the cost of litigation are relevant factors to think about. We discussed the prevalence of image and photography as art. We found that photography criticism can be relevant to legal analysis.

## Chapter Two

# Understanding Intellectual Property

## Introduction

There are four general areas of intellectual property—copyright, trademark, patents, and trade secrets. Patents are essentially government-issued monopolies that protect an idea that is useful and novel. Design patents apply to ornamental as opposed to functional features and would not apply to photographs. Trade secrets protect proprietary information. Generally speaking, you will not be concerned with patent or trade secret issues in most of your activity as a photographer. We cannot cover all of these in depth. This chapter is meant to highlight the relevant legal and practical issues.

## Copyright

### What May Be Copyrighted

Copyright is simultaneously the photographer's friend and enemy. Photographers want the protection of the copyright laws to prevent infringement and unauthorized use of their photographs. On the other hand, photographers want the freedom to be creative and not be claimed to be infringing themselves when they utilize aspects of others' intellectual property.

The copyright law of the United States has constitutional roots. Article I, Section 8, of the Constitution states: "The Congress shall have Power . . . To Promote the Progress of Science and useful Arts, by securing for limited Times to Authors and Inventors the exclusive Right to their respective

Writings and Discoveries." The Copyright Act of the United States is found within Title 17 of the U.S. Code. That statute preempts the field, so there are no state copyright laws. It is well beyond the scope of this book to provide a detailed discussion of the copyright law, but a few general principles and some practical applications, based on real cases addressing photographers, provide guidance. Unfortunately, for photographers seeking black-and-white answers, the range of cases demonstrates how critical the facts are of each situation and, in some cases, depend on which court is deciding the case.

The photographer does not have a copyright in the "reality" of the subject matter.[1] In other words, a photographer may have a copyright in her image of a bottle, but does not own a copyright in the bottle itself. Copyright protects the *expression* of an idea, but not the idea itself. It does not protect facts. There are only so many ways to say that "Abraham Lincoln was the 16th President of the United States," for example. Copyright law does apply to photographs, as we saw in the first chapter. To reiterate: in order to obtain copyright protection, only a low level of originality is needed. The holder of a copyright acquires a "bundle of rights" that basically include right of reproduction, right to prepare derivative works based on copyrighted image, and right to distribute, rent, lease copies, and display work publicly. The principal exception is the right of others to utilize the work in "fair use" under certain specified conditions based on a balancing of various factors.

The person who creates the work owns the copyright, unless an agreement in writing exists to the contrary or transfers that right to someone else. Since the Berne Convention, an international treaty governing copyright to which the United States is a party, it is not necessary to include a copyright notice. You have immediate copyright in a work fixed in a medium. So, for example, you have a copyright in your notes, even if not published.

1. *See* Leigh v. Warner Bros., 212 F.3d 1201, 1214 (11th Cir. 2000); Franklin Mint Corp. v. Nat'l Wildlife Art Exch., 575 F.2d 62, 64 (3d Cir.), *cert. denied*, 439 U.S. 880 (1978); Harney v. Sony Pictures Television, Inc., 704 F.3d 173, 181 (1st Cir. 2013) ("Where the photographer is uninvolved in creating his subject, that subject matter—whether a person, a building, a landscape or something else—is equivalent to an idea that the law insists be freely available to everyone.").

However, even though the copyright notice is option for post-1989 works, it has benefits because, as the Copyright Office states:

> [I]t informs the public that the work is protected by copyright, identifies the copyright owner, and shows the year of first publication. Furthermore, in the event that a work is infringed, if the work carries a proper notice, the court will not give any weight to a defendant's interposition of an innocent infringement defense—that is, that he or she did not realize that the work was protected. An innocent infringement defense may result in a reduction in damages that the copyright owner would otherwise receive.[2]

The Copyright Act contains a series of statutory definitions in 17 U.S.C. § 101, which need to be consulted to understand the scope of the operative provisions of the law. Section 102 sets forth what may be copyrighted, and tells us that it covers (1) "original works of authorship" (2) "fixed in a tangible medium of expression" (3) that can be perceived, reproduced, or communicated (4) directly or by aid of machine or device. The section then lists eight specific categories that are deemed works of authorship. You then have to go back to the definitions of those in § 101 to understand the scope. Further sections define other subject-matter areas, such as compilations and derivate works. Thus, copyright protection in a photograph also applies to "derivatives" of that photograph.

A derivative work is defined in the Copyright Act as

> a work based upon one or more preexisting works, such as a translation, musical arrangement, dramatization, fictionalization, motion picture version, sound recording, art reproduction, abridgment, condensation, or any other form in which a work may be recast, transformed, or adapted. A work consisting of editorial revisions,

2. *Copyright Office Circular* 3, available on U.S. Copyright Office website, http://www.copyright.gov/circs/circ03.html (last visited April 15, 2014).

> annotations, elaborations, or other modifications which, as a whole, represent an original work of authorship, is a "derivative work."[3]

This is important to read, because it is the starting point for any analysis of what a derivative work is. "Photograph" is not separately defined but is included within the definition of "pictorial, graphic, and sculptural works." Notably, though, such works can include "artistic craftsmanship insofar as their form but not their mechanical or utilitarian aspects are concerned."[4] A photograph is considered a "work of visual art" only to the extent it is "a still photographic image produced for exhibition purposes only, existing in a single copy that is signed by the author, or in a limited edition of 200 copies or fewer that are signed and consecutively numbered by the author."[5] Under § 102, a photograph would be accorded protection as an appropriate subject matter of copyright as a "pictorial, graphic, and sculptural work." Section 103 extends the § 102 protection for compilations and derivative works. "Unpublished" works—that is, undistributed copies to the public by sale or otherwise—are also protected, pursuant to § 104(a).

A principal point as to what may be copyrighted is that copyright applies to expression, not underlying ideas or facts themselves. Ownership of the "image" is not the same as ownership of the physical print. Copyright of a photograph is distinct from ownership of the material object—that is, the photographic print.[6] In other words, a photographer that makes a print owns the copyright in the image and controls the derivative and reproductive uses of the image, but as to the physical two-dimensional print on paper, that physical object is not within the scope of the photographer's copyright.

## Bundle of Rights

Generally speaking, copyright protection occurs upon images fixed in tangible expression. The duration of the copyright for post-1978 works is

3. 17 U.S.C. § 101.
4. *Id.*
5. *Id.*
6. *Id.* § 202.

the author's life plus 70 years.[7] The exclusive rights given to the copyright holder (here, the photographer) are the right

> (1) to reproduce the copyrighted work in copies or phonorecords; (2) to prepare derivative works based upon the copyrighted work; (3) to distribute copies or phonorecords of the copyrighted work to the public by sale or other transfer of ownership, or by rental, lease, or lending;
>
> (4) in the case of literary, musical, dramatic, and choreographic works, pantomimes, and motion pictures and other audiovisual works, to perform the copyrighted work publicly; and (5) in the case of literary, musical, dramatic, and choreographic works, pantomimes, and pictorial, graphic, or sculptural works, including the individual images of a motion picture or other audiovisual work, to display the copyrighted work publicly.[8]

## Can a Photograph Be Both Copyrighted and Trademarked?

The same image may be able to take advantage not only of the copyright statute but also protections under trademark law (discussed in the next section), depending upon it use. Copyright, as just noted, has a limited life; trademarks may be renewed indefinitely for as long as they are used in proper fashion.

Trademark and copyright claims may be found in the same case, and even regarding the same photograph. For example, in *Bach v. Forever Living Products U.S., Inc.*,[9] the defendant was alleged to have taken one of the plaintiff's copyrighted photographs and used it as a corporate logo, as well as in advertising, thus violating copyright laws as well as trademark laws in terms of false endorsement. The *Bach* court permitted both sets of claims to stand as independent, though it referenced the concern that trademark law did not provide a back door for perpetual copyright claims. It explained the differences and found no overlap between the claims at issue:

7. *Id.* § 302(a).
8. *Id.* § 106.
9. 473 F. Supp. 2d 1110 (W.D. Wash. 2007).

> Trademark and copyright law have fundamentally different purposes. "Trademark law is concerned with the protection of symbols; elements or devices used to identify a product in the marketplace and to prevent confusion as to its source." . . . In contrast, copyright law "protects the artist's right in an abstract design or other creative work." Therefore, trademark law protects the distinctive source-distinguishing mark, while copyright law protects the work as a whole.[10]

In *Armstrong v. Virgin Records, Ltd.*,[11] an American musician claimed that the defendant record company and musicians, individually and as a band, misappropriated his composition in an album they recorded in England. He brought both copyright and trademark claims. It is possible for the same set of facts to give rise to both sets of claims since both involve a failure to credit the original author. For a trademark claim to survive facts supporting a copyright claim, the plaintiff must show more than just a protected copyright and unauthorized profit; "[t]he author must make a greater showing that the designation of origin was false, was harmful, and stemmed from 'some affirmative act whereby [the defendant] affirmatively represented itself as the owner.'"[12] In *Armstrong*, the court found the claims duplicative and dismissed the trademark claim.

## Photographic Creativity and Originality

As noted in § 102, copyright requires "original" work. There is no statutory definition of "original." Photographs will be afforded copyright protection as works of expression, but that protection will not apply to the underlying subject matter if that subject matter is not original. For example, you may copyright your photograph of a cup, but you cannot stop anyone else from photographing a cup. You may be able to stop from photographing the cup someone who duplicates exactly all your photographic decisions—that is, your expression. We will explore examples of this below when we talk about "substantial similarity."

10. *Id.* at 1117.
11. 91 F. Supp. 2d 628 (S.D.N.Y. 2000).
12. *Id.* at 633 (citations omitted).

"Originality is a constitutional requirement."[13] It means there must be "at least some minimal degree of creativity."[14] As the Supreme Court explained in *Feist*:

> Originality does not signify novelty; a work may be original even though it closely resembles other works so long as the similarity is fortuitous, not the result of copying. To illustrate, assume that two poets, each ignorant of the other, compose identical poems. Neither work is novel, yet both are original and, hence, copyrightable.[15]

In *Schiffer Publishing, Ltd. v. Chronicle Books, LLC*,[16] Schiffer hired four photographers to take photographs of fabrics for various books on textiles. Defendants published a book called *1000 Patterns* that published 118 photos from 13 of the plaintiff's books, along with photographs from other sources. Defendants actually scanned the Schiffer images and then reproduced them. Co-defendant Ivy "packaged" these for Chronicle's book *1000 Patterns*. The court initially found questions of fact raised by defendant as to factors relating to "minimal creativity" and denied summary judgment. Later, at trial, the court examined the process by which each of the photographs was made, discussing what each of the four photographers did in terms of film choice, camera choice, lighting, and choice of highlights—which factors were not consistently employed among the photographers.[17] The court found that Ivy had directly copied the plaintiff's photographs. The court further found that the Schiffer photographs were entitled to copyright protection because the photographic elements established minimal creativity by virtue of camera choice, film choice, lens choice, lighting to highlight texture or patterns, and use of bracketing techniques.[18] The court rejected defendants' argument that such choices were "chimerical"

13. Feist Publ'ns, Inc. v. Rural Tel. Serv. Co., 499 U.S. 340, 346 (1991).
14. *Id.* at 345.
15. *Id.* at 345–46.
16. 350 F. Supp. 2d 613 (E.D. Pa. 2004).
17. Schiffer Publishing, Ltd. v. Chronicle Books, LLC, No. 03-4962, 2004 U.S. Dist. LEXIS 23052 (Nov. 12, 2004, E.D. Pa.).
18. *Id.* at *24.

and reflected pure functionality.[19] The court rejected as well the defense of fair use. At a later date, the court entered final judgment for statutory damages as well as injunctive relief. Of interest was the court's refusal to find the defendants' conduct wilful for purposes of additional damages, finding that defendants had a good faith belief that the Schiffer photographs were not copyrightable, and once notified of plaintiff's claims, stopped shipment and attempted to resolve the issue.[20]

As *Schiffer* shows, a court will look at the totality of photographic decisions, such as framing, lighting, camera angle, lens, and filer selection. In *SHL Imaging, Inc. v. Artisan House, Inc.*,[21] the plaintiff was a company owned by a photographer who was hired "to photograph mirrored picture frames manufactured and offered for sale by defendants . . . with the understanding that the photographs would be used as color slides by defendants' sales force." The defendants instead reproduced the images in a catalog, in brochures, and as magazine publicity releases. The plaintiff sued; the defendants claimed the photographs were not original, or if they were, the defendants were joint authors or the photographs were "work for hire" and therefore the copyright belonged to the defendants. The plaintiff photographer prevailed. As to originality, the court noted the creative decisions involved selection of camera; choice of lens, film type, paper type; use of diffusers, reflectors, and lighting equipment; and the angles and configuration of the lighting. The derivative work "must recast, transform or adopt the authorship contained in the preexisting work"[22] in order to be derivative. Here, there was no such recasting, as the plaintiff simply photographed the defendants' mirrored picture frames. Although the photographs were not derivative works, the court analyzed them to see if they satisfied originality and found that they did, based on the choices made in the making of the image. Interestingly, the court gave a short history of photography

19. *Id.* at 27, distinguishing Bridgeman Art Library, Ltd. v. Corel Corp., 25 F. Supp. 2d 421 (S.D.N.Y. 1998), where the photographs were exact copies of public domain artworks and which also decided under United Kingdom, not United States, copyright law.

20. Schiffer Publishing, Ltd. v. Chronicle Books, LLC, No. 03-4962, 2005 U.S. Dist. LEXIS 416 (Jan. 11, 2005, E.D. Pa. 2005).

21. 117 F. Supp. 2d 301, 303 (S.D.N.Y. 2000).

22. *Id.* at 306.

to highlight the creativity involved and put to rest any assumptions that a photographer simply presses a button. Having decided, though, that the plaintiff's pictures met the originality test set forth in *Feist*, that copyright is only for plaintiff's "incremental contribution" and plaintiff cannot prevent others from photographing the same mirror frames.[23]

Layout and computerized image enhancement are also indications of originality.[24] On the other hand, if the court finds that the photographs "lack any artistic quality, and neither the nature and content of such photographs, nor plaintiffs' description of their preparation," then the court may refuse to find "that any 'creative spark' was required to produce them."[25] Similarly, purely descriptive photographs of a product may not be copyrightable.[26] Recall the cup example.

In *FragranceNet.com, Inc. v. FragranceX.com, Inc.*,[27] the court held that photographs of third parties' intellectual property are not *per se* not copyrightable, although such images "may receive less protection than a completely original work." *FraganceNet.com* noted that there was a split in the courts over whether "photographs of a copyrighted work are properly considered derivative works."[28]

The Zapruder film of the Kennedy assassination was held original enough to be entitled to copyright.[29] On the other hand, in *Horgan v. MacMillan,*

23. *Id.* at 311.

24. E. Am. Trio Prods., Inc. v. Tang Elec. Corp., 97 F. Supp. 2d 395, 417–18 (S.D.N.Y. 2000).

25. Oriental Art Printing, Inc. v. Goldstar Printing Corp., 175 F. Supp. 2d 542, 546 (S.D.N.Y. 2001).

26. Custom Dynamics, LLC v. Radiantz LED Lighting, Inc., 535 F. Supp. 2d 542 (E.D.N.C. 2008).

27. 679 F. Supp. 2d 312, 322–23 (E.D.N.Y. 2010).

28. *Id.* at 618. *See also* Atari, Inc. v. North American Philips Consumer Electronics Corp., 672 F.2d 607, 618 n.12 (7th Cir. 1982) (infringement may be made out even if the "work is transferred into a different medium"); *but see* Ty, Inc. v. Publ'ns Int'l Ltd., 292 F.3d 512 (7th Cir.), *reh'g denied en banc*, 2002 U.S. App. LEXIS 14205 (7th Cir. 2002), *cert. denied*, 537 U.S. 1110 (2003) (holding that in the case of collectors' guides to Beanie Babies that utilized photographs of them, such were not derivative works).

29. Time, Inc. v. Bernard Geis Assocs., 293 F. Supp. 130, 143 (S.D.N.Y. 1968) ("The Zapruder pictures in fact have many elements of creativity. Among other things, Zapruder selected the kind of camera (movies, not snapshots), the kind of film (color), the kind of lens (telephoto), the area in which the pictures were to be taken, the time they were to be taken, and (after testing several sites) the spot on which the camera would be operated."). On the

*Inc.*,[30] the Second Circuit held that still photographs of ballet dancers in a performance, which were published in a book on the particular ballet, infringed the copyright held by the choreographer. The issue was whether the book and photographs could be a copy of the choreographed work since it either portrayed the "essence" of the *Nutcracker* at issue or, alternatively, it was an infringing derivative work.[31] In reversing the trial court and finding infringement, the appellate court stated the test to be whether the copy is substantially similar to the original and not whether it is possible to reproduce the original work from the copy.[32] The trial court had found no infringement because it found that the photographs caught "dancers in various attitudes at specific instances of time" and not "the flow of the steps in a ballet." Rejecting this, the Second Circuit appellate panel looked to substantial similarity, applying the long accepted test of the ordinary observer.[33] Since infringement across different mediums of expression defies re-creation of the original from the infringing copy, that does not provide a defense to infringement. The court conceded that "[i]t may be that all of the photographs mentioned above are of insufficient quantity or sequencing to constitute infringement; it may also be that they do copy but also are protected as fair use," but the proper test should have been substantial similarity.[34] Even if not all the photographs infringed, all that was needed was a small amount of the original in the material—in this case, the book of photographs. The court rejected the argument that "since each photograph in the book captures only a fraction of an instant, even the combined effect of 60 color photographs does not reproduce the choreography itself, nor provide sufficient details of movement to enable a choreographic work to be reproduced from the photographs."[35]

---

other hand, at least one court disagreed with *Bernard Geis* that consideration of the seriousness of the work is relevant in establishing fair use. *See, e.g.*, Haberman v. Hustler Magazine, Inc., 626 F. Supp. 201, 209–10 (D. Mass. 1986).

30. 789 F.2d 157 (2d Cir. 1986).
31. *Id.* at 161.
32. *Id.*
33. *Id.* at 162.
34. *Id.* at 163.
35. *Id.* at 162.

Another example is *Bill Diodato Photography, LLC v. Kate Spade, LLC*,[36] in which the plaintiff photographer shot a bathroom stall that showed a woman's feet in stylish shoes, with her underwear at the ankles and a handbag nearby. He submitted to the defendant, which denied having seen the image, but nonetheless defendant later ran a photograph showing the same elements. The plaintiff sued for copyright infringement and unfair competition. The court denied the plaintiff's motion for summary judgment, finding that "although the idea of using a woman sitting on a toilet to showcase stylish shoes and other fashion accessories is a clever one, it is an idea that has been used often in popular culture. Hence, Diodato's photograph contains elements that are not protected by the copyright laws." The court found that the common elements derived from the uncopyrightable idea, and that the concept and execution itself were not so unique as to justify the misappropriation claim.

The parameters are not always clear. If they were, we would not have this panoply of cases. It is one thing to generally say that ideas and facts cannot be copyrighted. As we see, it is not easy to predetermine how it will play out.

### *Scenes a Faire* and Thematic Concepts

A related issue involves "scenes a faire." We will discuss infringement analysis and defense later, but one of the common issues that faces photographers is the extent to which photographers can "rephotograph" a scene they find in another's photograph.

Copyright law does recognize that ideas cannot be copyrighted and that there are only certain ways to express certain facts. Indeed, when comparing two works—a book and a film—about police, one court noted that "[e]lements such as drunks, prostitutes, vermin and derelict cars would appear in any realistic work about the work of policemen in the South Bronx" and "therefore are unprotectible as 'scenes a faire,' that is, scenes that necessarily result from the choice of a setting or situation."[37]

36. 388 F. Supp. 2d 382 (S.D.N.Y. 2005).

37. Walker v. Time Life Films, Inc., 784 F.2d 44, 50 (2d Cir. 1986); *see also* Atari, Inc. v. N. Am. Philips Consumer Elecs. Corp., 672 F.2d 607, 616 (7th Cir. 1982) ("*Scenes a faire* refers to incidents, characters or settings which are as a practical matter indispensable, or at

In *Nichols v. Universal Pictures Corp.*,[38] the court articulated a set of parameters:

> Upon any work . . . a great number of patterns of increasing generality will fit equally well, as more and more of the incident is left out. The last may perhaps be no more than the most general statement of what the [work] is about, and at times might consist only of its title; but there is a point in this series of abstractions where they are no longer protected, since otherwise the [author] could prevent the use of his 'ideas,' to which, apart from their expression, his property is never extended.

least standard, in the treatment of a given topic. Such stock literary devices are not protectable by copyright. Thus, similarity of expression, whether literal or nonliteral, which necessarily results from the fact that the common idea is only capable of expression in more or less stereotyped form will preclude a finding of actionable similarity.") (internal quotations and citations omitted); Cain v. Universal Pictures, 47 F. Supp. 1013, 1017 (S.D. Cal. 1942) ("The other small details, on which stress is laid, such as the playing of the piano, the prayer, the hunger motive, as it called [sic], are inherent in the situation itself. They are what the French call "scènes à faire". Once having placed two persons in a church during a big storm, it was inevitable that incidents like these and others which are, necessarily, associated with such a situation should force themselves upon the writer in developing the theme. Courts have held repeatedly that such similarities and incidental details necessary to the environment or setting of an action are not the material of which copyrightable originality consists."); Kisch v. Ammirati & Puris, Inc., 657 F. Supp. 380, 382 (S.D.N.Y. 1987) ("The copyrightable elements of a photograph have been described as the photographer's original conception of his subject, not the subject itself.") (internal quotations and citations omitted); Reed-Union Corp. v. Turtle Wax, Inc., 77 F.3d 909, 911 (7th Cir. 1996) ("[no infringement when the] central elements—laboratory test results, the revival of a weatherbeaten car, the imperviousness of the polish to many car washes—are scenes a faire outside the scope of copyright protection."); Herzog v. Castle Rock Entm't, 193 F.3d 1241, 1248 (11th Cir. 1999) ("scenes a faire, sequences of events which necessarily follow from a common theme, are not protectible. Incidents, characters, or settings that are indispensable or standard in the treatment of a given topic are not copyrightable.") (internal quotations and citations omitted); Satava v. Lowry, 323 F.3d 805, 813 (9th Cir.), *cert. denied*, 540 U.S. 983 (2003) ("Nature gives us ideas of animals in their natural surroundings: an eagle with talons extended to snatch a mouse; a grizzly bear clutching a salmon between its teeth; a butterfly emerging from its cocoon; a wolf howling at the full moon; a jellyfish swimming through tropical waters. These ideas, first expressed by nature, are the common heritage of humankind, and no artist may use copyright law to prevent others from depicting them. An artist may, however, protect the original expression he or she contributes to these ideas. An artist may vary the pose, attitude, gesture, muscle structure, facial expression, coat, or texture of animal. An artist may vary the background, lighting, or perspective. Such variations, if original, may earn copyright protection.")

38. 45 F.2d 119, 121 (2d Cir. 1930), *cert. denied*, 282 U.S. 902 (1931).

A good example of this is in *Kaplan v. Stock Market Photo Agency, Inc.*[39] Kaplan's picture *Wing Tips over the Edge* was made in 1988 and showed "a businessperson standing perilously on the ledge or roof of a tall building looking down onto a car-lined street, and is taken from the viewpoint of the businessperson."[40] The defendant sought to create its own comparable advertisement and they engaged another photographer to take such an image, which "depicts a businessperson standing perilously on the ledge or roof of a tall building looking down onto a car-lined street, and is taken from the viewpoint of the businessperson."[41] *Kaplan* revolved around the substantial-similarity prong of the analysis. The court noted that "substantial dissimilarity" is not necessarily enough in itself.[42] Citing the doctrine of scenes a faire, the court noted that certain sequences are a matter of necessity and may be indispensable or standard.[43] The test is not exact and may depend on "the level or abstraction or generalization of the works being compared."[44] The *Kaplan* court found the two photographs were not substantially similar, finding the subject matter of the idea not copyrightable.[45] The *Kaplan* court engaged in an extended discussion into the various purposes of the photographs to determine what the underlying "facts" were, as well as analyzing the different elements, components, and perspective and other photographic decisions. It then eliminated the "unfair competition" claim by finding no "reverse passing off"—that is, by trying to pass off someone else's product as one's own—nor did it find straight passing off—that is, trying to pass of one's own product as someone else's.

39. 133 F. Supp. 2d 317 (S.D.N.Y. 2001).

40. *Id.* at 319.

41. *Id.* at 320.

42. *Id.* at 322. *See also* Rogers v. Koons, 960 F.2d 301, 308 (2d Cir.), *cert. denied*, 506 U.S. 974 (1992) ("It is only where the points of dissimilarity exceed those that are similar, and those similar are—when compared to the original work—of small import quantitatively or qualitatively that a finding of no infringement is appropriate.").

43. *Id.* at 323.

44. *Id.*

45. *See also* Kisch v. Ammirati & Puris, Inc., 657 F. Supp. 380, 382 (S.D.N.Y. 1987) ("Therefore, in cases involving photographs, a plaintiff's copyrights cannot monopolize the various poses used and can protect only [p]laintiff's particular photographic expression of these poses and not the underlying ideas therefor. . . . The copyrightable elements of a photograph have been described as the photographer's 'original' 'conception' of his subject, not the subject itself.") (internal quotations and citations omitted).

In *Sahuc v. Tucker*,[46] two photographs were at issue, both of the St. Louis Cathedral in New Orleans. The court described the images: "The St. Louis Cathedral, a worldwide recognized symbol of the City of New Orleans, appears in both photographs, along with the fence that borders Jackson Square, including the Decatur Street gate. Both photographs include fog rolling off the Mississippi River into Jackson Square in the morning hours."[47] Sahuc, a photographer, made his image in February 1999, and involved illuminated lamps, an open gate, no people, prominent banana leaves, the statue of Andrew Jackson, the urn, Mediterranean palms, and fog that partially covered the Cathedral; he sought a "spectral and mysterious look." Tucker, a painter as well as photographer, made his image in December 2001. There was no question of access; he had seen Sahuc's picture. Tucker's picture also involved fog, an open gate, lights on the fences, the Andrew Jackson statue, urn, banana leaves, Mediterranean palms, and no people, but puddles of water at the bottom were included, a distinguishing feature from the Sahuc photograph.

Finding that Tucker had access to Sahuc's work, the court noted that it did not need to evaluate whether Tucker actually used Sahuc's material, since not all legal copying is actionable, citing *Peel*, and proceeded directly to the substantial similarity analysis. Looking at both images on eases, the court found that while similar ideas were depicted, those ideas are not copyrightable; it distinguished the images as follows:

> *Decatur Street Gate* [Sahuc's image] is perfectly centered and every element contained in the photograph comes together to form the artistic vision expressed by it. The banana leaves frame the shot, protruding more boldly than even the Cathedral in the background, which is muted by the fog. All objects appear to be perfectly placed by Sahuc: the urn, the Mediterranean palms, the gates, and the Cathedral. There are no pedestrians present in *Decatur Street Gate*. Neither the street nor the curb are part of the scene. Decatur Street Gate is a timeless

46. 300 F. Supp. 2d 461 (E.D. La. 2004), *aff'd*, 166 F. App'x 157 (5th Cir. 2006).
47. *Id.* at 463.

> photograph; there is no sense of what year or what time of day it was taken. It is a special piece. Plaintiff's counsel artfully and clearly portrayed Sahuc's exceptional talent.
>
> * * *
>
> *Breaking Mist* [Tucker's image] is not, in the Court's opinion, substantially similar. It is a photograph of Jackson Square taken around dawn. The elements of the urn, the statue of Andrew Jackson, the Mediterranean palms, and the Cathedral appear to be off center. Banana leaves are heavy on one side but barely apparent on the other. Mr. Sahuc admitted that, looking at the photographs side-by-side, there is an apparent difference in the positioning of the elements that compose the pictures. The St. Louis Cathedral is hazy at the middle but visible at the top and bottom of the picture. The Cabildo juts out on the left side of the frame. The street and the curb appear at the bottom of the picture, along with puddles of water and what appears to be left over trash.[48]

The court also considered and cited testimony as to each photographer's purposes and assessed the "feeling" generated by each photograph as well. Despite the plaintiff's going "to considerable lengths to demonstrate to this Court that Tucker was an unethical artist out to make a quick dollar by defrauding the public and pirating Sahuc's life work. This notwithstanding, it should be noted that copying is an issue to be determined by the comparison of works, not credibility."[49]

The Andrew Jackson statue is an immoveable part of this landscape. The *Sahuc* court, though, never used the phrase "scenes a faire" and did not specifically address it. Other courts seem to have resolved the issue in

48. *Id.* at 465–66.
49. *Id.* at 467 (internal citation and quotation omitted).

On left: *Decatur Street Gate*, © Louis Sahuc. On right: *Breaking Mist*, © Lee Tucker.

comparable fashion even if not applying the doctrine. Courts have held that objects appearing as they occur or in the reality of the subject matter are not protectable, including a statue or its setting.[50] *Fournier v. Erickson*[51] is another example of a claim of copyright infringement based on another photographer's re-creation of a scene. Addressing the issues on summary judgment, the court found that "the total concept and feel of Fournier's photograph and the allegedly infringing one are unmistakably similar," as were the posing of the models.[52] The court also noted certain differences but found the similarities and differences were balanced enough—more so than in *Kaplan*, which the court discussed—so as to preclude summary judgment and allow the claim to go to trial. It did, however, dismiss the unfair competition and tortious misappropriation claims.

*Sahuc* is perhaps more problematic than *Fournier* or *Kaplan*, in that the courts actually undergo substantial similarity analysis based not on re-creations of the subject matter but the photographing of a natural landscape. Certain facts can be expressed in only so many ways. If writer A states that "X was born on January 1, 1941," there are only so many other ways to state that fact. Similarly, if one described by way of a list the elements

50. Leigh v. Warner Bros., Inc., 212 F.3d 1210, 1214 (11th Cir. 2000) (although not resolving *scenes a faire* issue as to cemeteries); Franklin Mint Corp. v. Nat'l Wildlife Art Exch., Inc., 575 F.2d 62, 65 (3d Cir.), *cert. denied*, 439 U.S. 880 (1978) ("Since copyrights do not protect thematic concepts, the fact that the same subject matter may be present in two paintings does not prove copying or infringement. Indeed, an artist is free to consult the same source for another original painting.").

51. 202 F. Supp. 2d 290 (S.D.N.Y. 2002).

52. *Id.* at 296.

seen in Jackson Square from a particular vantage point, that is an expression of fact. Photographers "speak" through their image, and the catalog of items in each of the above images is an expression of reality. Tucker did not photograph Sahuc's image. Tucker did not pass off Sahuc's image as his own. He simply photographed the same viewpoint. If that can be protected by copyright, then it would seem a very precarious business, since someone could "lock in" a particular landscape view from, say, a scenic overlook and preclude anyone else from photographing and publishing an image from that same place. In *Time Inc. v. Bernard Geis Associates*,[53] the court rejected the argument that by granting copyright protection to the Zapruder film it would be creating an "oligopoly" over the facts concerning the Kennedy assassination. No copyright was claimed in the events, only the particular form of expression. While news itself cannot be copyrighted, courts distinguish between the substance of the information and the way it has been expressed.[54]

If Tucker had not included puddles, would the court then have found substantial similarity?

A related concept is that of merger, which recognizes that there is a limited number of ways of expressing the same thing. In *Gentieu v. Tony Stone Images/Chicago, Inc.*,[55] involving the photographing of babies in a certain way, the court held: "It is not enough to establish infringement that the accused photographs were of naked babies in various poses. Rather Gentieu must show that the accused images are substantially similar to particular compositional elements of her expression that do not necessarily flow from the idea of photographing naked babies."[56] The court noted that "[s]ome ideas, however, can be expressed only in a limited number of ways, and where the gap between the idea of a work and its expression merge so the two become nearly inseparable, copyright protection must likewise narrow to avoid granting an effective monopoly of the idea itself."[57] This

53. 293 F. Supp. 130 (S.D.N.Y. 1968).
54. *Id.* at 143.
55. 255 F. Supp. 2d 838, 847–48 (N.D. Ill. 2003).
56. *Id.*
57. *Id.* at 849–50.

is known as the doctrine of merger, in which the issue is whether there are only a limited number of ways to express the idea. This case is discussed in more detail in the following section concerning ways to prove infringement.

In the *Sahuc* situation, I would suggest the better analysis is under unfair competition—that is, whether someone is attempting to fool the public into thinking his or her image is that of another. To do so under copyright is to place an unfair burden on the second photographer. There should be a per se rule, or at least a rebuttable presumption, that no photograph of subject matter can be deemed to infringe another photograph of the same subject matter in the same manner that one cannot copyright facts. It also seems somewhat arbitrary to focus on the access issue. Two photographers standing side by side at the overlook photographing a landscape would not be infringing since neither saw the other's image, but if the second saw the first image and two years later, standing at the same overlook on a comparable day and making a completely independent image, should not be found to be actionably infringing.

## Graffiti

Graffiti is another area of some developing controversy. Many photographers take pictures of graffiti. Is that copyrightable? The court in *Villa v. Brady Publishing*[58] assumed it could be, without deciding the question; the graffiti artist's mural was photographed and published in a book. The case was dismissed due to lack of copyright registration. To the extent one photographs graffiti, provided it is part of a transformative final photograph, it should not be an infringement. The so-called graffiti artist may have a hard time enforcing rights, if the expression itself were a trespass or defacement of private property. In *Cohen v. G&M Realty LP*,[59] the plaintiff sought to protect his "aerosol art" on a building set for demolition, relying on the Visual Artists Rights Act (VARA). Applying *Carter, supra,* the trial court found that the work was "art," but not "a *work* of visual art" under VARA, and the court had no authority under VARA to preserve the site as a tourist

58. No. 2-cv-570, 2002 U.S. Dist. LEXIS 11753, at *7 (N.D. Ill. June 27, 2002).
59. No. 12-cv-5612 (E.D.N.Y. Nov. 20, 2013).

attraction.[60] Of course, any analysis in the initial instance of the graffiti will have to consider whether it is more than just a title, or a common phrase, or other types of "expression" that are not sufficient to qualify for copyright protection. As such, photographing such graffiti would not be a violation of copyright (though it might conceivably be a kind of misappropriation tort; see Chapter 3). Another issue is whether spraying graffiti on a wall is fixation in a permanent form, particularly if it is vandalism and there is an assumption that it can, and will, be cleaned, although transitory expression may still be sufficient fixation.[61]

A related and also developing issue is the ability to obtain copyright protection over a tattoo. S. Victor Whitmill, the tattoo "artist" responsible for fighter Mike Tyson's facial tattoo, claimed copyright protection and sued Warner Brothers for its use of that tattoo on actor Ed Helms in the movie *The Hangover: Part II*. The case settled before ultimate resolution, but press reports indicated that Whitmill might ultimately prevail.[62] According to the complaint, Tyson had signed a release that acknowledged "that all artwork, sketches and drawings related to [his] tattoo and any photographs of [his] tattoo are property of Paradox-Studio of Dermagraphics," which was the plaintiff's company. The plaintiff actually registered the copyright of the tattoo.

In *Gonzales v. Kid Zone, Ltd.*,[63] Gonzales owned copyrights for designs used on T-shirts; defendant Kid Zone contacted defendant Transfer Technologies and asked it to create designer tattoos "in the same flavor" as Gonzales's for use as temporary tattoos. The plaintiff became aware of the potential infringement when the tattoos appeared in an advertisement. The trial court ruled for the plaintiff on infringement. There was no question as to literal infringement; the images were the same. On appeal, the court vacated and remanded, *Gonzales v. Transfer Technologies, Inc.*,[64] on the issue of attorneys' fees.

60. *Id.* at *35 (emphasis in original).

61. Advanced Computer Servs. of Mich., Inc. v. MAI Sys. Corp., 845 F. Supp. 356 (E.D. Va. 1994).

62. *See* Whitmill v. Warner Bros. Entm't, Inc., No. 4:11-cv-752 (E.D. Mo. 2011).

63. No. 00-cv-3969, 2001 U.S. Dist. LEXIS 12008 (N.D. Ill. Aug. 15, 2001).

64. 301 F.3d 608 (7th Cir. 2002).

One has to wonder where all this will end. If the photographer photographs a person on the street, she may survive privacy challenges (as discussed later in this chapter), but if the subject has a tattoo, is there now a copyright infringement? It may well be that First Amendment considerations, as noted below, will trump the copyright issue, but it is something else to think about. On the other hand, is a tattoo fixed in the medium of someone's skin any different than any other copyrightable graphic? As such, use of the tattoo as part of a portrait of someone should be acceptable fair use; what may have been more of an issue in the *Whitmill* case was its commercial exploitation for its own sake, as a gratuitous element.

### Derivative Works

As noted above, a copyright holder has rights to derivative uses. The contours of what constitutes a derivative work are not always clear-cut. The issue revolves around the difference between the original and the subsequent work to constitute sufficient originality.[65] In *Schrock v. Learning Curve International, Inc.*,[66] the Seventh Circuit clarified *Gracen*. The defendant was a licensee of the copyright to Thomas and Friends train characters, and hired Schrock to make photographs of the toys for advertising items. When the licensee continued to use the photographs after Schrock was no longer employed, he sued both the licensee and licensor for copyright infringement. The trial court found the photographs as derivative works, and therefore he had no case for copyright infringement. On appeal, the court reversed, assuming that the district court's classification of the works as derivate was correct but that that status was a matter of law, not contract. When the contract right to the derivative work expired, so did the photographer's rights: "Schrock created the photos with permission and therefore owned the copyright to the photos provided they satisfied the other requirements for copyright and the parties did not contract around the default rule."[67] The court found that there is no heightened standard for originality in a derivative work and found there was enough here to qualify for copyright,

65. Gracen v. Bradford Exch., 698 F.2d 300, 305 (7th Cir. 1983).
66. 586 F.3d 513, 516 (7th Cir. 2009).
67. *Id.* at 516.

but the record was insufficient to determine the extent of the contractual variation.[68]

Elements that go to assessing originality of photographs in derivative works are "posing the subjects, lighting, angle, selection of film and camera, evoking the desired expression, and almost any other variant involved."[69]

In *Fragrancenet.com, Inc. v. FragranceX.COM, Inc.*,[70] the plaintiff and defendant both sold perfume products online. The defendant used over 900 copyrighted images from the plaintiff's website and inserted the plaintiff's registered trademarks into "metatags" to facilitate search results. On the copyright issues, the defendant claimed the plaintiff's images lacked originality to sustain copyright protection and were simply photographs of third-party products without creative elements. The court rejected the first argument, relying on the copyright registration that provided a presumption of originality, that such threshold is "modest," and that sufficient allegations of photographic creativity were alleged in the complaint as to "background, arrangement, lighting, use of shadow, angle, and selection of products within each line to be included within the images are among the original elements contributing to the [i]mages."[71]

The second argument, based on the photographs being considered derivative works, was also rejected in this case. The court noted that "to be copyrightable, a derivative work must contain original elements that make the derivative work distinct from its original work," and added that there is no rule that "photographs of third-parties' intellectual property are per se not copyrightable."[72] The test is "[w]here the quantum of originality is slight

68. *See also* Latimer v. Roaring Toyz, Inc., 601 F.3d 1224, 1234 (11th Cir. 2010) (the standard of originality for photographs is "generous," citing and quoting *Schrock*; the court also noted: "[T]he copyright in a derivative work is defeated only when the underlying work has been misappropriated. Whether the copyright owner of an original work of authorship has granted a license to create a derivative work is a threshold question that must be answered before turning to the more difficult question of whether the derivative work qualifies as such.").

69. Rogers v. Koons, 960 F.2d 301, 307 (2d Cir.), *cert. denied*, 506 U.S. 934 (1992); Harney v. Sony Pictures Television, Inc., 704 F.3d 173, 181 (1st Cir. 2013) ("Alternatively, subject matter that the photographer did not create could be viewed as 'facts' that, like ideas, are not entitled to copyright protection.").

70. 679 F. Supp. 2d 312 (E.D.N.Y. 2010).

71. *Id.* at 320.

72. *Id.* at 323.

and the resulting copyright is 'thin,' infringement will be established only by very close copying because the majority of the work is unprotectable."[73] *Fragrancenet.com* was decided at the stage of a motion to dismiss, so there was greater tolerance based on the pleadings; at summary judgment or trial, the factual inquiry would have to be satisfied.

Recalling the cup example, photographs are not derivative of the subject that is found in the photograph as long as the subject was not independently capable of copyright.[74] Note, though, that in this area there is still disagreement over the extent of the inquiry. The District Court within the Second Circuit in *SHL Imaging* criticized the Ninth Circuit in *Ets-Hokin v. Skyy Spiritis, Inc.* for not also evaluating whether the derivative work changing the *authorship* of the previous work:

> Although the Ninth Circuit concluded that a photograph of a vodka bottle was not a derivative work of the bottle, it reached that holding only after determining that the bottle was not independently copyrightable. Thus, the Ninth Circuit reasoned that the bottle was not a preexisting work. *Ets-Hokin*, at 1077-1082. This Court respectfully believes that the *Ets-Hokin* court misconstrued the nature of derivative works. While the *Ets-Hokin* court correctly noted that a derivative work must be based on a "preexisting work," and that the term "work" refers to a "work of authorship" as set forth in 17 U.S.C. § 102(a), it failed to appreciate that any derivative work must recast, transform or adopt the authorship contained in the preexisting work. . . . In short, the authorship of the photographic work is entirely different and separate from the authorship of the sculpture.[75]

When considering what is and is not a derivative work, courts will look to the particular elements to see what has been added and whether it is novel.

73. Beaudin v. Ben & Jerry's Homemade, Inc., 95 F.3d 1, 2 (2d Cir. 1996).

74. Ets-Hokin v. Skyy Spirtis, Inc., 225 F. 3d 1068, 1077–82 (9th Cir. 2000); SHL Imaging, Inc. v. Artisan House, Inc., 117 F. Supp. 2d 301, 305–06 (S.D.N.Y. 2000); Oriental Art Printing v. Goldstar Printing Corp., 175 F. Supp. 2d 542 (S.D.N.Y. 2001) (photographs of direct depictions of Chinese menu dishes lack creativity).

75. *SHL Imaging*, 117 F. Supp. 2d at 305–06.

## Registration

One has automatic copyright protection as soon as the expression is fixed in form. However, it is a predicate to filing the copyright suit to have registered the work. Registration also has the advantage of establishing a date on which there was at least constructive notice to the world of the expression and, if the registration is made within five years of the original publication, it provides the copyright holder prima facie evidence of the copyright's validity. Publication is defined, essentially, as distribution to the public. Importantly, if the registration occurs within three months of publication, then certain attorneys' fees are available, in addition to actual damages and profits. Registration also provides a basis to enlist the aid of U.S. Customs to prevent infringing imports. This can have import in gray market cases. A good place to begin in understanding the rudiments of the Copyright Act is to go to www.copyright.gov and review the circulars, particularly Circular 1, titled "Copyright Basics."

It is not necessary to place the © designation on the photograph in order to obtain copyright protection. It is useful, though, because it does provide public notice of the owner's copyright and identity, creates a date of first use, and helps in the proof of access and to defeat innocent replication.

Publication of a photograph similarly requires the distribution to the public. While copyright protection exists in it, the lack of publication will preclude recovery of attorneys' fees under the statute. Publication by the infringer does not count as publication by the photographer of the original photograph.[76]

## Infringement

The Copyright Act provides for a federal cause of action to the copyright holder against those that infringe copyright. Remedies include injunctive relief, impounding and disposition of the infringing articles, as well as damages and profits, and in certain cases costs and attorneys' fees.[77] As noted above, there are also criminal sanctions for infringement done "willfully and

76. Zito v. Steeplechase Films, Inc., 267 F. Supp. 2d 1022 (N.D. Cal. 2003); *see also* Barrera v. Brooklyn Music, Ltd., 346 F. Supp. 2d 400 (S.D.N.Y. 2004).

77. 17 U.S.C. §§ 501–505.

for purposes of commercial advantage or private financial gain."[78] Infringement requires proof of ownership of a valid copyright and the unauthorized copying of the copyrighted work.[79]

"Actionable copying" requires further analysis:

> Two separate inquiries must be made to determine whether actionable copying has occurred. The first question is whether the alleged infringer copied, or "actually used the copyrighted material in his own work." Copying can be proven by direct or circumstantial evidence. Circumstantial evidence may support an inference of copying if the defendant had access to the copyrighted work and there is "probative similarity" between the copyrighted work and the allegedly infringing work."
>
> The second question is whether "substantial similarity" exists between the copyrighted work and the allegedly infringing work. To answer this question, "a side-by-side comparision must be made between the original and the copy to determine whether a layman would view the two works as 'substantially similar.'"[80]

### *Access*

You prove access by proving that the infringer had a "reasonable possibility" of access to the copyrighted work; this must be more than a "real possibility" and not the basis of "mere speculation or conjecture."[81] The plaintiff bears the burden of proof in the nature of "significant, affirmative

78. 17 U.S.C. § 506(a).

79. Feist Publ'ns, Inc. v. Rural Tel. Serv. Co., 499 U.S. 340, 361 (1991).

80. Bridgmon v. Array Sys. Corp., 325 F.3d 572, 576 (5th Cir. 2003) (citations omitted); *see also* Sahuc v. Tucker, 300 F. Supp. 2d 461, 464 (E.D. La. 2004), *aff'd*, 166 F. App'x 157 (5th Cir. 2006); Balsley v. LFP, Inc., 691 F.3d 747, 757–58 (6th Cir. 2012) (direct infringement is where the plaintiff needs to show ownership of a valid copyright and copying of the constituent elements of a work that are original); MiTek Holdings, Inc. v. Arce Eng'g Co., 89 F.3d 1548, 1554 (11th Cir. 1996) (indirect evidence shows that defendant had access to the copyrighted work and that there are legally sufficient similarities between the "original" and the "infringing" work).

81. Jorgensen v. Epic/Sony Records, 351 F.3d 46, 51 (2d Cir. 2003) (internal quotations and citations omitted).

and probative evidence."[82] Determination of access can involve examination into the working relationship between the owner and the alleged infringer.[83]

### Substantial Similarity

Substantial similarity may be found through one of several different approaches. The Second Circuit articulates the test as whether "an average lay observer would recognize the alleged copy as having been appropriated from the copyrighted work."[84] The Ninth Circuit employs dual examination based on an intrinsic/extrinsic test analysis that looks first to an objective review of the individual elements and then to a subjective analysis of the reasonable person.[85] Other circuits employ different tests or variations on these themes. Within the Fifth Circuit, proof of substantial similarity requires that "a side-by-side comparison must be made between the original and the copy to determine whether a layman would view the two works as 'substantially similar.'"[86]

Expert testimony as to substantial similarity is not permitted since it is the standard of the "layperson," although "probative similarity" may utilize such testimony.[87] Substantial similarity is the threshold for actionable copying; proof of actionable, as opposed to de minimis or trivial copying, is meant to require something more substantive. As explained in *Ringgold v. Black Entertainment Television, Inc.*:

> At first glance, it might seem odd to pursue an inquiry as to "substantial similarity" even after copying as a factual matter has been established. However, the superficial anomaly reflects only a lack of appreciation of the difference between factual copying and actionable

82. Scott v. Paramount Pictures Corp., 449 F. Supp. 518, 520 (D.D.C. 1978), *aff'd*, 607 F.2d 494 (D.C. Cir. 1979), *cert. denied*, 449 U.S. 849 (1980).

83. Lessem v. Taylor, 766 F. Supp. 2d 504, 509 (S.D.N.Y. 2011).

84. Knitwaves, Inc. v. Lollytogs, Ltd. (Inc.), 71 F.3d 996, 1001 (2d Cir. 1995) (internal quotes and citations omitted).

85. Sid & Marty Krofft Television Prods., Inc. v. McDonald's Corp., 562 F.2d 1157 (9th Cir. 1977).

86. Peel & Co. v. The Rug Market, 238 F.3d 391, 395 (5th Cir. 2001) (citations omitted).

87. Interplan Architects, Inc. v. CL Thomas, Inc., No. 08-cv-03181, 2010 U.S. Dist. LEXIS 107941, at *30 (S.D. Tex. Oct. 9, 2010).

> copying. The former (probative similarity) requires only the fact that the infringing work copies something from the copyrighted work; the latter (substantial similarity) requires that the copying is quantitatively and qualitatively sufficient to support the legal conclusion that infringement (actionable copying) has occurred. The qualitative component concerns the copying of expression, rather than ideas, a distinction that often turns on the level of abstraction at which the works are compared. See Nimmer § 13.03[A][1]. The quantitative component generally concerns the amount of the copyrighted work that is copied, a consideration that is especially pertinent to exact copying, see Nimmer § 13.03[A][2].[3] In cases involving visual works, like the pending one, the quantitative component of substantial similarity also concerns the observability of the copied work—the length of time the copied work is observable in the allegedly infringing work and such factors as focus, lighting, camera angles, and prominence. Thus, as in this case, a copyrighted work might be copied as a factual matter, yet a serious dispute might remain as to whether the copying that occurred was actionable. Since "substantial similarity," properly understood, includes a quantitative component, it becomes apparent why the concept of de minimis is relevant to a defendant's contention that an indisputably copied work has not been infringed. See id. at 13–46 & n. 92.2.[88]

Without evidence of direct copying, courts analyze the second element of copying in terms of whether the alleged infringer had access and there was substantial similarity in the works.[89] Other courts have expressed it in terms of "(1) whether the defendant copied from the plaintiff's work and (2) whether the copying, if proven, went so far as to constitute an improper appropriation."[90] In other words, would a reasonable observer believe there

88. 126 F.3d 70, 75 (2d Cir. 1997).

89. Gentieu v. Tony Stone Images/Chicago, Inc., 255 F. Supp. 2d 838, 847–48 (N.D. Ill. 2003).

90. Atari, Inc. v. N. Am. Philips Consumer Elecs. Corp., 672 F.2d 607, 614 (7th Cir.), *cert. denied*, 459 U.S. 880 (1982).

had been in appropriate misappropriation. Even when underlying elements are in the public domain, if the aggregation or compilation of them is original, copyright protection to that expression is obtained.[91]

In *Gentieu*, a photographer sued two stock-photo agencies for copyright infringement, breach of contract, and breach of fiduciary duty. She took pictures of babies in a particular way using particular lighting techniques. Getty instructed other of its photographers to shoot in the same way, essentially making derivative copies of her images, and also exceeding the scope of her licenses. The court found that access certainly existed but that Gentieu failed to prove substantial similarity. The court noted that to find substantial similarity, the court must look to the "total concept and feel: of the work, rather than dissecting it into parts, and conducts that inquiry in the manner of how the 'ordinary observer' would view the works."[92] The court further noted that the Copyright Act protects the expression, not the idea. Consequently, "Gentieu cannot claim a copyright in the idea of photographing naked or diapered babies or in any elements of expression that are intrinsic to that unprotected idea."[93]

Another example involved a photograph and stained-glass artwork.[94] On the right is the 1992 stained-glass portrait *Nohe* by Marylee Leialoha Colucci. On the left is the original photograph titled *Makanani* by Kim Taylor Reece and made in 1988.

Reece sued the art gallery that displayed Colucci's work, seeking an injunction against further display or sale. Reece lost.

The subject is a hula performance, a significant cultural ritual, and in particular, they are showing the "ike" movement. The analysis went as follows: The court first identified the elements of proof: ownership and infringement. To find ownership, the court found originality, copyrightability, and compliance with the statutory requirements. To find copying (infringement), the court first found access. It then turned to the substantial similarity analysis and employed two tests—extrinsic and intrinsic.

91. Schroeder v. William Morrow & Co., 566 F.2d 3, 5 (7th Cir. 1977).
92. *Id.* at 848.
93. *Id.* at 849.
94. Reece v. Island Treasures Art Gallery, Inc., 468 F. Supp. 2d 1197 (D. Haw. 2006).

On the left: *Makanani*, © Kim Taylor Reece. On the right: *Nohe*, © Mary Lee Leialoha Colucci.

The extrinsic test is "analytic dissection" that focuses on the isolated elements without regard to the combination or other elements.[95] The court looked to the source of the similarity, the copyrightability of the element, and the scope of the protection to the element. In *Reece*, the court found "thin" protection. The copyrightable elements of the photograph were identified to include "lighting, selection of film and camera, angle of photograph, and determination of the precise time when the photograph is to be taken."[96] The unprotectable element here was the idea of the performance of the ike movement. Under a scenes a faire analysis, the movements were standard forms and not copyrightable. Comparison of the isolated elements showed sufficient dissimilarity. The court went through a variety of other factors.

The court then employed the "intrinsic test," essentially a subjective comparison that looks to "whether the ordinary, reasonable audience would find the works substantially similar in the total concept and feel of the

95. *See* Dr. Seuss Enters., LP v. Penguin Books USA, Inc., 109 F.3d 1394 (9th Cir.), *cert. denied*, 521 U.S. 1146 (1997).

96. *Id.* at 1206 (citations omitted).

works."[97] While the central figure was the same, the court did not find substantial similarity.

In *Mannion v. Coors Brewing Co.*,[98] the plaintiff photographer made an image of a basketball star, and the photograph appeared in a magazine. The defendant ad company, with authorization for use of the image in an internal corporate merchandising catalog, "used a manipulated version of the [image] and superimposed on it" words and a Coors Light beer can for use on billboard. The court held that the derivative nature of the work was irrelevant on the basis that if not there was no infringement, there was no derivative use. It noted that copyright protects only the originality in the photo, not the subject—and copyright would not protect "slavish copying" of the subject, as such would not be "original." Here, though, the photograph was found to be original and copyrightable. It noted that the idea/expression dichotomy in the photography context was less relevant. Since the case was before the court on summary judgment, however, the court found a fact question as to whether there was substantial similarity, noting that the focus would not be on individual. The court declined to focus on the items in isolation.

Similarly, even if one work resembles another, if that similarity if fortuitous, there is no infringement.[99]

It is important to remember that simply claiming one's photograph was copied is not, in and of itself, sufficient; the copied work must be "substantially similar" to the original.[100] In *Harney*, the plaintiff, a professional photographer on assignment for a local newspaper, took a picture of a young girl and her father, which turned out to be particularly newsworthy since the father was charged with abduction in a case that became internationally publicized. The photograph was published with its original purpose of

97. *Id.* at 1209 (citation and internal quotations omitted).

98. 377 F. Supp. 2d 444 (S.D.N.Y. 2005).

99. Feist Publ'ns, Inc. v. Rural Tel. Serv. Co., Inc., 499 U.S. 340, 345–46 (1991); *see also* Echevarra v. Warner Bros. Pictures, Inc., 12 F. Supp. 632, 634 (D. Cal. 1935) ("[A] substantial similarity founded on coincidence, or the use of old or stock situations, or common sources, and not the result of piracy, direct or indirect, is insufficient to establish infringement; nor is the taking of a general idea or scheme sufficient.").

100. Harney v. Sony Pictures Television, Inc., 704 F.3d 173, 178 (1st Cir. 2013).

highlighting neighborhood activity; a year later the photograph was used on the FBI's Wanted poster, and later, Sony re-created the photographic scene with actors and used that new photo in a documentary to show its importance in the investigation. The inquiry into substantial similarity as laid out in *Harney* is a two-step process. First, the original work is dissected into its separate expressive elements as distinct from any unprotected content, and then the derivative work is compared with it for purposes of substantial similarity by giving weight only to the protected aspects of the original work.[101] In considering the subject matter and its reality, and the dissected elements of the "creative" versus "factual" elements of the two images, the *Harney* court applied the test for summary judgment as to whether a reasonable person would find the two works substantially similar. It concluded to the contrary:

> Sony copied little of Harney's original work—only the placement of Gerhartsreiter and Reigh in the photograph—and no jury could conclude that the similarity resulting solely from that copying is substantial. Moreover, given the differences in background, lighting and religious detail, a reasonable jury comparing the entirety of the two works could not conclude that the ordinary observer would "regard their aesthetic appeal as the same."[102]

Finally, as cold comfort to the photographic community, the court did add: "We can understand the frustration of photographers such as Harney whose works are afforded a limited copyright because they are comprised substantially of unprotected content. As the Supreme Court has emphasized, however, 'this is not "some unforeseen byproduct of a statutory scheme."'"[103]

101. *Id.* at 179.
102. *Id.* at 188.
103. *Id.* (citations omitted).

Although registration of the copyright is necessary to sue for a particular copyright, once infringement is found, the court may enjoin future infringements of any of the plaintiff's copyrights, whether registered or not.[104]

## Public Domain

No copyright protection will be given to an image that is in the public domain or that simply replicates public domain "reality."[105] While not relevant to works governed by the 1976 Copyright Act, public domain issues can be relevant, as well as its publication history, when reviewing older images for purposes of the infringement analysis.[106]

## Fair Use

The exclusive rights detailed in § 106—the "bundle of rights" that provide various derivative applications and rights of reproduction—are limited by a statutory doctrine of "fair use" that permits that others may utilize otherwise copyrighted material in certain statutorily defined circumstances constituting "fair use."[107] There are limits to the notion of derivative works.[108]

---

104. Perfect 10, Inc. v. Amazon.com, Inc., 508 F.3d 1146, 1154 n.1 (9th Cir. 2009); Olan Mills, Inc. v. Linn Photo Co., 23 F.3d 1345, 1349 (8th Cir. 1994); Pac. & S. Co. v. Duncan, 744 F.2d 1490, 1499 n.17 (11th Cir. 1984), *reh'g denied en* banc, 749 F.2d 733 (11th Cir. 1984), *cert. denied*, 471 U.S. 1004 (1985).

105. Harney v. Sony Pictures Television, Inc., 704 F.3d 173, 182 (1st Cir. 2013) ("A photograph that consists of public-domain subject matter may thus be protected from copying because it involves creative expression, but with the protection limited to the work's original elements."); *see also* Bridgeman Art Library, Ltd. v. Corel Corp., 36 F. Supp. 2d 191, 195 (S.D.N.Y. 1999) ("[P]laintiff's exact photographic copies of public domain works of art would not be copyrightable under United States law because they are not original.").

106. *See, e.g.*, Jim Marshall Photography, LLC v. John Varvatos Enters., Inc., No. 11-cv-6702, 2013 U.S. Dist. LEXIS 92471, at *7 (N.D. Cal. July 2, 2013) ("publication history of an image may be central to the question of whether the image has become part of the public domain").

107. *See, e.g.*, Núñez v. Caribbean Int'l News Corp., 235 F.3d 18, 25 (1st Cir. 2000) ("Unauthorized reproduction of professional photographs by newspapers will generally violate the Copyright Act of 1976; in this context, however, where the photograph itself is particularly newsworthy, the newspaper acquired it in good faith, and the photograph had already been disseminated, a fair use exists under 17 U.S.C. § 107.").

108. Sony Computer Entm't, Inc. v. Connectix Corp., 203 F.3d 596, 607–08 (9th Cir.), *cert. denied*, 531 U.S. 871 (2000); Twin Peaks Prods., Inc. v. Publ'ns Int'l, Ltd., 996 F.2d 1366, 1377 (2d Cir. 1993) ("[T]he author of 'Twin Peaks' cannot preserve for itself the entire field of publishable works that wish to cash in on the 'Twin Peaks' phenomenon.").

Section 107 of the Copyright Act states:

> Limitations on exclusive rights: Fair use
> Notwithstanding the provisions of sections 106 [exclusive rights] and 106A [visual artists' rights] the fair use of a copyrighted work, including such use by reproduction in copies or phonorecords or by any other means specified by that section, for purposes such as criticism, comment, news reporting, teaching (including multiple copies for classroom use), scholarship, or research, is not an infringement of copyright. In determining whether the use made of a work in any particular case is a fair use the factors to be considered shall include—
> (1) the purpose and character of the use, including whether such use is of a commercial nature or is for nonprofit educational purposes;
> (2) the nature of the copyrighted work;
> (3) the amount and substantiality of the portion used in relation to the copyrighted work as a whole; and
> (4) the effect of the use upon the potential market for or value of the copyrighted work.
> The fact that a work is unpublished shall not itself bar a finding of fair use if such finding is made upon consideration of all the above factors.

There is of course much litigation over fair use and many applications of these particular factors. Regarding the first factor, the purpose and character of use, the inquiry focuses on whether there has been a new work of originality. The "central purpose" of the inquiry is "whether and to what extent the new work is 'transformative'."[109]

109. Campbell v. Acuff-Rose Music, Inc., 510 U.S. 569, 579 (1994) (citations omitted); *see also* Núñez v. Caribbean Int'l News Corp., 235 F.3d 18 (2000) ("Unauthorized reproduction of professional photographs by newspapers will generally violate the Copyright Act of 1976; in this context, however, where the photograph itself is particularly newsworthy, the newspaper acquired it in good faith, and the photograph had already been disseminated, a fair use exists under 17 U.S.C. § 107.").

The Second Circuit importantly held in *Cariou v. Prince*[110] that fair use is not dependent upon the allegedly infringing work being commentary on the original work. At least one other circuit has adopted the *Prince* test. Citing *Prince*, the Ninth Circuit held that "an allegedly infringing work is typically viewed as transformative as long as new expressive content or message is apparent."[111]

The facts: A photographer, Cariou, published a book of portraits and landscapes in Jamaica; years later, Richard Prince "altered and incorporated several" of the "photographs into a series of paintings and collages" and exhibited them at the Gagosian Gallery. Cariou sued Prince and the gallery for copyright infringement. Defendants claimed the Prince works were "transformative" and fair use. The Second Circuit noted that Prince "is a well-known appropriation artist" and "a leading exponent of the genre." The size and amount of usage of the Cariou images varied; no permission for use was given. The district court had held that fair use was dependent upon a secondary use that provided comment, historical context, or critical reference regarding the original work.

The appellate panel rejected that premise as not found in the Copyright Act or case law. The transformative nature was expressed this way: "Where Cariou's serene and deliberately composed portraits and landscape photographs depict the natural beauty of Rastafarians and their surrounding environs, Prince's crude and jarring works, on the other hand, are hectic and provocative" and differed in size, color, distortion, and composition. It appears to have been helpful not only because of Prince's reputation and artistic standing, as well as his aesthetic purpose in what he did, although the court expressly rejected that commentary as to the original work was not relevant.

Some may wonder how this differed from *Fairey v. Associated Press*,[112] filed in the Southern District of New York, involving the famous poster of

110. 714 F.3d 694 (2d Cir.), *cert. denied*, 134 S. Ct. 618 (2013).

111. Seltzer v. Green Day, Inc., 725 F.3d 1170, 1177 (9th Cir. 2013).

112. No. 09-cv-1123. On February 9, 2009, Fairey sued Associated Press for declaratory and injunctive relief "to vindicate" his rights in the Obama poster. On February 24, 2012, Fairey was charged with criminal contempt in a separate proceeding based on untrue factual allegations and subsequent destruction of some documents, and creation of other fake

Barack Obama as part of the "hope and change" campaign that was taken from an Associated Press photograph. Unfortunately, Fairey changed his story as to which Associated Press photograph he had actually used, and admitted to destroying certain evidence. The case settled. Whether that would have been fair use or not after *Prince v. Cariou* is unclear. In seeking certification to the U.S. Supreme Court, Cariou's lawyers cited the *Fairey* case as exemplifying the problem of striking the balance between "incentivizing creativity through copyright protection and permitting referential fair use of copyrighted materials in order to promote that very creativity."[113] In March 2014, Cariou and Prince settled.

In *Rogers v. Koons*,[114] the court decided in favor of the photographer and against the sculptor who had utilized a photograph of otherwise prosaic material. A sculptor can infringe your photograph; infringement can occur across different media. In this case, Koons acknowledged the source of his sculpture, *String of Puppies*, was Rogers's image of puppies being held in a photo called *Puppies*. The court found the photograph was "original" and entitled to copyright protection, even though all the elements of that original photograph were not. The court looked at the elements of originality in the photograph as involving the posing, lighting, angle, film and camera selection, evocation of expression, and other variants. The copyright of the photo was infringed because it was unauthorized and "blatantly apparent" copying. "Koons admittedly gave a copy of the photograph to the Italian artisans with the explicit instruction that the work be copied,"[115] which included the poses, shading, and expressions. The court found the sculpture to be substantially similar, even if not literally so. The court rejected a fair-use defense and rejected a defense of parody since (among other things) the actual object, as opposed to society, was not the purpose.

documents, to hide the falsity of the allegations and to obstruct discovery. On September 14, 2012, Fairey pleaded guilty to the information and was placed on probation.

113. Petition for a Writ of Certiorari, Cariou v. Prince, *available at* http://www.ipintelligencereport.com/wp-content/uploads/sites/139/2013/11/Cariou-Petition-for-Certiorari.pdf. That petition was denied. Cariou v. Prince, 134 S. Ct. 618 (2013).

114. 960 F.2d 301 (2d Cir.), *cert. denied*, 506 U.S. 934 (1992).

115. *Id.* at 307.

In another case involving Koons, Blanch v. Koons,[116] the court held that Koons's use of the plaintiff's photograph was fair use, in which he scanned the image and utilized part of the image in a collage painting he created. Blanch was no amateur; the court noted she was "an accomplished professional fashion and portrait photographer" with a track record of publication.[117] Her photograph at issue appeared in a magazine under the title "Silk Sandals by Gucci" in 2000; the photograph showed "a woman's lower legs and feet, adorned with bronze nail polish and glittery Gucci sandals, resting on a man's lap in what appears to be a first-class airplane cabin." Koons's painting, *Niagara*, as part of his *Easyfun-Ethereal* series, "consists of fragmentary images collaged against the backdrop of a landscape."[118] Koons made a scan of the Blanch photograph and incorporated "only the legs and feet," discarding the rest of the image, and "inverted the orientation."[119] On the issue of fair use, the court found for Koons. The work was transformative not because a photograph was used in a painting but because of the different purposes behind the use of the image, and the photograph was not used in the same way as in the painting. This was contrasted with a simple repackaging of the original work or using it in the same manner. That Koons earned money did not turn the commercial factor against him; where there has been "substantial" transformation, commercial gain is less important. It could not be said that Koons's painting replaced or competed with the original photograph in the marketplace. As for parody, satire, and justification for copying, the court found that the use did advance the artistic purpose and declined to be judgmental on whether it was necessary or not. Finally, the court noted that failure to ask permission in the initial instance was not per se bad faith. All factors favored Koons, and there was no finding of infringement.

Complementary copying of the original copyrighted work is fair use, but when it becomes a substitution for, or derivative of, the original work,

116. Blanch v. Koons, 467 F.3d 244 (2d Cir. 2006).
117. *Id.* at 247.
118. *Id.*
119. *Id.*

it is not fair use.[120] Complementary copying is considered a type of transformative use, whereas substitutional copying is more of a superseding by the copy of the original.[121]

The court recited the factors used to evaluate fair use under Section 107: "(1) the purpose and character of the use, (2) the nature of the copyrighted work, (3) the amount and substantiality of the work used, and (4) the effect of the use on the market for the original."[122]

Some other examples help at least give a sense of the variety of facts and shifting scope of fair use.[123]

On the other hand, in yet another Koons case, *United Feature Syndicate, Inc. v. Koons*,[124] Koons lost another case of copyright infringement. He had produced four sculptures that utilized unauthorized copies of the character Odie in the *Garfield* comic strip. The plaintiff alleged unfair competition under the trademark statute (the Lanham Act), copyright infringement, dilution under New York's General Business Law section 368-d, and common-law unfair competition. The sculpture, called *Wild Boy and Puppy*, utilized the Odie character and a cutout image of a stuffed doll for the boy.

---

120. Ty, Inc. v. Publ'ns Int'l, Ltd., 292 F.3d 512 (7th Cir.), *reh'g denied*, *en banc*, 2002 U.S. App. LEXIS 14205 (7th Cir. 2002), *cert. denied*, 537 U.S. 1110 (2003).

121. *Id.* at 518.

122. *Id.* at 112.

123. *See* Seltzer v. Green Day, Inc., 725 F.3d 1170 (9th Cir. 2013) (rock bands' use of artist's illustration in video backdrop was fair use after balancing the factors); Bill Graham Archives v. Dorling Kindersley, Ltd., 448 F.3d 605, 608–09 (2d Cir. 2006) (defendant's use of plaintiff's artistic concept posters in a cultural history of the Grateful Dead was fair use); L.A. News Serv. v. CBS Broad., Inc., 305 F.3d 924 (9th Cir.), *amended and reh'g denied*, 313 F.3d 1093 (9th Cir. 2002) (use of video clip in promotional materials was fair use); Hofheinz v. A&E Television Networks, 146 F. Supp. 2d 442 (S.D.N.Y. 2001), *aff'd*, 2002 U.S. App. LEXIS 13314 (2d Cir. 2002) (use of clips from movie was fair use in biography of actor appearing in movie); Gregerson v. Vilana Fin., Inc., 446 F. Supp. 2d 1053 (D. Minn. 2006) (defendant used plaintiff's photograph *Minneapolis Skyline at Night* from his website in an advertisement for a business directory; court rejected claim of fair use based on argument that the image "was only intended to inform potential customers that Defendants conduct business in both Minneapolis and St. Paul, and they did not try to reproduce, sell, or distribute the photograph"); Warner Bros. Entm't, Inc. v. RDR Books, 575 F. Supp. 2d 513 (S.D.N.Y. 2008) (rejecting fair use of characters and other information in *Lexicon* online encyclopedia based on Harry Potter series); Haberman v. Hustler Magazine, Inc., 626 F. Supp. 201 (D. Mass. 1986) (Hustler's publication of plaintiff's surrealist photographs in its "Bits and Pieces" section, reduced in size and with accompanying text that commented on the images, which included plaintiff's copyright notices, held to be fair use).

124. 817 F. Supp. 370 (S.D.N.Y. 1993).

The court found that the puppy was "virtually an exact reproduction of the 'Odie' character," despite the minor change of the length of the dog's tongue. As to the fair-use analysis, the court found the purpose and character was for sale as "high-priced art, the nature of the 'Odie' character imaginative and not factual, the amount and substantiality met by Koons' use of the character in its entirety, and the effect of the market on the original such that it impacts on the plaintiff's ability to exploit the market for sculptures. The fair-use analysis weighed in the plaintiff's favor. As to parody, as in *Rogers v. Koons*,[125] the parody defense was not established because "the sculpture is, at best, a parody of society at large, rather than a parody of the copyrighted 'Odie' character."

In *Calkins v. Playboy Enterprises International, Inc.*,[126] the plaintiffs owned a photography studio that photographed a future Playboy model when she was a high school senior. Seven years later, Playboy ran one of the senior portraits in an anniversary issue of its magazine without Calkin's permission. The photograph was slightly cropped and used to illustrate the "personal" life of the model. Playboy defended on fair-use grounds. On the first factor, purpose and character of use, the court found it was for commercial purpose, but the use was transformative since it was smaller and served a different purpose than the original, which outweighed the commercial use. On the second factor, nature of the copyrighted work, the court found the work was not previously published and not intended to be published, but it was creative, so this weighed in favor of Calkins. The amount and substantiality of the portion used favored neither, as the entire photo was used, but it was reasonable to do so in the context. Finally, the fourth factor, effect of use on the market, weighed in favor of Playboy since the image had no effect on Calkins's market and, if anything, publicized him. On the whole, therefore, the court found fair use.

125. 960 F.2d 301 (2d Cir.), *cert. denied*, 506 U.S. 974 (1992).
126. 561 F. Supp. 2d 1136 (E.D. Cal. 2008).

### Parody

A subset of the fair use defense is parody.[127] The degree of transformation in the parody relates to the first factor of the purpose and character of the work. The second factor—that is, the nature of the copyrighted work—is less relevant, "since parodies almost invariably copy publicly known, expressive works."[128] The third factor, amount and substantiality of the copying, looks to whether the parodist took only what was necessary to achieve the parody result. Finally, the fourth factor, focused on the potential market value, looks to whether there would be an adverse effect on the potential market of the original. In *Campbell*, the court held that 2 Live Crew's parody of Roy Orbison's *Oh, Pretty Woman* was entitled to fair use as parody, even though it was of a commercial nature, providing all the factors were met; the Court rejected a presumption against parody as fair use based on commercial use.

In *Leibovitz v. Paramount Pictures Corp.*,[129] photographer Annie Leibovitz sold the image of visibly pregnant Demi Moore to *Vanity Fair*, used on its cover. Paramount used a pregnant model photographed against a similar background, with similar lighting and pose, and computer manipulation of body configuration with the face of Leslie Nielsen to promote a *Naked Gun* movie. Leibovitz proved ownership of valid copyright and unauthorized copying (access or direct evidence, and substantial similarity). Citing the Supreme Court's decision in *Campbell*, the court found parody, and therefore fair use, notwithstanding the "commercial nature of Paramount's advertisement."[130]

In *Rogers v. Koons*,[131] discussed earlier in this chapter, the court defined parody or satire to be

> when one artist, for comic effect or social commentary, closely imitates the style of another artist and in so doing creates a new art work

127. Campbell v. Acuff-Rose Music, Inc., 510 U.S. 569 (1994).
128. *Id.* at 586.
129. 137 F.3d 109 (2d Cir. 1998).
130. *Id.* at 110.
131. 960 F.2d 301 (2d Cir.), *cert. denied*, 506 U.S. 974 (1992).

> that makes ridiculous the style and expression of the original. Under our cases parody and satire are valued forms of criticism, encouraged because this sort of criticism itself fosters the creativity protected by the copyright law.[132]

True parody affords greater leeway than otherwise allowed under a substantial similarity analysis, but it still has its limits. The rule is that "though the satire need not be only of the copied work and may . . . also be a parody of modern society, the copied work must be, at least in part, an object of the parody, otherwise there would be no need to conjure up the original work."[133] While the court concluded that Koons's sculpture satirized modern society, it did not parody the photograph itself, and was done in bad faith and purely for profit.[134] Therefore, the first factor for fair use was decided against Koons.

### *Appropriation Art*

The *Prince* case raises the issue of "appropriation art." For a general discussion, see the article on the Museum of Modern Art website.[135] Perhaps one of the most famous examples is the *Campbell's Soup Can* by Andy Warhol.

An interesting (if, at least to me, baffling) take on this issue is the work of Sherrie Levine. In an exhibit at the Metropolitan Museum of Art in New York, and as part of the museum's collection,[136] is a photograph of Allie Mae Burroughs. Like *Migrant Mother*, this is another iconic image of the Depression, and was made by Walker Evans. According to the description provided by the museum, a group of photographers "began using photography to reexamine the strategies and codes of representation." Levine in 1981 "photographed reproductions of Depression-era photographs of Walker Evans." The description calls the series "a landmark of postmod-

132. *Id.* at 309–10.
133. *Id.* at 310.
134. *Id.* at 310.
135. *Appropriation*, Museum of Modern Art, http://www.moma.org/learn/moma_learning/themes/pop-art/appropriation (last visited Jan. 25, 2014).
136. http://www.metmuseum.org/Collections/search-the-collections/190019034 (last visited April 18, 2014).

ernism. . . . Far from a high-concept cheap shot, Levine's works from this series tell the story of our perpetually dashed hopes to create meaning, the inability to recapture the past, and our own lost illusions." Levine was not passing this off as her own. Assuming, though, that the image were not in the public domain or otherwise covered by copyright, would a photographer be able to photograph the photograph and simply call it *After*? Should she be? At what point does this cease to be art and simply an example of the Emperor's New Clothes?

## Other Exceptions to Exclusive Rights

In addition to the defenses to copyright discussed, including fair use in § 107, there are certain statutory limitations on exclusive rights contained with §§ 107 through 122. Of potential relevance to photographers are § 108, which permits libraries and archives to make or distribute one limited copy; § 110, exempting from infringement certain performances or displays, such as in face-to-face classroom-type situations based on lawful copies; and § 113, exempting useful articles from the scope of protected rights.

However, § 113 provides that a photographer holding a copyright in a photograph has the exclusive right to reproduce it "in or on any kind of article, whether useful or otherwise," but does not afford any greater or lesser rights to the "making, distribution, or display of the useful article" that is the subject of the photograph than otherwise afforded by law, and the copyright does not preclude use of the photograph on the useful article as part of advertisements or commentaries. Section 113 further addresses situations where a work of visual art is incorporated or made part of a building, and procedures for its removal under certain circumstances.

## Web Issues

In *Kelly v. Arriba Soft Corp.*,[137] the court sustained the right of Arriba to maintain a search engine database of thumbnail images of pictures from other websites. The court held that "[t]he creation and use of the thumbnails

137. 336 F.3d 811 (9th Cir. 2001).

in the search engine is a fair use.[138] Secondary liability exists when "[o]ne infringes contributorily by intentionally inducing or encouraging direct infringement, and infringes vicariously by profiting from direct infringement while declining to exercise a right to stop or limit it."[139]

Similarly, Google's use of cached copies of Web pages to facilitate its searching functions is transformative fair use.[140]

## Joint Authorship

The Copyright Act provides for joint ownership and defines a joint work as "a work prepared by two or more authors with the intention that their contributions be merged into inseparable or interdependent parts of a unitary whole."[141] One joint author cannot sue the other joint author since the copyright is deemed unified and inseparable.[142] It is a question intention and whether the two or more alleged joint authors "entertain[ed] in their minds the concept of joint authorship, whether or not they understood precisely the legal consequences of their relationship."[143]

## Collective Works

According to 17 U.S.C. § 201(c):

> Copyright in each separate contribution to a collective work is distinct from copyright in the collective work as a whole, and vests initially in the author of the contribution. In the absence of an express transfer of the copyright or of any rights under it, the owner of copyright in the collective work is presumed to have acquired only the privilege of reproducing and distributing the contribution as part of that

138. *See also* Perfect 10, Inc. v. Amazon.com, Inc., 508 F.3d 1146 (9th Cir. 2007) (Google's thumbnail versions of plaintiff's images was fair use so as to not constitute direct infringement, but held that Google might be liable for secondary infringement based on its in-line linking to infringing full-size images).

139. Metro-Goldwyn-Mayer Studios Inc. v. Grokster, Ltd., 545 U.S. 913, 930 (2005) (internal citations omitted).

140. Field v. Google, Inc., 412 F. Supp. 2d 1106 (D. Nev. 2006).

141. 17 U.S.C. § 101.

142. Childress v. Taylor, 945 F.2d 500, 505 (2d Cir. 1991).

143. *Id.* at 508.

> particular collective work, any revision of that collective work, and any later collective work in the same series.

Note, also, that when a photographer contributes photographs as part of a collective work, the copyright in the individual photograph is distinct from and does not include copyright ownership of the entire collected work.

In *New York Times v. Tasini*,[144] the Supreme Court held that freelance authors held rights to their articles such that use by the New York Times Company in computer databases violated their copyrights. The New York Times had relied on "the privilege" in § 201(c) of "reproducing and distributing," but the Court rejected that on the grounds that "the databases reproduce and distribute articles standing alone and not in context" were not part of the collective work to which the author has contributed.[145]

*Tasini* governed the photographer's claim in *Greenberg v. National Geographic Society*.[146] Greenberg had photographs published in *National Geographic Magazine*. He objected to *National Geographic*'s reproduction of his images that had been in bound volumes, microfiche, and microfilm for back issues in a 30-disc CD-ROM titled *The Complete National Geographic*. The trial court found § 201(c)'s privilege applied and dismissed the complaint. Applying *Tasini*, the court nonetheless found that even though the Complete National Geographic was in a different medium, the photographs were "preserved intact . . . and can only be viewed as part of the original collective works in which they appeared."[147] The court expressed the *Tasini* holding to be based on "contextual fidelity to the original print publication as presented to, and perceivable by, the users of the revised version of the original publication."[148] The Second Circuit had come to the same conclusion in *Faulkner v. National Geographic Enterprises, Inc.*,[149] although it held that as to seven particular photographs, contractual provisions that

144. 533 U.S. 483 (2001).
145. *Id.* at 489.
146. 533 F.3d 1244 (11th Cir.), *cert. denied*, 555 U.S. 1070 (11th Cir. 2008).
147. *Id.* at 1258.
148. *Id.*
149. 409 F.3d 26 (2d Cir.), *cert. denied*, 546 U.S. 1076 (2005).

preserved electronic rights for the photographers governed the outcome in those cases.

## First Sale Doctrine

Section 109 embodies the "first sale" doctrine, which means that anyone buying a copyrighted work from the copyright holder has the right to resell that particular copy of the work. It does not protect sales of unauthorized reproductions of the purchased copy.

Holders of registered copyrights have the ability to utilize the services of U.S. Customs and Border Protection. Once registration occurs, holders can access the e-Recordation application for Customs at https://apps.cbp.gov/e-recordatons/. Infringing goods can be stopped at the border. In essence, so-called pirated copies that are identical or substantially identical to registered copyrighted works can be seized. Consequently, Section 106(3) gives the copyright holder the exclusive right to distribute copies of the copyrighted item, and Section 602(a) allows the prevention of the unauthorized importation of copies.

What about the first sale doctrine in Section 109? If the work is sold overseas, does the first sale doctrine render the sale legitimate and allow importation of the copy, even if the copyright holder objects? Since *Bobbs-Merrill Co. v. Straus,*[150] the Supreme Court endorsed the first sale doctrine and permitted resale of discounted books, holding that the distribution or right to "vend" applied only to the first sale of the particular item of the copyrighted work. This was codified in 17 U.S.C. § 109.

In *Quality King Distributors, Inc. v. L'Anza Research International, Inc.,*[151] the Supreme Court applied the doctrine to works sold overseas. In *Quality King,* L'Anza made shampoos and hair care products, with copyrighted labels. It sold to domestic distributors under restriction and in foreign markets through foreign distributors. All items are manufactured in the United States. The goods at issue were apparently sold outside normal or contractually authorized distribution channels and resold in the United

150. 210 U.S. 339 (1908).
151. 523 U.S. 135 (1998).

States. Such "gray market" goods are not counterfeit and are legitimate, but sold in breach of contractual territorial or other restrictions. Two principal defenses are copyright and trademark infringement allegations; in this case, copyright infringement was alleged. The Supreme Court reversed both the district and appellate courts and held that the first sale doctrine applied. In *Kirtsaeng v. John Wiley & Sons, Inc.*,[152] the Court expanded *Quality King* and applied the first sale doctrine to copies of the copyrighted work lawfully made abroad, and not simply those made in the United States and sent abroad. It rejected a reading of the phrase "lawfully made under this title" to be restricted to works made in the United States, and applied the "first sale" doctrine to copies of copyrighted items lawfully made outside the United States.[153]

In *Quality King*, the Court noted the difference between statutory and contractual rights. It is important to understand this—there may still be contractual remedies against distributors who violate their contracts, but the ability to rely on copyright law and claims of infringement to preclude importation is something else.

Of relevance to photographers is that unlike *Quality King*, the products expressly at issue in *Kirtsaeng* were books. John Wiley & Sons specifically included language in each of its Asian-produced books that exportation out of specified foreign territories without the publisher's permission was a violation of its rights. Kirtsaeng was a Thai citizen who studied in the United States and had asked family and friends in Thailand to buy the John Wiley books he needed and send them to him. When done, Kirtsaeng agreed to sell the books, reimburse his family, and retain any profit.

A photographer may sell a print to someone; that person has the right under the first sale doctrine to sell the physical photograph to someone else.

152. 133 S. Ct. 1351 (2013).

153. *See also* AFL Telecomms. LLC v. Surpluseq.com Inc., 946 F. Supp. 2d 928, 943 (D. Ariz. 2013) (citing both *Quality King* and *Kirtsaeng*, the court held plaintiffs did not have valid copyright infringement claims since "SurplusEQ sold Fujikura splicers that were manufactured and first sold outside the United States. Fujikura's authorization of that initial foreign sale triggered the first sale doctrine, which qualified its otherwise 'exclusive rights' 'to distribute copies . . . of [a] copyrighted work.' 17 U.S.C. § 106(3). All subsequent owners of those Fujikura splicers, including SurplusEQ, were 'entitled, without the authority of the copyright owner, to sell or otherwise dispose of the possession of that copy[.]' *Id.* § 109(a).")

The same principles apply to a foreign print or a book of photographs. After the first sale of the actual physical copy, that physical copy can be resold without infringement.

### Government and Copyright

Under 17 U.S.C. § 105, "Copyright protection under this title is not available for any work of the United States Government, but the United States Government is not precluded from receiving and holding copyrights transferred to it by assignment, bequest, or otherwise." Section 101 defines a "work of the United States Government" as "a work prepared by an officer or employee of the United States Government as part of that person's official duties."

### Sovereign Immunity

Sovereign immunity is a doctrine that prevents suit against governments, whether state, national, or foreign, unless authorized by statute. Principles of sovereign immunity affect the ability of a photographer to sue a government. In *Ingrassia v. Chicken Ranch Bingo and Casino*,[154] the plaintiffs produced images that appeared on souvenirs; eventually the plaintiffs learned that the purchasers—including a Native American tribe—were later selling allegedly infringing items without permission and sued for copyright infringement. The suit was barred against the tribe since there had been no express consent to be sued.

Prior to 1990, three circuit courts of appeal refused to find that the Copyright Act abrogates 11th Amendment immunity to the states from suit under that act.[155]

In *Richard Anderson Photography v. Brown*,[156] the court held that the Copyright Act did not abrogate sovereign immunity of states and did not find any "constructive consent" or "implied waiver." In this case, the pho-

154. 676 F. Supp. 2d 953 (E.D. Cal. 2009).

155. *See* BV Eng'g v. Univ. of Cal., 858 F.2d 1394 (9th Cir. 1988), *cert. denied*, 489 U.S. 1090 (1989); Richard Anderson Photography v. Brown, 852 F.2d 114 (4th Cir. 1988), *cert. denied*, 489 U.S. 1033 (1989)); Lane v. First Nat'l Bank of Bos., 871 F.2d 166 (1st Cir. 1989).

156. 852 F.2d 114 (4th Cir. 1988).

tographer was hired to produce photographs for a student prospectus for a university. He later learned of unauthorized use of his images and sued the school's director of public information and relations individually, as well as the university and others. Brown argued her conduct was in her official capacity; plaintiff argued that since it was illegal, it could not have been within her authority. When a claim for money damages against a state official can be paid by the individual independent of her state official status without consequences to the state's treasury, it is not immune.[157] The court stated:

> The mere fact that her conduct was undertaken in the course of her state employment does not of course relieve her of individual liability, even if her employer could not be sued for it. A state may no more than an individual principal give its agent authority to commit torts without civil recourse.[158]

In 1990, the Copyright Remedy Clarification Act added § 511 to the statute, which now makes clear that states, and officers acting in official capacity, are not immune under the 11th Amendment or "any other doctrine of sovereign immunity," from copyright claims.

Under 28 U.S.C. § 1498(b), sovereign immunity against the United States is waived for copyright claims, subject to certain conditions. The United States, and its contractors acting for the federal government, may be sued for copyright infringement. A government employee may also sue *except* where he or she "was in a position to order, influence, or induce use of the copyrighted work by the Government." In addition there is no right of action

> on any copyright owner or any assignee of such owner with respect to any copyrighted work prepared by a person while in the employment or service of the United States, where the copyrighted work was prepared as a part of the official functions of the employee, or in the preparation of which Government time, material, or facilities were used.[159]

157. *Id.* at 122.

158. *Id.* (citing Larson v. Domestic & Foreign Commerce Corp., 337 U.S. 682, 694 n.15 (1948)).

159. 28 U.S.C. § 1498(b).

No action may be maintained as well where government time, material or facilities were utilized.[160]

Copyright infringement by the United States or such suits must be brought in the Court of Federal Claims. The federal government is immune from copyright claims unless it has expressly waived that immunity, and any such claims against the federal government must be brought in the Court of Federal Claims.[161]

In *Gaylord v. United States*,[162] the sculptor who created *The Column* war memorial succeeded in his copyright suit against the United States' use of an image of *The Column* on a postage stamp without permission, rejecting a fair-use defense.

## Remedies

Copyright remedies are statutory and are only available if found within the statute.[163] These are injunctive relief against infringement (§ 502), impoundment and disposition of infringing articles (§ 503), either actual damages and the infringer's additional profits *or* statutory damages of between $750 to $30,000 (§ 504), and in the case of proven willful infringement, statutory damages up to $150,000 (§ 504). Attorneys' fees and costs are also recoverable (§ 505). Attorneys' fees and costs are not automatic but within the court's discretion, based on the level of frivolousness on the part of the losing party, motivation, objective unreasonableness of the behavior, and deterrent effect.[164] Baker had prevailed in the liability portion of the case, based on photographs he took and published in a book and that were later used by defendant without authorization as the picture insert in frames for sale.[165]

Actual damages may be proved by showing "lost sales, lost opportunities to license, or diminution in the value of the copyright," and when those

160. Blueport Co., LLC v. United States, 533 F.3d 1374 (Fed. Cir. 2008), *cert. denied*, 555 U.S. 1153 (2009).

161. O'Rourke v. Smithsonian Inst. Press, 296 F. Supp. 2d 434, 436 (S.D.N.Y. 2003), *aff'd*, 399 F.3d 113 (2d Cir.), *cert. denied*, 546 U.S. 814 (2005).

162. 595 F.3d 1364, 1381 (Fed. Cir. 2010).

163. Sony Corp. of Am. v. Universal City Studios, Inc., 464 U.S. 417 (1984).

164. Baker v. Urban Outfitters, Inc., 431 F. Supp. 2d 351 (S.D.N.Y. 2006), *aff'd*, 249 F. App'x 845 (2d Cir. 2007).

165. *See* Baker v. Urban Outfitters, Inc., 254 F. Supp. 2d 346 (S.D.N.Y. 2003).

cannot be established, by "the fair market value of a license covering the defendant's use," based on a hypothetical arm's-length negotiation.[166]

Criminal offenses are also provided in § 506 for willful infringement of copyright if the infringement was committed:

> (A) for purposes of commercial advantage or private financial gain;
> (B) by the reproduction or distribution, including by electronic means, during any 180-day period, of 1 or more copies or phonorecords of 1 or more copyrighted works, which have a total retail value of more than $1,000; or
> (C) by the distribution of a work being prepared for commercial distribution, by making it available on a computer network accessible to members of the public, if such person knew or should have known that the work was intended for commercial distribution.[167]

Certain other remedies exist for alteration of programming by cable systems.[168]

The statute of limitations for civil copyright infringement actions is five years after the cause of action accrued.

## Digital Millennium Copyright Act

The Digital Millennium Copyright Act (DMCA) has several sections incorporated into Title 17, the Copyright Act, that are relevant to photographers. Section 1202 precludes anyone, without permission of the copyright holder, from intentionally removing or altering "copyright management information" or distributing works knowing that such has occurred. "Copyright management information" is defined in the statute as the copyright owner's or author's name "and other identifying information about either." Upon violation of the statute, the photographer can obtain actual damages and additional profits, or statutory damages per violation of between $2,500

166. Gaylord v. United States, 678 F.3d 1339, 1343 (Fed. Cir. 2012) (internal citations and quotations omitted).
167. 17 U.S.C. § 506.
168. 17 U.S.C. § 510.

and $25,000. The photographer does not have to register the photograph in advance, as is a necessary predicate for an infringement action, to bring an action under the DMCA.

Other provisions of the DMCA contain prohibitions on circumvention of technology controlling access to protected works. The On-Line Copyright Infringement Liability Limitation Act contained a provision that is now codified as part of the DMCA at 17 U.S.C. § 512 that provides immunity for Internet service providers (ISPs) provided someone other than the ISP initiated the material, transmission is carried out automatically and without input by the ISP, the ISP does not select the material's recipients, no copy is maintained by the ISP that is ordinarily accessible to anyone other than anticipated recipients and maintained only for a reasonable period for such transmission, and the material is transmitted without modification. The ISP is also not liable for temporarily cached items under certain conditions. Those who claim infringement can notify the ISP under § 512, and there are safe harbors for the ISP to remove the material based on the information received and its satisfaction of statutory criteria.

The DMCA also provides a statutory mechanism for issuance of a subpoena to obtain identification of the alleged infringer. In *Recording Industry Association of America, Inc. v. Verizon Internet Services, Inc.*,[169] a subpoena by the plaintiff seeking the identity of copyright infringers served on the ISP was quashed; § 512 was held to authorize a subpoena "only to an ISP engaged in storing on its servers material that is infringing or the subject of infringing activity" and not regardless of whether or not it acts as a conduit.[170]

Note that the rights under the DMCA belong to the copyright owner and not the subject of the photograph, so the individual cannot necessarily utilize the DMCA procedures. Other remedies, as discussed below, are available.

169. 351 F.3d 1229 (D.C. Cir. 2003).
170. *Id.* at 1233.

## Plagiarism

Plagiarism is the taking of someone else's ideas or means of expression and passing them off as your own work. It can rise to the level of fraud. It is not the same as copyright infringement, which is more specific to its statutory roots, and renders one liable for copying another's copyrighted work without permission. Copyright also does not protect ideas, only the expression of them. Copyright, as noted above, has specific elements. Plagiarism is commonly defined in the academic context, where definitions may vary. For example, in *Seitz-Partridge v. Loyola University of Chicago*,[171] plagiarism was defined in Loyola's student handbook as

> the appropriation of gain of ideas, language or work of another without sufficient public acknowledgment that the material is not one's own. The following acts are regarded as such violations:
> — Submitting another person's unpublished work or examination as one's own;
> — Submitting a rewritten or paraphrased version of another person's work.

In *Mehta v. Ohio University*,[172] the court noted a definition as provided by an expert witness, a writing director at Rochester Institute of Technology, who "defined plagiarism as the deliberate use of someone else's ideas expressed as one's own without proper attribution. According to Dr. Scanlon, plagiarism requires a finding of an attempt to deceive the reader by not directing the reader to the original source."

Suppose someone discovered a little known 19th-century novel and passed it off today as his or her own. The novel, in the public domain, would not permit a copyright infringement suit, but would constitute plagiarism. Similarly, an idea itself cannot be copyrighted, but passing off someone else's idea as one's own could be plagiarism. In photography, if one took an anonymous photograph from the 19th century and claimed

171. 2013 Ill. App. (1st) 113409 (2013) at p 24, appeal denied, 2013 Ill. LEXIS 801 (Ill. May 29, 2013).

172. 2012 Ohio 3677, *aff'd*, 2012 Ohio 6201 (2012).

it was one's own, that would be plagiarism, even if not legally constituting copyright infringement.

Outside of the academic context, it is not clear that plagiarism provides a cause of action. As a violation of university policy, it may be relevant to claims of discipline regarding faculty or students. As a separate legal cause of action, its viability is limited. To the extent that the facts present a copyright claim, an attempt to circumvent those proofs by claiming "conversion" or plagiarism is like to fail as preempted by copyright law.[173] Generally speaking, most prior state law remedies for plagiarism have been deemed preempted, although at least in California, one may seek to bring an action based on implied in fact contract where there is a claim for theft of literary or artistic ideas.[174] *Benay v. Warner Brothers Entertainment, Inc.* added that "[s]imilar to the inference of copying in copyright law, California contract law permits actual use of a plaintiff's idea to be inferred from evidence of access and similarity."[175]

The Supreme Court has declined to read a plagiarism cause of action into Section 43(a) of the Lanham Act—that is, it did not recognize a cause of action as a matter of trademark law for plagiarism for "the use of otherwise unprotected works and inventions without attribution."[176]

## Internet Search Engines

Another common issue that arises is the use of someone else's image as a thumbnail. The maintenance of thumbnail images of another's photographs posted on the Internet, for use in search engines, has been held fair use and not an infringement of the photographer's copyright.[177]

173. U.S. *ex rel.* Berge v. Bd. of Trustees of Univ. of Alabama, 104 F. 3d 1453, 1464 (4th Cir.) *cert. denied*, 522 U.S. 916 (1997).

174. Benay v. Warner Bros. Entm't, Inc., 607 F. 3d 620, 629 (9th Cir. 2010).

175. *Id.* at 630.

176. Dastar Corp. v. Twentieth Century Fox Film Corp., 539 U.S. 23, 36 (2003); *see also* Andela v. Univ. of Miami, 692 F. Supp. 2d 1356, 1376 (S.D. Fla.) *aff'd in part app. dismissed in part,* 461 Fed. Appt 832 (11th Cir. 2010) (unpublished).

177. Kelly v. Arriba Soft Corp., 336 F.3d 811 (9th Cir. 2003); *see also* Perfect 10, Inc. v. Amazon.com, Inc., 508 F.3d 1146 (9th Cir. 2007).

## Architectural Works

An architect can obtain copyright protection in blueprints. However, that copyright protection will not preclude a photographer from taking pictures of the building:

> 17 U.S.C. § 120. Scope of exclusive rights in architectural works
> (a) Pictorial Representations Permitted.—The copyright in an architectural work that has been constructed does not include the right to prevent the making, distributing, or public display of pictures, paintings, photographs, or other pictorial representations of the work, if the building in which the work is embodied is located in or ordinarily visible from a public place.

An architectural work is defined in 17 U.S.C. § 101 as "the design of a building as embodied in any tangible medium of expression" and "includes the overall form as well as the arrangement and composition of spaces and elements in the design, but does not include individual standard features."

The Manhattan Bridge.

Copyright Circular 41 defines a building as an intended permanent and stationary structure "habitable by humans."[178] For post–December 1, 1990 architectural works, copyright protection lasts the lesser of 95 years from date of publication of the work or 120 years after creation of the work. Under 17 U.S.C. § 102(a)(8), added in 1990, specifically includes "architectural works" as copyrightable subject matter.

The Flatiron Building, NYC.

The Code of Federal Regulations amplifies and states "[t]he term building means humanly habitable structures that are intended to be both permanent

178. http://www.copyright.gov/circs/circ41.pdf (last visited April 18, 2014).

and stationary, such as houses and office buildings, and other permanent and stationary structures designed for human occupancy, including but not limited to churches, museums, gazebos, and garden pavilions."[179] However, works excluded and which cannot be registered are "[s]tructures other than buildings, "that is, "[s]tructures other than buildings, such as bridges, cloverleafs, dams, walkways, tents, recreational vehicles, mobile homes, and boats."[180] In addition, standard features that are "[s]tandard configurations of spaces, and individual standard features, such as windows, doors, and other staple building components" also cannot be registered.[181]

So I can take a picture of the Manhattan Bridge.

I am also entitled to make this image of the Flatiron Building in New York.

In *Tiffany Design, Inc. v. Reno-Tahoe Specialty, Inc.*,[182] the plaintiff hired a photographer to take aerial photographs of the Las Vegas Strip. Using image-processing software, the photographer made an artistic image of the strip that altered the size of certain buildings and colors and added illumination. The image was sold as posters and the plaintiff and the photographer documented the conveyance of any of the photographer's rights to Tiffany. Defendant Reno-Tahoe created its own photographic image, though that product utilized certain scanned buildings from the Tiffany image. Tiffany sued for infringement. In addressing the predicate issue of whether the plaintiff's copyright was valid, the defendant argued that under § 120, scanning and manipulation of the six buildings was not actionable since these were pictorial representations of buildings. The court rejected this, holding that "while an architect may not prevent a photographer from producing pictures of her buildings . . . that photographer may in turn certainly copyright those pictures."[183]

As long as structures can be considered part of an architectural work, even if they have independent artistic elements, they may be covered by § 120.[184] On the other hand, statues were held to be not architectural works under

179. C.F.R. § 202.11(b)(2).
180. C.F.R. § 202.11(d)(1).
181. C.F.R. § 202.11(d)(2).
182. 55 F. Supp. 2d 1113 (D. Nev. 1999).
183. *Id.* at 1119 (citations omitted).
184. Leicester v. Warner Bros., 232 F.3d 1212 (9th Cir. 2000).

§ 120.[185] It is irrelevant whether the copyright holder has a copyright in either the actual building or the technical drawings; a photograph of that structure is still exempt under § 120.[186]

In *Robinson v. HSBC Bank USA*,[187] the plaintiffs sued a bank that used a photograph of the plaintiffs' distinctive Victorian-style houses in an advertising brochure. By the photo appeared the caption "A Mortgage to Match Your Ambitions. Wherever the World Takes You." The plaintiffs complained that their neighbors and others had formed certain opinions as to the plaintiffs' economic circumstances and banking relationships. Among a variety of theories in the case, the court held that the Copyright Act did not prevent other common-law claims, such as misappropriation (discussed in Chapter 3), meaning that the federal copyright law was not meant to preclude state-court claims, such as use of the photograph of a building, inasmuch as the plaintiffs could not have asserted a copyright claim based on the photograph of the building.

There are other issues concerning photographs of buildings relating to proprietary and privacy rights, which are addressed later.

### Mannequins and Dolls

In *Ty, Inc. v. Publications International, Ltd.*,[188] a publisher published photographs of Beanie Babies in books geared toward fans and collectors. Conceding the photographs were derivative works, the publisher nonetheless claimed they were fair use. The Seventh Circuit agreed that at least some of the books might meet that defense and reversed. It preferred to speak of "complementary" and "substitutional" copying as opposed to the "transformative" and "superseding" language used by the Supreme Court in *Campbell*.[189]

185. Gaylord v. United States, 595 F.3d 1364 (Fed. Cir. 2010) (holding that *The Column*, a series of sculptures of Korean War soldiers on the Washington Mall, were not architectural works such that would permit photographs of them).

186. Builders Mut. Ins. Co. v. Donald A. Gardner Architects, Inc., 856 F. Supp. 2d 773 (D.S.C. 2012).

187. 732 F. Supp. 2d 976 (N.D. Cal. 2010).

188. 292 F.3d 512 (7th Cir. 2002).

189. *Id.* at 518.

In a 2–1 decision, the majority held in *Carol Barnhart, Inc. v. Economy Cover Corp.* that the "plaintiff's mannequins of partial human torsos used to display articles of clothing are utilitarian articles not containing separable works of art, and thus are not copyrightable." [190] On the other hand, the Second Circuit distinguished taxidermy mannequins that mount animal skins, and that they had certain utilitarian function was not enough to deny protection.[191] That level of detail and creativity as a separable element from utilitarian elements led the court in *Pivot Point International, Inc. v. Charlene Products, Inc.*,[192] in its own 2–1 decision, to afford copyright protection to mannequin heads, slip-on faces, and hair pieces. The dissent was unpersuaded and the court found the mannequin in this case not copyrightable.[193] Not all courts, though, follow the *Pivot Point* test, and at least one has noted there are "at least six distinct variations" of the "conceptual separability test" seeking to determine if the usefulness of an article can be separated from its artistic elements.[194] You need to understand, first, that copyright will not protect utilitarian components but that there is not necessarily unanimity of the approach of courts in attempting to resolve that issue.

However, this is not to say that a photograph of someone else's copyrighted mannequin would be dispositive as to infringement. There remains fair use, and if the image were part of another use that embodied creative effort, as in the Koons painting, it would seem to provide a defense. How a particular court would deal with it is another matter.

190. 773 F.2d 411, 412 (2d Cir. 1985).

191. Hart v. Dan Chase Taxidermy Supply Co., Inc., 86 F.3d 320 (2d Cir. 1996); *see also* Superior Form Builders, Inc. v. Dan Chase Taxidermy Supply Co., Inc., 74 F.3d 488 (4th Cir.), *cert. denied*, 519 U.S. 809 (1996).

192. 372 F.3d 913 (7th Cir. 2004), *reh'g, en banc, denied*, 2004 U.S. App. LEXIS 16553 (7th Cir. Aug. 10, 2004).

193. *Id.* at 932.

194. Galiano v. Harrah's Operating Co., Inc., 416 F. 3d 411, 417–18 (5th Cir. 2005).

## Moral Rights

VARA (the Visual Artists Rights Act) protects the integrity of an artist's work and applies to photographers. It is embodied in section 106A of the Copyright Act, 17 U.S.C. § 106A:

> § 106A. Rights of certain authors to attribution and integrity
>
> (a) RIGHTS OF ATTRIBUTION AND INTEGRITY.—Subject to section 107 [fair use] and independent of the exclusive rights provided in section 106, the author of a work of visual art—
>
> (1) shall have the right—
>
> (A) to claim authorship of that work, and
>
> (B) to prevent the use of his or her name as the author of any work of visual art which he or she did not create;
>
> (2) shall have the right to prevent the use of his or her name as the author of the work of visual art in the event of a distortion, mutilation, or other modification of the work which would be prejudicial to his or her honor or reputation; and
>
> (3) subject to the limitations set forth in section 113(d), shall have the right—
>
> (A) to prevent any intentional distortion, mutilation, or other modification of that work which would be prejudicial to his or her honor or reputation, and any intentional distortion, mutilation, or modification of that work is a violation of that right, and
>
> (B) to prevent any destruction of a work of recognized stature, and any intentional or grossly negligent destruction of that work is a violation of that right.

Certain state statutes may provide alternative relief, though copyright law is generally preemptive where its law is meant to cover the field. So while no one can draw mustaches on your physical photographic portrait, this will not necessarily prevent them from making a copy and engaging in parody.

In *Lilley v. Stout*,[195] the photographer plaintiff claimed, among other theories, that his moral rights under VARA had been violated when the defendant took six of his photographs and incorporated them without attribution into another artwork. The two had collaborated, in which the defendant was to have used the photographs as the basis for paintings. Instead, she incorporated the images into the artwork. The photographer was unsuccessful because, although his photographs met the definition of "still photographic image," he failed to prove an intent to produce the photographs for exhibition purposes only. That intent is determined not at the moment the photograph is taken but when the work was "produced"—that is, when the print is made. In this case, the primary purpose was to assist his artist friend. Other relevant factors included "plaintiff's acts of reviewing the photographs with defendant and turning over possession to her. It is difficult to conceive how plaintiff could have exhibited these prints once they were incorporated into" the final product of defendant.[196]

In *Berrios Nogueras v. Home Depot*,[197] plaintiff claimed violation of VARA when Home Depot used a poster of his in promotional brochures without attribution of authorship, and that his right of integrity was violated by reproduction of his artwork without his "knowledge, compensation or consent."[198] The court denied relief, finding that "VARA does not afford a right of action to plaintiff for the unauthorized reproduction of his work upon the 'posters' or 'shoppers' i.e. 'advertising or promotional material' that were printed or published by defendants in their stores."[199]

Note, though, that VARA will not apply to work that is "embodied" in the architectural work under 17 U.S.C. § 120(b), and the owner of the building does not need consent of the copyright holder before making alterations to the building or even destroying it. VARA also has a "public presentation" exception that states "[t]he modification of a work of visual art which is the result of conservation, or of the public presentation, including lighting

195. 384 F. Supp. 2d 83 (D.D.C. 2005).
196. *Id.* at 88.
197. 330 F. Supp. 2d 48 (D.P.R. 2004).
198. *Id.* at 49.
199. *Id.* at 51.

and placement, of the work is not a destruction, distortion, mutilation, or other modification described in subsection (a)(3) unless the modification is caused by gross negligence."[200]

Certain states may also have statutes that impact on the integrity of an artwork, particularly regarding "site specific" work.[201] In *Phillips v. Pembroke Real Estate, Inc.*,[202] plaintiff sought injunctive relief under both VARA and the Massachusetts Art Preservation Act (MAPA)[203] in federal court. The plaintiff sculptor had contracted with defendant for sculptures to be placed in a public park; after completion, defendant needed to alter the par and, based on a new landscape design, needed to remove and relocate the plaintiff's work, which plaintiff opposed. After the district court initially enjoined the removal, it certified the question to the state court to construe the Massachusetts statute. The Massachussetts Supreme Court held that MAPA did not protect placement of site-specific art. It concluded that the prohibitions against "any physical defacement, mutilation, alteration, or destruction of a work of fine art" did not include or extend to "conceptual destruction."[204] It found that the legislature was also concerned with property owners' rights, and that to find a legislative intent to include this type of site-specific art would dramatically affect landowners. Consequently, it would not infer legislative intent to so extend MAPA. The district court then applied VARA to the work but found applicable the public presentation exception, refusing plaintiff's request for an injunction. Following the certification of the question and its answer by the Massachusetts Supreme Court, the district court vacated its previous injunction and permitted removal. On appeal, the First Circuit held that VARA does not apply to site-specific art (disagreeing with the District Court on that issue) but otherwise affirming its decision allowing defendant to remove the plaintiff's work from the park.[205]

---

200. 17 U.S.C. § 106A(c)(2).

201. *See, e.g.*, N.Y. Arts & Cult. Aff. § 14.03: Artists Authorship Rights.

202. 288 F. Supp. 2d 89 (D. Mass. 2003).

203. Mass. Gen. Laws ch. 231, § 85S (1984).

204. Phillips v. Pembroke Real Estate, Inc., 443 Mass. 110, 115–116 (2004).

205. Phillips v. Pembroke Real Estate, Inc., 459 F.3d 128, 129 (1st Cir. 2006) ("Although we disagree with the district court's reasoning (we hold that VARA does not apply to site-specific art at all), we affirm the decision of the district court permitting Pembroke to remove Phillips' works from the Park").

## Work for Hire

If the photographer is employed by someone or a legal entity, then it is deemed "work for hire" and owned by the employer, unless the parties agree otherwise in writing.[206] Otherwise, the initial ownership of the copyright vests in the photographer.[207]

The test for determining if a work is a work prepared by an employee in the initial instance was laid out by the Supreme Court in *Community for Creative Non-Violence v. Reid* [208]:

> In determining whether a hired party is an employee under the general common law of agency, we consider the hiring party's right to control the manner and means by which the product is accomplished. Among the other factors relevant to this inquiry are the skill required; the source of the instrumentalities and tools; the location of the work; the duration of the relationship between the parties; whether the hiring party has the right to assign additional projects to the hired party; the extent of the hired party's discretion over when and how long to work; the method of payment; the hired party's role in hiring and paying assistants; whether the work is part of the regular business of the hiring party; whether the hiring party is in business; the provision of employee benefits; and the tax treatment of the hired party."

If there is an independent contractor and the facts of the relationship do not otherwise fit certain statutory definitions, then the work is not work for hire unless agreed otherwise in writing. The duration of work for hire is shorter of 95 years from publication or 120 years from creation.

In *Aymes v. Bonelli*,[209] the Second Circuit adopted five of the thirteen *Reid* factors as most important, noting that each of the other eight factors may have more or less importance depending upon the subject matter and the case. The five essential factors to be considered, per the *Aymes* court

206. 17 U.S.C. § 201(b).
207. 17 U.S.C. § 201(a).
208. 490 U.S. 730, 739–40 (1989).
209. 980 F.2d 857, 860–64 (2d Cir. 1992).

are "(1) the hiring party's right to control the manner and means of creation; (2) the skill required; (3) the provision of employee benefits; (4) the tax treatment of the hired party; and (5) whether the hiring party has the right to assign additional projects to the hired party."[210]

In *Carter v. Helmsley-Spear, Inc.*,[211] a tenant had commissioned the plaintiffs' artwork to be in the lobby of a commercial building. Although there were separate elements, each (with some exceptions) built upon the others and was deemed an integrated, single work of art. That there were "applied art" elements was not enough to remove them from the definition of protected visual art. On appeal, though, the court reversed on the issue of work for hire. Applying the *Reid* test, noted above, the court found that the work was made for hire and therefore vacated the injunction against alternation of artwork.

The contract negotiated between the photographer and the owner therefore has significance.[212]

## Putting It in Perspective

The photographer is concerned with copyright as both sword and shield. The sword is the copyright protections the photographer wants to assert in his or her own photographs. The ability to maintain copyright in a photograph will depend to a certain extent on the subject matter and the originality of the image; as noted, the standard is relatively low. The shield is the photographer's ability to claim fair use or otherwise defend against claims of infringement against him or her in the initial instance. While general principles are easily stated, the extent of copyright litigation and fact-sensitivity makes it difficult to offer dispositive legal advice in any particular situation.

210. *Id.* at 861.
211. 71 F.3d 77 (2d Cir. 1995), *cert. denied*, 517 U.S. 1208 (1996).
212. *See* Serra v. U.S. Gen. Servs. Admin., 847 F.2d 1045 (2d Cir. 1988).

# Trademark

## Overview

A trademark (for goods) and a service mark (for services) is a brand identifier. Its purpose is to identify source, even if that source is unknown. For example, whether or not you know the actual company that owns a brand name, you recognize a brand name and associate it with a certain level of quality or product. Trademarks are covered by federal law, under the Lanham Act,[213] but not exclusively, as copyrights or patents. States also have trademark statutes, and the right to a name or mark is also a common-law right. Trademarks are based on actual use and may be limited to areas of actual use. The advantage of a federal registration of a trademark is to afford certain presumptions of entitlement, and other benefits as to preventing infringing products from being imported.

The test for infringement is either evidence of actual confusion or whether there is substantial likelihood of confusion. Defenses include the nature of the product, the types of customers, and a variety of other factors. A mark that has achieved a level of fame can also be deemed a famous mark and can be infringed if it is diluted or tarnished.

As discussed, it is possible for the same item to have both copyright and trademark protection. For example, wallpaper can be copyrighted as well as its pattern being a logo that is trademarked.

The statutory definition of a trademark

> includes any word, name, symbol, or device, or any combination thereof—
>
> (1) used by a person, or
>
> (2) which a person has a bona fide intention to use in commerce and applies to register on the principal register established by this chapter, to identify and distinguish his or her goods, including a unique product, from those manufactured or sold by others

213. 15 U.S.C. §§ 1051–1141n.

> and to indicate the source of the goods, even if that source is unknown.[214]

Unlike copyright, it is not necessary to register a trademark in order to bring an action for infringement of a mark under the Lanham Act. Nonetheless, there are advantages to a registration on what is called the Principal Register. These are public notice of ownership, legal presumption of your ownership and exclusive rights to use the mark nationally, federal court jurisdiction, use of the mark for foreign registrations, ability to register with Customs and prevent certain imported goods, right to use the ® symbol, and a listing in the U.S. Patent and Trademark Office's online database.

### Types of Trademarks

Trademarks are divided into four general types:

> Arranged in ascending order of strength, these categories are: (1) generic, (2) descriptive, (3) suggestive, and (4) arbitrary or fanciful. A generic term can never become a valid trademark and cannot be registered. A descriptive term can be registered as a mark only if it has "become distinctive of the applicant's goods in commerce," 15 U.S.C. § 1052(f), that is, in the unfortunate parlance of the cases, only if it has acquired "secondary meaning." Suggestive marks, falling between the merely descriptive and the arbitrary or fanciful, are entitled to registration without proof of secondary meaning, as are fully arbitrary or fanciful terms. (citing *Abercrombie & Fitch Co. v. Hunting World, Inc.*, 537 F.2d 4, 9 (2d Cir. 1976)[215]

The purpose of these categories is to justify the kind of protection that trademarks afford. For example, someone manufacturing a high-quality pen called, say, Dowego would be arbitrary or fanciful. Over time, someone buying a Dowego pen would know what to expect. It is such an arbitrary

214. 15 U.S.C. § 1127.

215. McGregor-Doniger Inc. v. Drizzle Inc., 599 F.2d 1126, 1131 (2d Cir. 1979).

or fanciful mark that a competitor who tried to market its pens under the Dowego name would clearly be attempting to trade on the original owner's goodwill. A suggestive mark might be Smooth, so it is not quite descriptive of the pen itself but does have certain qualities that you might associate with a pen so as to not qualify as actually arbitrary or fanciful. Again, it is not counterintuitive to afford protection to someone who builds up a brand name around such a mark, as it does not preclude others from marketing pens. Both of these categories may be registered on the Principal Register as a trademark. A descriptive mark is generally not entitled to registration, as it essentially "conveys an immediate idea of the ingredients, qualities or characteristics of the goods."[216] An example might be Easywrite Pens. The last category, generic, is essentially the species of the product. You could not trademark, for example, "Ballpoint" for pens.

Trademarks are not limited to words or logos. They can also take the form of trade dress, either in terms of packaging (which, e.g., itself can include the interior look of a chain restaurant)[217] or the shape of an item, provided that that form of "trade dress" requires secondary meaning; that is, while not inherently distinctive, its use has led the consuming public to otherwise associate the product with the particular shape.[218]

Defenses raised to trademark infringement matters include, as in copyright, a certain type of fair use, as well as challenges to the category. A trademark held to be generic, for example, would not be enforceable such as to establish infringement. Unlike copyrights or patents, that have specified terms, trademark rights depend on use; a trademark can be deemed to be abandoned and there are requirements for renewal to maintain federal trademark registrations.

## Passing Off and Reverse Passing Off

A trademark is used to identify source, even if the source is not known to the general public. When a consumer is familiar with a trademark, such as a logo, and sees it on a product, the consumer has an understanding

216. *Id.* at 11 (citations omitted).
217. *See* Two Pesos, Inc. v. Taco Cabana, Inc., 505 U.S. 763 (1992).
218. Wal-Mart Stores, Inc. v. Samara Bros., Inc., 529 U.S. 205 (2000).

as to the quality of the product based on that logo. This is based on the identification of the mark with the product. Trademark claims take several forms. "Passing off" exists when one party uses another's trademark for the parties' own goods in an attempt to pass off its goods as those of, or at least affiliated with, the rightful trademark owner. As described by the Supreme Court, "[p]assing off (or palming off, as it is sometimes called) occurs when a producer misrepresents his own goods or services as someone else's. . . . 'Reverse passing off,' as its name implies, is the opposite: The producer misrepresents someone else's goods or services as his own."[219] The bottom line issue for trademark analysis is whether there would be a likelihood of confusion by a consumer by the use of one party of another's trademark.[220] In *Medic Alert*, the court found no likelihood of confusion as to endorsement of Corel's software product by Medic Alert when Corel used the words "Medic Alert" as a clip art image constituting "one graphic among thousands in the clipart library."[221]

## Distinctiveness

The key element of a trademark is its distinctiveness. Distinctiveness can be established either inherently by the mark itself or by secondary meaning—that is, an acquired distinctiveness based on public awareness. Secondary meaning means "words which have a primary meaning of their own, such as bug, may by long use in connection with a particular product, come to be known by the public as specifically designating that product."[222] In other words, if your mark is not distinctive enough to qualify as an arbitrary, fanciful, or suggestive mark, it can nonetheless establish distinctiveness by proving secondary meaning—that is, that the public associates your mark with a particular product or service.

The test for inherent distinctiveness is whether the mark is either generic, descriptive, suggestive, arbitrary, or fanciful.[223] The first two are

219. Dastar Corp. v. Twentieth Century Fox Film Corp., 539 U.S. 23, 27 n.1 (2003).
220. Medic Alert Found. U.S., Inc. v. Corel Corp., 43 F. Supp. 2d 933, 937 (N.D. Ill. 1999).
221. *Id.* at 939.
222. Volkswagenwerk Aktiengesellschaft v. Wheeler, 814 F.2d 812, 816 (1st Cir. 1987).
223. *Two Pesos*, 505 U.S. at 768; Abercrombie & Fitch Co. v. Hunting World, Inc., 537 F.2d 4, 9 (2d Cir. 1976).

not inherently distinctive, but the last three are. The rationale is that generic or descriptive words by themselves do not identify a source but the object.

In *Jeffrey Milstein, Inc. v. Greger, Lawlor, Roth, Inc.*,[224] the plaintiff designed and made greeting cards by using die-cut photographs in the shape of the objects depicted. The defendant made die-cut gift bags, stand-ups, and note pads, and expanded into die-cut greeting cards. The plaintiff's cards only showed the image on the front, and the defendant used three panels on the cards. Note that the issue was not copying the photographs but the die-cut formation. The court essentially found that the design was generic and refused to allow the plaintiff to monopolize essentially an idea for that kind of die-cut product, which trademark law does not protect.

## Trade Dress

Trademark protection attaches to trade dress. Trade dress can be the packaging, as with the box in which something comes, or it can be the actual shape of the product itself, as a Coca-Cola bottle. In the latter case, a product's design is distinctive, and therefore protectable, when secondary meaning is shown.[225] This means that even if the design by itself would not establish recognition sufficient for trademark protection, you can prove that the public nonetheless associates the particular design with your product and thereby establish registration. On the other hand, secondary meaning is not necessary, and there is inherent distinctiveness where the trade dress is not the design of the product itself but the packaging of the product.[226] The Supreme Court distinguished between the decor of the restaurant in *Two Pesos* as packaging from the actual product design itself of the clothing at issue in *Samara.*

## Need for Use as Trademark

In *Leigh v. Warner Brothers, Inc.*,[227] the photographer of the image of the Bird Girl Statue in the Bonaventure Cemetery in Savannah, Georgia—used

224. 58 F.3d 27 (2d Cir. 1995).
225. Wal-Mart Stores, Inc. v. Samara Bros., Inc., 529 U.S. 205 (2000).
226. Two Pesos, Inc. v. Taco Cabana, Inc., 505 U.S. 763 (1992).
227. 212 F.3d 1210 (11th Cir. 2000).

not only on the cover of the book *Midnight in the Garden of Good and Evil* but also in the movie—did not have a claim for trademark infringement. The photographer claimed the image was a "source identifier" for his workshop and artwork.[228] The court found he failed to establish prior use of that image as a trademark, and even if he did use it, it was deemed "descriptive" of his work and therefore not entitled to protection.[229]

### State Trademark Laws

Unlike copyright, which is exclusively federal, states can have their own trademark laws. The state trademark does not give the national presumption that a federal trademark does but can be useful for proving first use.

### Factors Constituting Likelihood of Confusion

Trademark infringement is a function of the likelihood of confusion. Different circuits define the test for likelihood of confusion in slightly different terms, but essentially the analysis encompasses a variety of factors. For example, "Cadillac" applies to both dog food and automobiles; traditionally, no one has confused those as being the same company as the source of the product. (There is of course the concept of product expansion, and in an age of diversified conglomerate corporations, the assumption may no longer hold, but that is beyond the scope of this introductory set of remarks.) The classic formulation of the various factors, and the one often cited by the Trademark Office examiners, is found in *Application of EI DuPont DeNemours & Co.*:

> (1) The similarity or dissimilarity of the marks in their entireties as to appearance, sound, connotation and commercial impression.
> (2) The similarity or dissimilarity and nature of the goods or services as described in an application or registration or in connection with which a prior mark is in use.

228. *Id.* at 1217.
229. *Id.* at 1218.

(3) The similarity or dissimilarity of established, likely-to-continue trade channels.
(4) The conditions under which and buyers to whom sales are made, i. e. "impulse" vs. careful, sophisticated purchasing.
(5) The fame of the prior mark (sales, advertising, length of use).
(6) The number and nature of similar marks in use on similar goods.
(7) The nature and extent of any actual confusion.
(8) The length of time during and conditions under which there has been concurrent use without evidence of actual confusion.
(9) The variety of goods on which a mark is or is not used (house mark, "family" mark, product mark).
(10) The market interface between applicant and the owner of a prior mark:
 (a) a mere "consent" to register or use.
 (b) agreement provisions designed to preclude confusion, i. e. limitations on continued use of the marks by each party.
 (c) assignment of mark, application, registration and good will of the related business.
 (d) laches and estoppel attributable to owner of prior mark and indicative of lack of confusion.
(11) The extent to which applicant has a right to exclude others from use of its mark on its goods.
(12) The extent of potential confusion, i.e., whether de minimis or substantial.
(13) Any other established fact probative of the effect of use.[230]

For the photographer, trademark issues can arise in the subject matter of the photograph.

## Buildings

In *Rock and Roll Hall of Fame v. Gentile Productions*,[231] the defendant photographer took a picture of a museum against a sunset and sold the

230. *Application of EI DuPont DeNemours & Co.*, 476 F.2d 1357, 1361 (C.C.P.A. 1973).
231. 134 F.3d 749 (6th Cir. 1998).

images as posters. The museum plaintiff claimed its logo and building shape as trademarks. The museum itself also marketed a poster, but the image in that poster was different from the one at issue. The trial court found infringement. The appellate court reversed, holding that defendant's photograph of the museum was not a trademark use of building design, and the use of the words to describe the photograph "ROCK N' ROLL HALL OF FAME" was "a non-trademark use which simply and accurately describes his non-infringing photograph of the Museum."[232] The court stated, "When we view the photograph in Gentile's poster, we do not readily recognize the design of the Museum's building as an indicator of source or sponsorship."[233]

While someone can own a trademark in a person's name, it cannot claim ownership of every image of that person.[234] In *Pirone*, the court rejected an argument that the owner of the trademarked words "Babe Ruth" was entitled to claim infringement based on use by others of certain photographs of the baseball player. Recognizing that words and pictorial representations are not equatable as a matter of law, the cases where protection was granted involved a single, repeated image that designated origin. The court distinguished cases and situations like those involving Pegasus, discussed previously, and stated:

> Unlike a stylized flying horse or similar picture marks, an individual's likeness is not a consistently represented fixed image—different photographs of the same person may be markedly dissimilar. Thus a photograph of a human being, unlike a portrait of a fanciful cartoon character, is not inherently 'distinctive' in the trademark sense of tending to indicate origin.[235]

232. *Id.* at 753.
233. *Id.* at 754.
234. Pirone v. MacMillan, Inc., 894 F.2d 579, 582 (2d Cir. 1990).
235. *Id.* at 583; *see also* ETW Corp. v. Jireh Publ'g, Inc., 332 F.3d 915 (6th Cir. 2003).

## Artistic Expression

The leading analytical framework is the so-called *Rogers* test, expressed in *Rogers v. Grimaldi*.[236] The court held:

> [I]n general the Act should be construed to apply to artistic works only where the public interest in avoiding consumer confusion outweighs the public interest in free expression. In the context of allegedly misleading titles using a celebrity's name, that balance will normally not support application of the Act unless the title has no artistic relevance to the underlying work whatsoever, or, if it has some artistic relevance, unless the title explicitly misleads as to the source or the content of the work.[237]

In order to claim a false-endorsement case, one need not be a celebrity; what is needed is a reasonable commercial interest in the marks sought to be protected.[238] The issue is one of false endorsement, and while it is perhaps easier to establish that when the plaintiff is a known celebrity,[239] the *Arnold* court did not find that celebrity status was a prerequisite for such a Lanham Act claim.

To see how this can play out, consider *Mattel, Inc. v. Walking Mountain Productions*.[240] The photographer, Thomas Forsythe (another defendant) took pictures of plaintiff Mattel's Barbie doll in a particular way, most of his photographs "portray[ing] a nude Barbie in danger of being attacked by vintage household appliances."[241] Mattel claimed infringement of copyright, trademark, and trade dress. Forsythe prevailed at both the trial and appellate level. He argued that his images had political overtones and addressed "the objectification of women . . . and . . . the conventional beauty myth . . . ."[242]

---

236. 875 F.2d 994 (2d Cir. 1989).
237. *Id.* at 999.
238. Arnold v. Treadwell, 632 F. Supp. 2d 723 (E.D. Mich. 2009).
239. *See, e.g.*, Parks v. LaFace Records, 329 F.3d 437 (6th Cir.), *cert. denied*, 540 U.S. 1074 (2003).
240. 353 F.3d 792 (9th Cir. 2003).
241. *Id.* at 796.
242. *Id.*

The work was publicly shown at two art festivals, and to some extent on promotional postcards as well as business cards. His proofs included evidence from an art history expert and curator at the San Francisco Museum of Modern Art that put Forsythe's work in context. The trial court held the use of Mattel's copyright in the doll as fair use. It also found, regarding the trademark and trade dress claims, that there was "no likelihood of confusion as to Mattel's sponsorship of Forsythe's works" and found the use was noncommercial.[243]

The court set out the standard:

> [T]o assess whether a defendant has infringed on a plaintiff's trademark, we apply a "likelihood of confusion" test that asks whether use of the plaintiff's trademark by the defendant is "likely to cause confusion or to cause mistake, or to deceive as to the affiliation, connection, or association" of the two products.[244]

What was of particular relevance here, though, was the First Amendment implication:

> [W]hen marks "transcend their identifying purpose" and "enter public discourse and become an integral part of our vocabulary," they "assume[] a role outside the bounds of trademark law." Where a mark assumes such cultural significance, First Amendment protections come into play. In these situations, "the trademark owner does not have the right to control public discourse whenever the public imbues his mark with a meaning beyond its source-identifying function.[245]

Conducting a balancing test, the court weighed the public interest against consumer confusion on the one hand with the public interest in free expression on the other, and here found the latter triumphed.[246] As for trade dress,

243. *Id.* at 798.
244. *Id.* at 806–07.
245. *Id.* at 807 (citation omitted).
246. *Id.* at 807.

the court found fair use in its "classic" sense, which in the trademark context meant that the defendant did not use the mark to describe the plaintiff's product but only to describe his own product.[247] The other type of fair use is nominative use:

> First, the plaintiff's product or service in question must be one not readily identifiable without use of the trademark; second, only so much of the mark or marks may be used as is reasonably necessary to identify the plaintiff's product or service; and third, the user must do nothing that would, in conjunction with the mark, suggest sponsorship or endorsement by the trademark holder.[248]

As is evident, there was no effort by the artist to pass of the Barbie product as his own.

Finally, the court rejected dilution claims because "Forsythe's artistic and parodic work is considered noncommercial speech and, therefore, not subject to a trademark dilution claim."[249]

More common are circumstances in which photographers capture, as part of the scenery of the image, whether rural or urban, well-known signs or other objects. For example, in *Roxbury Entertainment v. Penthouse Media Group, Inc.*,[250] the defendants' photograph of two topless women standing on a roadmap was used on the cover of a Penthouse DVD. In the photograph appeared the words "Route 66" as well as a California highway sign showing Route 66. The DVD was "hard core" pornography, and the plaintiff, owner of the mark Route 66 based on the prior television programs, sued

247. *Id.* at 809 (citations omitted).

248. *Id.* at 810.

249. *Id.* at 812; *see also* Hoffman v. Capital Cities/ABC, Inc., 255 F.3d 1180 (9th Cir. 2001) (Dustin Hoffman lost a suit against a magazine that used digitally altered image of him as "Tootsie" in a designer dress as part of a "Grand Illusions" article; this was protected non-commercial speech, finding that any commercial aspects were "inextricably intertwined" with expressive elements and non-separable from the protected whole). *But see* Jordan v. Jewel Food Stores, Inc., 743 F.3d 509, 521 (7th Cir. 2014) (criticizing *Hoffman's* application of the "inextricably intertwined" doctrine, since "[n]o law of man or nature compelled Jewel to combine commercial and noncommercial messages as it did here.").

250. 669 F. Supp. 2d 1170 (C.D. Cal. 2009).

for trademark infringement among other claims. Acknowledging that First Amendment defenses can defeat trademark infringement claims for artistic works, the court nonetheless noted that noncommercial speech's protection is less "robust." Applying the *Rogers* test, the court first analyzed whether the plaintiff's trademark is relevant to the underlying work, even if minimally, and second, if so, whether the use explicitly misleads consumers as to the source or content; if not, then there is no Lanham Act claim.[251] The court found that this was an expressive work, and therefore the claim for trademark infringement failed. There was some relevance to the Route 66 mark, and no one buying the pornographic video, the court found, would think they were buying anything related to the old television show.

## Celebrities

If you take a picture of a celebrity, regardless of whatever other rights that celebrity may have, he or she does not have the right to claim trademark violation by use of his or her image. "As a general rule, a person's image or likeness cannot function as a trademark."[252]

In *Downing v. Abercrombie & Fitch*, the court identified eight factors to be addressed in determining if there has been a trademark infringement of a trademark in a celebrity case relating to the star's persona:

> 1. the level of recognition that the plaintiff has among the segment of the society for whom the defendant's product is intended; 2. the relatedness of the fame or success of the plaintiff to the defendant's product; 3. the similarity of the likeness used by the defendant to the actual plaintiff; 4. evidence of actual confusion; 5. marketing channels used; 6. likely degree of purchaser care; 7. defendant's intent on selecting the plaintiff; and 8. likelihood of expansion of the product lines.[253]

251. *Id.* at 1175.

252. ETW Corp. v. Jireh Publ'g, Inc., 332 F.3d 915, 922 (6th Cir. 2003) (no trademark protection in the use of the likeness of Tiger Woods); *see also* Pirone v. MacMillan, Inc., 894 F.2d 579, 586 (2d Cir. 1990) (no trademark infringement claim for use by calendar publisher of photographs of Babe Ruth's likeness).

253. 265 F.3d 994, 1007–08 (9th Cir. 2001).

Note that this is addressing only the trademark issue and not other issues as to statutory rights regarding celebrity, as discussed in Chapter 3.

## Trademark Fair Use

Just as in copyright law, trademark law also accommodates a certain "fair use." "Nominative fair use" provides a defense to use of trademark to describe the mark holder's product, provided (1) the product must be one not readily identifiable without use of the trademark; (2) only so much of the mark or marks may be used as is reasonably necessary to identify the product; and (3) the user must do nothing in conjunction with the mark to suggest sponsorship or endorsement.[254] In *Standard Process*, defendant Total Health used Standard Process's name placed prominently as a paid advertiser in search engine results and used first-person pronouns "we" or "our" to refer to Standard Process products; since this suggested sponsorship, Total Health failed to establish the fair-use defense. In other words, fair use will produce the right to sell products lawfully acquired in stream of commerce but will not necessarily suffice if the acquirer conspired to violate a franchise or distribution agreement. Courts have limited the fair-use defense to instances where there is no other conduct of infringement or where the defendant is only reselling product, and not tortiously interfering with the trademark holder's products.

To establish fair use of a trademark, the defendant's use of the plaintiff's mark must be "(1) other than as a mark, (2) in a descriptive sense, and (3) in good faith."[255]

254. Standard Process, Inc. v. Total Health Disc., 559 F. Supp. 2d 932, 938 (E.D. Wis. 2008).

255. EMI Catalogue P'ship v. Hill, Holliday, Connors, Cosmopulos, Inc., 228 F.3d 56, 64 (2d Cir. 2000); *see also* Downing v. Abercrombie & Fitch, 265 F.3d 994, 1009 (9th Cir. 2001) ("[W]here the defendant uses a trademark to describe the plaintiff's product rather than its own product, a commercial user is entitled to a nominative fair use defense provided the defendant meets three requirements: 1. the product or service in question must be one not readily identifiable without use of the trademark; 2. only so much of the mark or marks may be used as is reasonably necessary to identify the product or service; and 3. the user must do nothing that would, in conjunction with the mark, suggest sponsorship or endorsement by the trademark holder.").

In *The New Kids on the Block v. News America Publishing, Inc.*,[256] the plaintiff pop-music group attempted to control all aspects of the use of its name and sought to enjoin two newspaper defendants from running popularity polls as to individual members of the band. Among other claims, the plaintiff raised a Lanham Act trademark claim.[257] The basis of the defense is fair use; that is, the trademarks are not being used in a traditional sense of utilizing a trademark to identify the source of a product.[258]

In *Car-Freshner Corp. v. Getty Images, Inc.*,[259] the plaintiff sued the stock-photo agency because various of its images contained the plaintiff's "Tree Marks." It sued under eight separate theories: "(1) federal trademark infringement; (2) federal false designation of origin; (3) common law trademark infringement; (4) common law unfair competition; (5) contributory trademark infringement, unfair competition and dilution; (6) vicarious trademark infringement, unfair competition and dilution; (7) federal dilution; and (8) dilution under New York State law."[260] On the relevant issue here—that is, whether defendants "used" the Tree Marks as trademarks—the court found that Getty had used the Tree Marks in their images in order to sell the particular images—that is, as a trademark. With regard to nominative fair use—that is, even if the marks were used as a trademark—their use being incidental and descriptive and not capitalizing on consumer confusion, the court noted that Getty was not a seller or trader in the branded product, and "these factual allegations plausibly suggest that the purpose of using the Tree Marks in the pictures was to capitalize on the popularity of the marks."[261]

256. 971 F.2d 302 (9th Cir. 1991).

257. *See also* Volkswagenwerk Aktiengesellschaft v. Church, 411 F.2d 350 (9th Cir. 1969) (an automobile repair shop could use Volkswagen's trademark to advertise its repair of Volkswagen automobiles; defendant had not indicated it was affiliated with the Volkswagen company or that it was sponsored by it); WCVB-TV v. Bos. Athletic Ass'n, 926 F.2d 42, 46 (1st Cir. 1991); Smith v. Chanel, Inc., 402 F.2d 562 (9th Cir. 1968).

258. *But see* Tiffany (N.J.), Inc. v. eBay, Inc., 600 F.3d 93, 102 (2d Cir. 2010) ("We have referred to the doctrine, albeit without adopting or rejecting it," and declining to "address the viability of the doctrine [of nominative fair use] to resolve Tiffany's claim").

259. 822 F. Supp. 2d 167 (N.D.N.Y. 2011).

260. *Id.* at 171.

261. *Id.* at 179.

In *Volkswagen AG v. Dorling Kindersley Publishing, Inc.*,[262] the defendant's use of plaintiff's VW emblem and Beetle trademark design in photographs and illustrations in a children's book were fair use, but found an issue of fact as to infringement regarding the New Beetle trade dress design and the shape of the book.

## Trademark, Copyright, and the Public Domain

While it is possible to assert both trademark and copyright claims based on the same item, if the material was either copyrighted or subject to copyright, but has passed into the public domain, trademark law cannot be used to circumvent the copyright law.[263] Generally, trademark law will not be extended to cover an act provided by a character—in this case, the use of a limited segment of a *Three Stooges* clip in the background in a scene in a movie. This was contrasted with *White v. Samsung Electronics America, Inc.*,[264] in which a commercial likeness of celebrity Vanna White as used in a television commercial for the purpose of selling the defendant's products. Similarly, taking a work already in the public domain and copying it, even with only minor changes, and producing it as one's own is not actionable under trademark law.[265] The Court gave this example:

> It forbids, for example, the Coca-Cola Company's passing off its product as Pepsi-Cola or reverse passing off Pepsi-Cola as its product. But the brand-loyal consumer who prefers the drink that the Coca-Cola Company or PepsiCo sells, while he believes that that company produced (or at least stands behind the production of) that product, surely does not necessarily believe that that company was the "origin" of the drink in the sense that it was the very first to devise the formula. The consumer who buys a branded product does not automatically

262. 614 F. Supp. 2d 793 (E.D. Mich. 2009).
263. Comedy III Prods., Inc. v. New Line Cinema, 200 F.3d 593 (9th Cir. 2000).
264. 971 F.2d 1395 (9th Cir. 1992), *cert. denied*, 508 U.S. 951 (1993).
265. Dastar Corp. v. Twentieth Century Film Corp., 539 U.S. 23, 32 (2003) (as used in Lanham Act, origin does not refer to entity that originated the ideas contained in the goods, but "prohibits actions like trademark infringement that deceive consumers and impair a producer's goodwill").

> assume that the brand-name company is the same entity that came up with the idea for the product, or designed the product—and typically does not care whether it is. The words of the Lanham Act should not be stretched to cover matters that are typically of no consequence to purchasers.[266]

### Contributory Trademark Infringement

Contributory trademark infringement exists where

> a manufacturer or distributor intentionally induces another to infringe a trademark, or if it continues to supply its product to one whom it knows or has reason to know is engaging in trademark infringement, the manufacturer or distributor is contributorially responsible for any harm done as a result of the deceit.[267]

### Hyperlinks and Metatags

A hyperlink has been defined as "highlighted text or images that, when selected by the user, permit[s][her] to view another, related Web document."[268] The definition of metatag is

> hypertext markup language ("HTML") code, invisible to the Internet user, that permits web designers to describe their webpage. There are two different types of metatags: keyword and description. The keyword metatag permits designers to identify search terms for use by search engines. Description metatags allow designers to briefly describe the contents of their pages. This description appears as sentence fragments beneath the webpage's listing in a search result.[269]

266. *Id.* at 32–33.

267. Inwood Labs., Inc. v. Ives Labs., Inc., 456 U.S. 844, 854 (1982); Tiffany (N.J.), Inc. v. eBay, Inc., 600 F.3d 93, 103–04 (2d Cir.), *cert. denied*, 131 S. Ct. 647 (2010).

268. Bensusan Rest. Corp. v. King, 126 F.3d 25, 27 n.1 (2d Cir. 1997).

269. Bihari v. Gross, 119 F. Supp. 2d 309, 312 n.3 (S.D.N.Y. 2000).

Use of a photograph as the source of a hyperlink or metatag can be an infringement of trademark if it is used "as a conduit, steering potential customers away from [one company] and toward its competitors."[270]

Again, we see the distinction between the taking of the image and its subsequent use. The more someone else's trademark is used for commercial purposes as opposed to forming an element of a more artistic, or less opportunistic purpose that suggests unfair competition, the more suspect that use becomes.

### First Sale Doctrine

The first sale doctrine, discussed above in terms of copyright, also applies in the trademark context, such that a trademark holder does not control the sale of its product beyond the first sale of the product.[271] However, the first sale doctrine will not protect affirmative misuse, such as passing off or otherwise attempting to "give the impression that they are favored or authorized dealers for a product when in fact they are not."[272] In *Australian Gold*, the 10th Circuit held that use of goodwill caused consumers to be lured to the competitor's goods. But in *Designer Skin, LLC v. S&L Vitamins, Inc.*, the court held:

> [T]here is a meaningful distinction between (1) using a mark to attract potential customers to a website that only offers products of the mark holder's competitors and (2) using a mark to attract potential customers to a website that offers the mark holder's genuine products as well as the products of competitors.[273]

270. *Id.* at 318; *see also* Gov't Emps. Ins. Co. v. Google, Inc., 330 F. Supp. 2d 700 (E.D. Va. 2004); 1-800 Contacts, Inc. v. WhenU.com, Inc., 414 F.3d 400 (2d Cir.), *cert. denied*, 546 U.S. 1033 (2005).

271. Sebastian Int'l v. Longs Drug Stores Corp., 53 F.3d 1073, 1074 (9th Cir.), *cert. denied*, 516 U.S. 914 (1995); Standard Process, Inc. v. Total Health Disc., 559 F. Supp. 2d 932 (E.D. Wis. 2008).

272. Austl. Gold, Inc. v. Hatfield, 436 F.3d 1228, 1241 (10th Cir. 2006).

273. 560 F. Supp. 2d 811, 820 (D. Ariz. 2008).

## False Advertising

There is a private remedy for false advertising in violation of 15 U.S.C. § 1125(a). It entails proof of (1) false (literally or implicitly) statement, (2) actually deceived or tendency to deceive substantial audience segment, (3) material deception, (4) interstate commerce, and (5) damages. A claim for common-law fraud may also be made out by proving (1) a false statement, (2) knowingly made, (3) relied upon, and (4) damages.

A related claim may be made for "initial interest confusion" in which a Lanham Act claim may be brought when "a consumer is lured to a product by its similarity to a known mark, even though the consumer realizes the true identity and origin of the product before consummating a purchase."[274]

A set of issues also exists of particular relevance to photographers in that extensive image manipulation that may falsely indicate the effect of cosmetics may violate advertising standards. There were rulings in the United Kingdom regarding digital manipulation of images of actresses used by Christian Dior and L'Oreal. Within the United States, the National Advertising Division, which self-regulates advertising, issued a ban regarding misleading use of image processing, resulting from a CoverGirl ad by Procter and Gamble. In an age when class actions are used to challenge misleading claims, this may well become an area fraught with litigation.

On the other hand, "puffing" is not actionable; it is "exaggerated advertising, blustering, and boasting upon which no reasonable buyer would rely."[275]

More about the ethics of image processing later.

## Putting It in Perspective

On page 132 is an image I made in Dallas, Texas.

Mobil Oil Corp. used the Pegasus symbol since 1931 and displayed it, in varying colors, on its products. Pegasus Petroleum Corp. was formed in

274. Eli Lilly & Co. v. Natural Answers, Inc., 233 F.3d 456, 464 (7th Cir. 2000); *see also* Brookfield Commcn's, Inc. v. W. Coast Entm't Corp., 174 F.3d 1036, 1062 (9th Cir. 1999); JK Harris & Co., LLC v. Kassel, 253 F. Supp. 2d 1120 (N.D. Cal. 2003).

275. Southland Sod Farms v. Stover Seed Co., 108 F.3d 1134, 1145 (9th Cir. 1997).

The ExxonMobil Pegasus.

1981 and, unlike Mobil, is engaged in oil trading and does not sell directly to consumers; it did not use the flying horse but only the name. Mobil sued for trademark infringement and prevailed; in this case, balancing all the factors that go into a likelihood of confusion analysis, the court found infringement.[276]

My photograph includes the famous trademark of the Pegasus (flying horse) currently owned by ExxonMobil. This is a fair use of this mark. This is artistic, noncommercial use (even if I were to sell the photograph), as it is an element of a broader composition. Several creative decisions were made in the photograph. It is tightly cropped to focus only on the detailed architecture of the buildings. The Pegasus fixture is part of that scene; to restrict the ability to photograph otherwise freely available buildings from public spaces would have a contrary effect to First Amendment rights of photographers. Applying the *Rogers* test, and as other courts have applied it, it is obvious that the use of the mark has at least minimal relationship to the overall image and purpose of the underlying work, and second, this use of the trademark in this image does not explicitly mislead a consumer into thinking that I am ExxonMobil.

## Trade Secrets

Trade secrets are confidential information that a person or company seeks to protect. They are not generally known or otherwise easily able to be re-created, and you take appropriate steps to ensure their confidentiality. Perhaps the most famous example of a trade secret is the recipe for Coca-Cola. Its trade secret status is not subject to a term limit; it persists for as long as you can keep it secret. The common-law definition of a trade secret is

276. Mobil Oil Corp. v. Pegasus Petrol. Corp., 818 F.2d 254 (2d Cir. 1987).

> any formula, pattern, device or compilation of information which is used in one's business, and which gives him an opportunity to obtain an advantage over competitors who do not know or use it. It may be a formula for a chemical compound, a process of manufacturing, treating or preserving materials, a pattern for a machine or other device, or a list of customers.[277]

The Uniform Trade Secrets Act, which has been adopted by a variety of states, has its own definition, and there are issues as to whether that statute preempts other trade secret cases.

Note also that there can be criminal repercussions for photographing trade secrets. Knowingly photographing a trade secret with intent to convert it is a federal crime under 18 U.S.C. § 1832(a). In *United States v. Howley*,[278] two engineers were convicted of violating this statute, among other wire fraud statutes. Howley, on a visit to a competitor plant and in violation of the "secrecy agreement" and "no camera" rules, "used his cell-phone camera to take seven photos of a swabbing-down device on one of Goodyear's tire-assembly Machines," and sent them to others at his company. A concerned company manager blew the whistle.[279] Defendants argued that the information in the photographs did not rise to the level of trade secret. They lost; as the Court of Appeals held, "[i]t was no stretch for the jury to conclude that Roberts and Howley knew the machines they photographed constituted trade secrets and, by extension, that the photographs would help a Goodyear competitor."[280]

277. Kewanee Oil Co. v. Bicron Corp., 416 U.S. 470, 474–75 (1974) (quoting RESTATEMENT OF TORTS § 757, comment b (1939)).
278. 707 F.3d 575 (6th Cir. 2013).
279. *Id.* at 578–79.
280. *Id.* at 580.

## Chapter Three

# Torts, Privacy, Defamation, and Related Statutory Claims

## Overview

When people seek to recover money from another party, they need to do so by placing their particular facts into a legal theory. You may not like a hat that someone is wearing, but you cannot obtain money from them based on that dislike. There is no acceptable claim that may be pleaded that would require someone to pay you simply because you do not like that person's hat. You need a recognized cause of action. In common-law jurisdictions, like the United States, those causes of action may be developed at com mon law, by courts, or they may be provided by statute, by legislatures. In civil-law jurisdictions, causes of action are provided exclusively by statute or accepted rules or regulations.

We will focus on the United States in this chapter, and discuss those claims that are raised against photographers. Whereas photographers may be on both the receiving end as well as the delivering end of an intellectual property claim discussed in Chapter 2, the claims in this chapter place certain limitations on photographers and may subject them to damages as well as injunctive relief against further practice. While we will note First Amendment defenses as appropriate, First Amendment issues are discussed in more detail in Chapter 6. The purpose here is to forewarn the photographer and, to the extent it is possible, provide some parameters or "best practices." If one thing is clear, it is that there can be no real dispositive advice that applies in every circumstance. Most books discussing legal rights and obligations of photographers set forth general principles. I will do that here, and provide real case examples, often using the courts' own language. However, not only does law vary or differ from state to state in the United States, but application of the same law will depend upon the facts of a particular case. While facts may be similar, they are in most cases not exactly identical, and where the lines are drawn provides the uncertainty.

## Torts in General

As noted in Chapter 1, law has a great divide between torts and contracts. Claims based on contract as they affect photographers are discussed in Chapter 4. Essentially, a contract claim is based on an agreement, written or oral, express or implied, that sets forth the terms of a relationship. Model releases and licensing agreements are contracts and define the scope of what is and is not permissible. Torts are "civil wrongs," meaning they have developed at common law as a policy matter to provide redress in certain defined circumstances where one party has wronged the other party A tort is "a civil wrong, other than breach of contract, for which the court will provide a remedy in the form of an action for damages."[1] Among the most commonly experienced torts is that of negligence, in which a party that owes a legal duty to another fails to exercise an appropriate level of care, which has caused damage or harm to the other party. You will note the particular facets of this definition; various courts will define it differently, and there are levels of negligence (gross negligence as opposed to plain negligence) that entail different levels of proof and, to an extent, different levels of recovery.

1. United States v. Burke, 504 U.S. 229, 234 (1992) (citation omitted).

## Defamation

Defamation is concerned with the damage to a person's reputation. Specific definitions of what is and is not defamatory will differ from jurisdiction to jurisdiction, but the one in New Jersey will serve our purposes here. A defamatory statement in that state is "one that is false and 'injurious to the reputation of another' or exposes another person to 'hatred, contempt or ridicule' or subjects another person to 'a loss of the good will and confidence' in which he or she is held by others."[2] To prove defamation, the plaintiff must prove "(a) a false and defamatory statement concerning another; (b) an unprivileged publication to a third party; (c) fault amounting at least to negligence on the part of the publisher;' and (d) damages, unless the statement is actionable irrespective of special harm."[3] The key point is "what the person . . . to whom the communication was published reasonably understood as the meaning intended to be expressed."[4]

A succinct explanation of common-law defamation is provided by Supreme Court Justice Byron White, concurring in the judgment in *Dun & Bradstreet, Inc. v. Greenmoss Builders, Inc.*:

> Until *New York Times Co. v. Sullivan*, 376 U. S. 254 (1964), the law of defamation was almost exclusively the business of state courts and legislatures. Under the then prevailing state libel law, the defamed individual had only to prove a false written publication that subjected him to hatred, contempt, or ridicule. Truth was a defense; but given a defamatory false circulation, general injury to reputation was presumed; special damages, such as pecuniary loss and emotional distress, could be recovered; and punitive damages were available if common-law malice were shown. General damages for injury to reputation were presumed and awarded because the judgment of history was that "in many cases the effect of defamatory statements is so subtle and indirect that it is impossible directly to trace the effects thereof in

2. Romaine v. Kallinger, 109 N.J. 282, 289 (1988) (citations omitted).
3. Swerdlick v. Koch, 721 A.2d 849, 859–60 (R.I. 1998).
4. *Id.* at 860.

> loss to the person defamed." Restatement of Torts § 621, Comment a, p. 314 (1938). The defendant was permitted to show that there was no reputational injury; but at the very least, the prevailing rule was that at least nominal damages were to be awarded for any defamatory publication actionable per se. This rule performed "a vindicatory function by enabling the plaintiff publicly to brand the defamatory publication as false. The salutary social value of this rule is preventive in character since it often permits a defamed person to expose the groundless character of a defamatory rumor before harm to the reputation has resulted therefrom" Id. § 569, Comment b, p. 166.[5]

Similar rules applied to slanderous statements that were actionable per se. The footnote relating to slanderous statements stated:

> At the common law, slander, unlike libel, was actionable per se only when it dealt with a narrow range of statements: those imputing a criminal offense, a venereal or loathsome and communicable disease, improper conduct of a lawful business, or unchastity of a woman. Restatement of Torts § 570 (1938). To be actionable, all other slanderous statements required additional proof of special damages other than an injury to reputation or emotional distress. The special damages most often took the form of material or pecuniary loss. Id., § 575 and Comment b, pp. 185–187.[6]

*New York Times Co. v. Sullivan*,[7] referred to by Justice White, applied a higher standard to proving defamation—a required showing of "actual malice"—when the plaintiff claiming defamation was actually a public figure. This standard was applied in *Time, Inc. v. Hill*,[8] in the context of private individuals involved in a matter of public interest asserting violation of privacy rights under the New York Civil Rights Act. In *Gertz v. Robert*

5. 472 U.S. 749, 765 (1985).
6. *Id.* at 765 n.1.
7. 376 U.S. 254 (1964).
8. 385 U.S. 374 (1967).

*Welch, Inc.*, the Supreme Court recognized that the *New York Times* standard might apply to a private figure who "may achieve such pervasive fame or notoriety that he becomes a public figure for all purposes and in all contexts" or "voluntarily injects himself or is drawn into a particular public controversy and thereby becomes a public figure for a limited range of issues. In either case such persons assume special prominence in the resolution of public questions."[9]

In other words, defamation depends upon whether the photographic subject involves a public figure or matter of public concern. It is a matter of state (or foreign) law. To see how this plays out in a courtroom, I will note the jury instructions applicable in New Jersey to show what a jury would be expected to apply. The New Jersey Model Jury Instructions for a plaintiff that is a public figure or private figure but matter of public concern require proof of (1) a defamatory statement of fact, (2) concerning the plaintiff, (3) which was false and (4) was communicated to a person or persons other than the plaintiff (5) with actual knowledge by the defendant that the statement was false or with reckless disregard by the defendant of the statement's truth or falsity.

When a private figure is involved, the standards are lower. New Jersey's Model Jury Instructions for a private figure where there is not a matter of public concern require proof of (1) a defamatory statement of fact, (2) concerning the plaintiff, (3) which was false, (4) was communicated to a person or persons other than the plaintiff and (5) with actual knowledge by the defendant that the statement was false, or with reckless disregard by the defendant of the statement's truth or falsity, or with negligence by the defendant in failing to determine the falsity of the statement.

The difference is that in the case of a private person and a situation that is not matter of public concern, all that is needed to be proved are the first four elements. In other words, lesser standard for purely private persons. Where public figures or matters of public concern are involved, the standard is higher and includes malice.

9. 418 U.S. 323, 351–52 (1974).

A variation on private or public defamation is commercial defamation, or trade libel. California, for example, defines trade libel as

> as an intentional disparagement of the quality of property, which results in pecuniary damage to plaintiff. . . . "Injurious falsehood, or disparagement, then, may consist of the publication of matter derogatory to the plaintiff's title to his property, or its quality, or to his business in general. . . . [T]he plaintiff must prove in all cases that the publication has played a material and substantial part inducing others not to deal with him, and that as a result he has suffered special damages. . . . Usually . . . the damages claimed have consisted of loss of prospective contracts with the plaintiff's customers."[10]

In *Times v. Sullivan*, the advertisement in question was not a commercial advertisement but rather a political statement that sought public support. When the alleged derogatory advertisement is meant solely to sell the newspaper, it does not fall within the *Sullivan* privilege.[11]

A photograph can give rise to a claim of defamation. In *Stanton v. Metro Corp.*,[12] the cover article of an issue of *Boston Magazine* was titled "Fast Times at Silver Lake High: Teen Sex in the Suburbs." A photograph in the article inside included the plaintiff, a teenage girl, with other teenagers at dance, some of whom are smoking or drinking. She was not. The caption contained a disclaimer indicating that those in the photograph were not related to the other people mentioned in the article. Stanton claimed damages based on the theory of defamation, as well as a claim based on invasion of privacy. Stanton alleged that the disclaimer was itself defamatory in falsely identifying her as a subject of the photographer's "project on teen sexuality," and "[t]he juxtaposition of [her] photograph and the

10. Erlich v. Etner, 224 Cal. App. 2d 69, 73 (1964).

11. Rinaldi v. Village Voice, 47 A.D.2d 180 (N.Y. App. Div. 1st), *cert. denied*, 423 U.S. 883 (1975).

12. 438 F.3d 119 (1st Cir. 2006).

text describing suburban teenage promiscuity . . . insinuated that [she] was engaged in the activity described in the article . . . ."[13] The court held that

> [t]o succeed on a defamation claim under Massachusetts law, a plaintiff must show that the defendant was at fault for the publication of a false statement of and concerning the plaintiff which was capable of damaging his or her reputation in the community and which either caused economic loss or is actionable without proof of economic loss.[14]

The trial court had accepted the disclaimer as a defense. The First Circuit reversed and held that the issue at the summary judgment stage was not whether the statement was ultimately defamatory but whether it was susceptible, for purposes of stating a claim as a matter of law, of defamatory meaning, and found that a reasonable reader could so conclude. In other words, a photograph may become defamatory based on the circumstances of its publication or display.

In *Doe v. Merck & Co.*,[15] the defendant used a photograph of the plaintiff as part of two brochures on HIV—one educational, the other to promote its products. The plaintiff had consented to the former but not the latter use, since she did not have the disease in terms of the commercial use. Defendants sought subpoenas to establish the plaintiff's status at the time of the picture, since truth is an absolute defense to a defamation claim, defendants could not establish that access to stored blood would be dispositive.

In *Knievel v. ESPN*,[16] the famed motorcyclist sued ESPN for publishing a photograph of him with one arm around his wife and the other around another woman, with the caption "Evel Knievel proves that you're never too old to be a pimp." On a motion to dismiss, the trial court held the photograph and caption were not defamatory, and the Ninth Circuit affirmed. Knievel had failed to prove that the photograph and caption were "reasonably capable of sustaining defamatory meaning," as opposed to just being

13. *Id.* at 123.
14. *Id.* at 124.
15. 283 A.D.2d 543 (2nd Dept. 2001).
16. 393 F.3d 1068 (9th Cir. 2005).

First Amendment–sanctioned comment.[17] To determine whether a statement was defamatory, the court looked to "the standpoint of the average reader" and not the statement in isolation.[18] The court applied a three-part test: the broad context, the specific context, and whether the statement was sufficiently factual to be able to evaluated as true or false.[19]

Under the "first publication rule" or "single publication rule," a single action for defamation accrues on the first publication of the defamatory material.[20] As noted in *Christoff v. Nestle USA, Inc.*, his was meant to prevent the unfairness of literally millions of repeated claims and a never-ending statute of limitations.[21] Christoff was a model who posed for a coffee label. The company used his image on a Taster's Choice label; he discovered that 16 years after the original photo was taken and sued, claiming use of his image without his consent. Despite the two-year statute of limitations, the jury found he did not know and could not have reasonably known, of the subsequent nonconsensual use of his image and awarded $15 million in damages. The appellate court reversed, based on the "single publication" rule, and the tolling would apply only if the jury found that Nestle had "hindered" plaintiff's discovery of the image. The Supreme Court of California agreed to the reversal but held that "single publication" was dependent upon whether the first publication was a "single integrated publication."[22] Whether the subsequent publications were simply later sales, or constituted a different type of publication for purposes of accrual of the statute of limitations (i.e., a republication), was a jury question.

17. *Id.* at 1073–74 (citation omitted).

18. *Id.* at 1074.

19. *Id.* at 1080 (citation omitted).

20. Roberts v. McAfee, Inc., 660 F.3d 1156, 1166–67 (9th Cir. 2011); Gregoire v. G.P. Putnam's Sons, 298 N.Y. 119, 123 (1948) ("[T]he publication of a defamatory statement in a single issue of a newspaper, or a single issue of a magazine, although such publication consists of thousands of copies widely distributed, is, in legal effect, one publication which gives rise to one cause of action and that the applicable [s]tatute of [l]imitation[s] runs from the date of that publication.").

21. Christoff v. Nestle USA, Inc., 47 Cal. 4th 468, 477–78 (2009).

22. *Id.* at 477. *See also* Rinaldi v. Viking Penguin, Inc., 52 N.Y.2d 422, 434–35 (1981) (distinguishing "a new edition and, as such, a republication" from "a delayed circulation of the original edition").

The single publication rule applies to publication on the Internet.[23] A court may still apply standards to see if there has been a republication based on a "separate aggregate publication from the original, on a different occasion," and not merely a "delayed" publication, but simply modifying a website is not legally sufficient.[24] In *Geary v. Town Sports International Holding, Inc.*,[25] a 1999 photograph of plaintiff while playing football, and displayed in various sports clubs, was held to be "republished" on the Internet in or after 2007 for purposes of triggering a new statute of limitations.[26] Similarly, using a hyperlink to direct someone to the original source is not a republication so as to avoid the single publication rule.[27]

Substantive defenses to defamation include truth,[28] fair comment (opinion),[29] consent,[30] official proceedings,[31] and reply.[32]

The publication of a photograph related to an official action or proceeding holds a qualified privilege known as the fair report privilege; it is not absolute and can be undone if the reporting was "inaccurate, incomplete, or an unfair abridgment of the proceeding."[33] In *Lavin v. New York News, Inc.*,[34] the plaintiff's photograph appeared next to a newspaper article about an organized-crime investigation; Lavin was briefly mentioned in the article as one of three police officers denying bribes. Of relevance here was the plaintiff's claim "that the combined effect of the headlines and the photograph is an accusation that plaintiff was guilty of taking

23. Firth v. New York, 98 N.Y.2d 365, 370 (2002).

24. *Id.* at 371.

25. 21 Misc. 3d 512 (N.Y. Cty. 2008).

26. *See also, e.g.*, Ladd v. Uecker, 780 N.W.2d 216, 220 (Wis. Ct. App. 2010); *In re* Phil. Newspapers, LLC, 690 F.3d 161, 174 (3d Cir. 2012), *cert. denied*, Gureghian v. Phil. Newspapers, LLC, 133 S. Ct. 1001 (2013).

27. Salyer v. S. Poverty Law Ctr., Inc., 701 F. Supp. 2d 912, 918 (W.D. Ky. 2009).

28. Carter v. Visconti, 233 A.D.2d 473 (N.Y. App. Div. 2d 1996), *app. denied*, 89 N.Y.2d 811 (1997).

29. Piscatelli v. Smith, 424 Md. 294 (Ct. App. 2012).

30. Mullenaux v. Graham Cnty., 82 P.3d 362, 368 (Ariz. Ct. App. 2004), *rev. denied*, 2004 Ariz. LEXIS 64 (Ariz. May 25, 2004).

31. Salzano v. N. Jersey Media Grp., Inc., 201 N.J. 500 (2010), *cert. denied*, 131 S. Ct. 1045 (2011).

32. Shenkman v. O'Malley, 2 A.D.2d 567 (N.Y. App. Div. 1st 1956).

33. Schiavone Constr. Co. v. Time, Inc., 735 F.2d 94, 96–97 (3d Cir. 1984).

34. 757 F.2d 1416 (3d Cir. 1985).

bribes . . . ."[35] The principle on which the case was resolved was whether "a reasonable fact-finder could conclude that the headline, photograph, and article, separately and together, are more pejorative than the FBI affidavit."[36] The dissent disagreed with the application of the principle by the majority, noting his belief

> that it would be equally reasonable for a reader to conclude on these facts that the allegations in the FBI affidavit concerning Lavin did not so nearly approximate in seriousness the charges or evidence against Sisk as to justify painting the two with the same brush or describing them with a common headline over their joint photograph.[37]

Statutory defenses would include timeliness in terms of a statute of limitations, whether by statute or if related to a contract, any proper contractual limitation. A court may also employ laches if it finds unreasonable delay in bringing an action. This will have primary import in seeking an injunction; it is hard to claim irreparable and immediate harm if someone has waited a long time. Similarly, estoppel and waiver may be available based on the conduct of the person alleging defamation.

Defamation may be pleaded in addition to claims for breach of privacy, addressed next. "Privacy" actually takes four basic forms. Complicating the discussion is that certain states—most notably New York and California—have specific statutes that address the issues, and each has developed a body of law based on those statutes.

35. *Id.* at 1418.
36. *Id.* at 1420.
37. *Id.* at 1426.

## Privacy

The common law "right" to privacy is often linked to an article published in 1890 by Samuel D. Warren and Louis D. Brandeis.[38] Georgia was the first state to recognize a common-law right to privacy.[39] Thereafter, noted tort authority William Prosser concluded, in 1960, that the right to privacy had four essential variations, each constituting its own tort. These are "(1) intrusion upon a person's seclusion or solitude; (2) public disclosure of private facts; (3) publicity that places a person in a false light; and (4) misappropriation of a person's name and likeness."[40] In *Ignat*, the court addressed a prior "requirement" under California law that a right of privacy could only be violated by a writing, and not word of mouth; the court rejected that stricture.[41] Privacy may also find its basis in a state constitution; the difference is that "[t]he constitutional variety focuses on institutional record keeping and does not require a wide dissemination of private information . . . . Liability for the common law tort requires publicity; disclosure to a few people in limited circumstances does not violate the right."[42]

The *Restatement (Second) of Torts* § 652A(1) (1977) states as a general principle that "(1) one who invades the right of privacy of another is subject to liability for the resulting harm to the interests of the other." In Section 652A(2), we are told that "(2) The right of privacy is invaded by: (a) unreasonable intrusion upon the seclusion of another, as stated in 625B; or (b) appropriation of the other's name or likeness, as stated in 652C; or (c) unreasonable publicity given to the other's private life, as stated in 652D; or (d) publicity that unreasonably places the other in a false light before the public, as stated in 652E." Each of the referenced sections then flesh out the particular elements.

38. Samuel D. Warren & Louis D. Brandeis, *The Right to Privacy*, 4 HARV. L. REV. 193 (1890).

39. Pavesich v. New England Life Ins. Co., 122 Ga. 190 (1905).

40. *See* Ignat v. Yum! Brands, Inc., 214 Cal. App. 4th 808, 812–14 (2013).

41. *Id.* at 819.

42. *Id.* at 820 (citations omitted).

The right of privacy is also referred to as a right of publicity. As of this writing, 19 states have statutes that govern the right of publicity or privacy; 28 states have addressed it as a matter of common law.[43]

Generally speaking, common-law jurisdictions recognize four types of tort involving privacy: (1) intrusion (e.g., intrusion upon a plaintiff's physical solitude or seclusion, as by invading his or her home, illegal search, eavesdropping, prying into personal affairs, etc.); (2) public disclosure of private facts (e.g., making public private information about a plaintiff); (3) placing a plaintiff in a false light in the public eye (which need not be defamatory, but must be something that would be objectionable to the ordinary reasonable man); and (4) appropriation, which is defined as an "appropriation, for the defendant's benefit, of the plaintiff's name or likeness."[44]

Some states define the claim by statute. For example, in California, "California Civil Code § 45a, Appellants may only prevail on a libel claim if the publication is (1) libelous on its face, or (2) if special damages have been proven."[45] In New York, the statute preempts the common-law remedy and is the exclusive remedy. The statute preempts the right of publicity at common law.[46]

California recognizes both common law and statutory grounds for misappropriation.[47]

---

43. *Statutes*, Right of Publicity, http://rightofpublicity.com/statutes (last visited Apr. 7, 2014).

44. Canessa v. J.I. Kislak, Inc., 97 N.J. Super. 327, 334 (Law Div. 1967); *see also, e.g.*, Dalley v. Dykema Gossett, P.L.L.C., 287 Mich. App. 296 (2010); Spellman v. Disc. Zone Gas Station, 975 So. 2d 44 (La. Ct. App. 2007).

45. Downing v. Abercrombie & Fitch, 265 F.3d 994, 1010 (9th Cir. 2001).

46. Pirone v. MacMillan, Inc., 894 F.2d 579 (2d Cir. 1990); Howell v. N.Y. Post Co., 81 N.Y.2d 115 (1993) (Civil Rights Law is exclusive remedy for rights of privacy and rejecting common law claims of unreasonable publicity given to another's private life (RESTATEMENT (SECOND) OF TORTS § 652D); unreasonable intrusion upon seclusion (*id.* § 652B); and publicity that unreasonably places another in a false light (*id.* § 652E)); Stephano v. News Grp. Publ'n, Inc., 64 N.Y.2d 174, 183 (1984); Arrington v. N.Y. Times Co., 55 N.Y.2d 433 (1982), *cert. denied*, 459 U.S. 1146 (1983).

47. Fraley v. Facebook, Inc., 830 F. Supp. 2d 785, 803 (N.D. Cal. 2011) ("California law provides two vehicles for asserting such a right: a common law cause of action for commercial misappropriation, and a statutory remedy for commercial misappropriation under California Civil Code § 3344.").

States vary in approach. In Minnesota, there is no common-law recognition of a false-light claim, but there is for intrusion upon seclusion, appropriation, and publication of private facts.[48] The *Lake* court stated that "[t]he right to privacy is an integral part of our humanity; one has a public persona, exposed and active, and a private persona, guarded and preserved. The heart of our liberty is choosing which parts of our lives shall become public and which parts we shall hold close."[49] It held that false light was too similar to defamation and declined otherwise to recognize it separately. Massachusetts, which has a statute with languages essentially identical to that of New York, nonetheless construes it less broadly, and does not rule out certain common law remedies.[50]

## The New York Statute

The New York Civil Rights Law provides:

> Sec. 50. Right of privacy. A person, firm or corporation that uses for advertising purposes, or for the purposes of trade, the name, portrait or picture of any living person without having first obtained the written consent of such person, or if a minor of his or her parent or guardian, is guilty of a misdemeanor.
>
> Any person whose name, portrait, picture or voice is used within this state for advertising purposes or for the purposes of trade without the written consent first obtained as above provided may maintain an equitable action in the supreme court of this state against the person, firm or corporation so using his name, portrait, picture or voice, to prevent and restrain the use thereof; and may also sue and recover damages for any injuries sustained by reason of such use and if the defendant shall have knowingly used such person's name, portrait, picture or voice in such manner as is forbidden or declared to be unlawful by section fifty of this article, the jury, in its discretion, may award exemplary damages. But nothing contained in this article

48. Lake v. Wal-Mart Stores, Inc., 582 N.W.2d 231, 232–33 (Minn. 1998).
49. *Id.* at 235.
50. Tropeano v. Atl. Monthly Co., 379 Mass. 745 (1980).

> shall be so construed as to prevent any person, firm or corporation from selling or otherwise transferring any material containing such name, portrait, picture or voice in whatever medium to any user of such name, portrait, picture or voice, or to any third party for sale or transfer directly or indirectly to such a user, for use in a manner lawful under this article; nothing contained in this article shall be so construed as to prevent any person, firm or corporation, practicing the profession of photography, from exhibiting in or about his or its establishment specimens of the work of such establishment, unless the same is continued by such person, firm or corporation after written notice objecting thereto has been given by the person portrayed; and nothing contained in this article shall be so construed as to prevent any person, firm or corporation from using the name, portrait, picture or voice of any manufacturer or dealer in connection with the goods, wares and merchandise manufactured, produced or dealt in by him which he has sold or disposed of with such name, portrait, picture or voice used in connection therewith; or from using the name, portrait, picture or voice of any author, composer or artist in connection with his literary, musical or artistic productions which he has sold or disposed of with such name, portrait, picture or voice used in connection therewith. Nothing contained in this section shall be construed to prohibit the copyright owner of a sound recording from disposing of, dealing in, licensing or selling that sound recording to any party, if the right to dispose of, deal in, license or sell such sound recording has been conferred by contract or other written document by such living person or the holder of such right. Nothing contained in the foregoing sentence shall be deemed to abrogate or otherwise limit any rights or remedies otherwise conferred by federal law or state law.

Section 51 therefore provides the civil remedy of injunctive relief to any person whose photograph (or other identifying features as defined) are used within New York "for advertising purposes or for the purposes of trade without the written consent" of the person. You can sue for injunction or damages but only if violates the above—that is, the offending use is for advertising or trade.

The key language involves the "commercial purpose." New York courts have recognized exception for newsworthiness and incidental use.[51] *Finger* involved a nonconsensual use of a photograph of plaintiffs (two adults and their six children) in an *Omni* magazine article on caffeine-aided fertilization. The opinion does not elucidate the circumstances of the taking of the photograph. The defendants argued that fertility was "a topic of legitimate public interest."[52] The court rejected the plaintiffs' claim and noted as well that such an image next to an article would be deemed not to be of public interest only if it had "no real relationship to the article . . . or unless the article is an advertisement in disguise."[53]

In *Arrington v. N.Y. Times, Co.*,[54] the plaintiff was photographed while walking on a New York City street, and the photograph was used without his consent as part of an article in the *Times*' Sunday magazine titled "The Black Middle Class: Making It." Arrington's name was not mentioned in the article, and he claimed he disagreed with the views made in the article and did not like his image used as an exemplar, and further contended it caused embarrassment to him for those who recognized him. The defendants included the freelance photographer hired to take the picture. The plaintiff sued under the New York statute, as well as common-law privacy violation and a claimed constitutional right to privacy (i.e., "an emerging 'right to be let alone'"). The court of appeals in *Arrington* rejected a common-law right to privacy in New York. The court also rejected a false-light invasion of privacy tort. However, while it affirmed the dismissal of the case against The New York Times, it allowed the statutory case to proceed against the other defendants, including the photographer, since

51. *See, e.g.*, Finger v. Omni Publ'ns Int'l, Ltd., 77 N.Y.2d 138, 141–42 (1990) ("Although the statute does not define 'purposes of trade' or 'advertising,' courts have consistently refused to construe these terms as encompassing publications concerning newsworthy events or matters of public interest.").

52. *Id.* at 141.

53. *Id.* at 142 (citations omitted); *see also* Arrington v. N.Y. Times, Co., 55 N.Y.2d 433 (1982).

54. 55 N.Y.2d 433, 439 (1982).

> unlike the position of the Times, none of the other three defendants played the part of publisher of the article which plaintiff's photograph accompanied. Were the plaintiff to establish the truth of his allegations, the acts in which one or more of these defendants will have been proved to have engaged will, plainly and simply, have included that of a nonconsensual selling of the photograph. Thus, operating independently from the publisher, each at that point would have "commercialized the photograph" in "furtherance of [his] trade."[55]

Written consent is necessary under sections 50 and 51 before the photograph can be used in trade or advertising, and oral consent is not a defense to liability.[56]

One of the more interesting cases in New York is *Nussenzweig v. diCorcia*.[57] DiCorcia was a respected photographer with a history of shows in New York museums. He photographed a *Heads* series of candid "street photography" shots of people at the same Times Square location. The images were exhibited in a gallery for sale. The image of the Nussenzweig was readily identifiable; there was no consent to diCorcia to use it. The exhibit was open to the public and was advertised. All ten photos of Nussenzweig, in a limited edition, sold for $20,000 to $30,000 each. Nussenzweig was an Orthodox Jew with deep religious beliefs against the use of his image. The trial court addressed two issues: whether the statute of limitations had run (finding it had) and the merits, noting the statute was the exclusive remedy, and held that "art" is an exception for use under the statute, and that this was art (free speech), and *not* trade or advertising. The appellate court affirmed expressly on the statute of limitations grounds, not reaching the privacy issue, although one judge in a concurring opinion did so reach it and agreed with the trial court on the merits. The highest court, the New

55. *Id.* at 443 (citations omitted).
56. Brinkley v. Casablancas, 80 A.D.2d 428 (N.Y. App. Div. 1st 1981).
57. 9 N.Y.3d 184 (2007), *aff'g* 38 A.D.3d 339 (N.Y. App. Div. 1st 2007), *aff'g* 2006 slip op. 50171U, 1 (N.Y. Cty. 2006).

York Court of Appeals, affirmed solely on the statute of limitations basis without addressing the lower court's findings on the merits.[58]

In *Yasin v. Q-Boro Holdings, LLC*,[59] Yasin was photographed by consent for promoting her career; the photograph ended up without consent and without a model release on the cover of a book. The court found this was not a use of the image to illustrate an article of public interest but, here, was solely for marketing purposes. This case should be contrasted with the facts noted in other cases cited in it, where the photographs had relationship to the content matter of the book[60] or use as a work of art.[61] The New York Civil Rights Law regarding privacy is to be strictly construed, and as long as it cannot be said that there is no "real relationship" between the article's contents and photograph, it will not be determined to be for trade or advertising.[62]

In *Gaeta v. Home Box Office*,[63] the plaintiff watched HBO filming of the defendant photographer as he shot nude models in New York City streets. The plaintiff herself was photographed as part of a crowd and featured in close-up in the program as publicly broadcast. Under the New York cases interpreting the Civil Rights statute, the court applied the "newsworthy or public interest" exception. Noting that while there is some law that the spectator cannot be singled out in crowd, such an exception is very limited, and in this case, the plaintiff was voluntarily part of the crowd.[64] The court commented that there are limits to one's expectation of privacy. In this case, the court had no difficulty with "essentially stock photos to be used, outside the context in which they were taken, to illustrate related topics."[65]

58. For a general discussion, *see* Ariella Goldstein, Note, *Privacy from Photography: Is There a Right Not to Be Photographed Under New York State Law?*, 26 CARDOZO ARTS & ENT. L.J. 233 (2008).

59. 2010 N.Y. slip op. 50742 (Kings Cty. 2010).

60. *See, e.g.*, Dallesandro v. Henry Holt & Co., 4 A.D.2d 470 (N.Y. App. Div. 1st 1957), *appeal dismissed*, 7 N.Y.2d 735 (1959).

61. *See, e.g.*, Hoepker v. Kruger, 200 F. Supp. 2d 340 (S.D.N.Y. 2002).

62. Finger v. Omni Publ'ns Int'l, Ltd., 77 N.Y.2d 138, 143 (1990); Murray v. N.Y. Magazine Co., 27 N.Y.2d 406 (1971).

63. 169 Misc. 2d 500 (N.Y. Cty. 1996).

64. *Id.* at 502–03.

65. *Id.* at 506. *See also* Alvarado v. K-III Magazine Corp., 203 A.D.2d 135 (N.Y. App. Div. 1st 1994) (magazine permitted to use nonconsensual photograph of young men next to an

Photographer Arne Svenson used a telephoto lens to take pictures from his own apartment of people in a neighboring apartment building, through large windows in those units. The photographs consisted of still lifes, people, and children; he did not ask permission and did not have permission to photograph the people. He exhibited them in a show. Various neighbors, for themselves and their children, sought an injunction against dissemination and sale, in particular two images showing plaintiff's children's faces and "partially-clad bodies." Analyzing sections 50 and 51 of New York's Civil Rights Law, the trial court found that the likenesses were protected by the First Amendment, and that "privacy rights yield to free speech rights in the context of newsworthy events." These particular images were "art" and "promote the enjoyment of art in the form of a displaced exhibition." The trial court found that "the value of artistic expression outweighs any sale that stems from the published photos."[66]

In *D'Andrea v. Rafla-Demetrious*,[67] a hospital resident permitted his photograph for use in a brochure about the hospital's internship and residency programs. Although the resident had insisted on prior notification,

---

article on Mexicans attending conferences; the men were not Mexican and did not attend the conferences of the kind in the article, but the newsworthiness exception to the statute applied).

66. Foster v. Svenson, 2013 N.Y. slip op. 31782(U) (N.Y. Cty. Aug. 5, 2013); *see also* Hoepker v. Kruger, 200 F. Supp. 2d 340 (S.D.N.Y. 2002); Friedan v. Friedan, 414 F. Supp. 77 (S.D.N.Y. 1976) (famed feminist Betty Friedan's use of former husband's name and photograph in an article she wrote for *New York Magazine* did not violate his right to privacy, as it was a matter of public interest and not used for trade or advertising, and the use of the same in commercials to promote the article falls within the privilege afforded to the article); Namath v. Sports Illustrated, 48 A.D.2d 487 (N.Y. App. Div. 1st 1975), *aff'd*, 39 N.Y.2d 897 (1976) (use of famed quarterback Joe Namath's photograph from 1969 Super Bowl without consent in promotional advertising for magazine not actionable as it did not indicate an endorsement of the magazine but suggested the content of the magazine); Booth v. Curtis Publ'g Co., 15 A.D.2d 343 (N.Y. App. Div. 1st), *aff'd*, 11 N.Y.2d 907 (1962) (collateral or incidental advertising not enough to remove newsworthy element; "so long as the reproduction was used to illustrate the quality and content of the periodical in which it originally appeared" it is not actionable). *But see* Flores v. Mosler Safe Co., 7 N.Y.2d 276 (1959) ("In view of the fact that defendant chose to reprint the entire original news coverage of the fire, including the entire news account which mentioned plaintiff's name several times and described how either he or the other person present started the fire by their carelessness or negligence, in a circular designed for the sole purpose of soliciting purchasers for the defendant's products . . . we do not believe that it can be said that this complaint fails to set forth a use of plaintiff's name which is a violation of his statutory right of privacy as a matter of law.").

67. 972 F. Supp. 154 (E.D.N.Y. 1997), *aff'd*, 146 F.3d 64 (2d Cir. 1998).

he did not object after initial publication and only did so in the context of claims brought years later. The court rejected his claim since the use was not unauthorized and his picture was incidental to the other information in the brochure. Similarly, in *Candelaria v. Spurlock*,[68] a use of a McDonald's employee's photograph for three to four seconds in the film *Super Size Me* was not violative of section 50 due to the "newsworthiness" and "incidental" exceptions.

What about look-alikes? In *Allen v. National Video, Inc.*,[69] a Woody Allen look-alike was used in an advertisement by a video rental club. Allen sued under the New York statute, claiming his identity was "usurped for another's commercial gain." The real issue was not whether people would be "reminded" of Allen but whether they would be likely to think it was him. Ultimately, the court found it to be a question of fact on the question:

> We are unable to conclude, however, that no reasonable jury could find that others would so interpret the advertisement, or at least recognize it to contain a look-alike, particularly in light of the distinctions noted above. Therefore, while the court finds that the advertisement at bar clearly makes reference to plaintiff, it hesitates to conclude that the photograph is, as a matter of law, plaintiff's portrait or picture.[70]

Finding the Lanham Act (dealing with trademarks) to be a better means of resolution, and the court found a likelihood of confusion as a matter of law.[71] The *Allen* court distinguished *Onassis* because, in the *Onassis* case, there was a more complex staged event with look-alikes that did more than just "remind" people of the aggrieved celebrity.

68. No. 08-civ-1830, 2008 U.S. Dist. LEXIS 51595 (E.D.N.Y. July 3, 2008).

69. 610 F. Supp. 612 (S.D.N.Y. 1985).

70. *Id.* at 624.

71. *Cf.* Onassis v. Christian Dior-New York, Inc., 122 Misc. 2d 603 (N.Y. Cty. 1984), *aff'd w/o*, 110 A.D.2d 1095 (1st Dept. 1985) (use for commercial purposes of a look-alike of a well-known personality violates the right of privacy legislatively granted by enactment of sections 50 and 41 of the Civil Rights Law).

### The California Statute

As noted, California also has a statutory privacy statute that does not preempt but complements common law rights of misappropriation:

> [a]ny person who knowingly uses another's name, voice, signature, photograph, or likeness, in any manner, on or in products, merchandise, or goods, or for purposes of advertising or selling, or soliciting purchases of, products, merchandise, goods or services, without such person's prior consent, or, in the case of a minor, the prior consent of his parent or legal guardian, shall be liable for any damages sustained by the person or persons injured as a result thereof.[72]

The statutory remedy applies to commercial use and also expressly references photographs.[73] Essentially, anyone (1) *knowingly* (2) using another's likeness (3) on a product or for commercial purposes (4) without prior consent (5) is liable for damages of the greater of $750 or actual damages plus (6) profits from the unauthorized use and (7) punitive damages may be awarded. The test of identification means that "[a] person shall be deemed to be readily identifiable from a photograph when one who views the photograph with the naked eye can reasonably determine that the person depicted in the photograph is the same person who is complaining of its unauthorized use."[74] Exceptions to use include use of the likeness "in connection with any news, public affairs, or sports broadcast or account, or any political campaign."[75] Notably, use in a commercial medium is not dispositive in itself, even if paid advertising; it has to be in connection with a sponsorship or other defined use that meets the criteria just outlined.

Claims for misappropriation under California Civil Code § 3344 are preempted by the federal Copyright Act to the extent the subject of the claim and the rights asserted are within the scope of the Copyright Act's

72. Cal. Civ. Code § 3344(a).
73. *Id.* § 3344.
74. *Id.* § 3344(b)(1).
75. *Id.* § 3344(d).

subject matter and exclusive rights sections.[76] However, that holding was limited to "the solid proposition that performers in a copyrighted film may not use their statutory right of publicity to prevent the exclusive copyright holder from distributing the film."[77] Where the exploitation of the work was unauthorized display of the work, such preemption did not apply. In *KNB Enterprises*, the plaintiff/owner of erotic photos (and their copyrights) of noncelebrity models posted them on its website; the defendant copied and displayed them on its own website without permission. The plaintiff relied on statutory misappropriation claim, which was not preempted in this case by copyright.

Copyright law preempts state-law unfair-competition claims where the claim is based on misappropriation of copyrighted items.[78] The core of the claim is taking and use of another's property. It is meant to be broad and flexible. In *Roy Export*, the court found that the compilation of film segments owned by the plaintiff was taken by the defendant and was not so "inextricably related" to the copyrighted material of the actual films, so there was no preemption.

In *Fraley v. Facebook, Inc.*,[79] the court found the allegations sufficient and a material factual dispute existed to sustain a claim that Facebook's use of members' names, photographs, likenesses, and identities in paid advertisements—the "Sponsored Stories"—violated California's privacy statute. The case ultimately settled.

In *Downing v. Abercrombie & Fitch*,[80] the defendant purchased from the photographer a photograph of the plaintiffs appearing in a photography book on surfers. The photograph was then used in the defendant's magazine, and the defendant made T-shirts identical to those in the photograph. The plaintiffs claimed misappropriation under the California statute and common law. On appeal, the court held that the defendant's use of the pho-

76. Fleet v. CBS, Inc., 50 Cal. App. 4th 911 (1996).

77. KNB Enters. v. Matthews, 78 Cal. App. 4th 362, 372 (2000), *review denied*, Supreme Court Minute, 06-14-2000, 2000 Cal. LEXIS 4906 (Cal. June 14, 2000)

78. Roy Exp. Co. Establishment of Vaduz v. Columbia Broad. Sys., 672 F.2d 1095 (2d Cir.), *cert. denied*, 459 U.S. 826 (1982).

79. 830 F. Supp. 2d 785 (N.D. Cal. 2011).

80. 265 F.3d 994 (9th Cir. 2001).

tograph was not protected First Amendment expression, since although an article about surfing culture was arguably public interest, there was only here "a tenuous relationship"; the catalog did not identify the plaintiffs as "legends," incorrectly identified the location and date of the image, and therefore the photograph did "not contribute significantly to a matter of the public interest."[81]

## The Massachusetts Statute

A national survey of each state is beyond the scope of this book. One other state statute will suffice by way of example.

In Massachusetts, two statutes are relevant: Massachusetts General Laws chapter 214, section 1B, which provides that "a person shall have a right against unreasonable, substantial or serious interference with his privacy," and Massachusetts General Laws chapter 214, section 3A, which provides a cause of action for "any person whose name, portrait or picture is used within the commonwealth for advertising purposes or for the purposes of trade without his written consent."

In *Peckham v. New England Newspapers, Inc.*,[82] plaintiff sued the newspaper for publication of a photograph of the injured plaintiff at the scene of an automobile accident claiming negligent infliction of emotional distress and violation of his right to privacy. The newspaper raised the defense that the photograph was "newsworthy"; the court, citing *Restatement (Second) of Torts*,[83] analyzed the issue under two factors: "(1) whether the subject matter at issue is properly considered a matter of legitimate public concern and (2) whether there is a substantial nexus between the publication and the alleged issue of concern."[84] The court also noted that the issue would turn on whether the photograph was part of "sociological commentary"

81. *Id.* at 1002; *cf.* Dora v. Frontline Video, Inc., 15 Cal. App. 4th 536 (1993) (found for defendant because the plaintiff was specifically identified as a surfing legend and use was in a documentary film).

82. 865 F. Supp. 2d 127 (D. Mass. 2012).

83. § 652D cmt. h (1977) ("[T]he extent of the authority to make public private facts is not . . . unlimited.").

84. 865 F. Supp. 2d at 131 (citation omitted).

or as part of a "means of soliciting sales."[85] The court denied defendant's motion to discmiss.

What can we make of these cases? They are not the universe of cases, again indicating the fact-sensitive nature of the analysis. More to the point, the cases also confirm the distinction between the taking of the image in the initial instance and the use of the image as a separate factor. In the latter regard, it is also obvious that a photograph standing by itself, as a purely artistic endeavor, might stand, but once it is attached to a caption or an article, other issues come into play. At least in New York, while the publisher itself may find a way out through the newsworthy exception, the photographer who has been paid for the work as a commercial act, at least in *Arrington*, may have a harder row to hoe.

We are also not addressing the particularized issues of photographs taken in the course of surveillance, particularly after an individual has filed a claim or court proceeding and subjected his or her activities to certain scrutiny.[86]

## Common Law Claims

We can now look to situations involving the different claims, to provide a sense of the parameters. Remember that different states may not recognize a particular claim or may frame the elements differently.

### Intrusion upon Seclusion

To prove intrusion upon seclusion, one must prove "(1) an intrusion into a protected zone of privacy that (2) was so unjustified and offensive as to constitute a privacy violation."[87] Note that this privacy tort in California

85. *Id.* at 132 (citing Tropeano v. Atl. Monthly Co., 379 Mass. 745 (1980)). In *Tropeano*, the court interpreted the statute by noting that "the crucial distinction under [section 3A] must be between situations in which the defendant makes an incidental use of the plaintiff's name, portrait or picture and those in which the defendant uses the plaintiff's name, portrait or picture deliberately to exploit its value for advertising or trade purposes." *Tropeano*, 349 Mass. at 749.

86. *But see* Kyllo v. United States, 533 U.S. 27 (2001) (thermal imaging of a home was an unlawful search under the Fourth Amendment).

87. Hernandez v. Hillsides, Inc., 47 Cal. 4th 272, 277 (2009).

was recognized as a matter of common law and not under the California Civil Code § 3344, discussed above. It is a defense, however, if the items are already either in the public record or otherwise required to be made available for public inspection.[88] Where a person is in plain sight, even in a privately owned building otherwise open to the public, there is no seclusion.[89] In *Stessman*, even though a woman eating in a restaurant told a reporter not to film her and the reporter did so, she had not proved she was "secluded." The *Stessman* court cited other cases that provide some guidance to photographers as to the scope of this:

> *See also Jackson v. Playboy Enters., Inc.*, 574 F.Supp. 10, 13–14 (S.D.Ohio 1983) (publication of photograph of plaintiffs on a city sidewalk); *Neff v. Time, Inc.*, 406 F.Supp. 858, 861 (W.D.Pa.1976) (publication of photograph of plaintiff at football stadium); *Jaubert v.Crowley Post-Signal, Inc.*, 375 So.2d 1386, 1387 (La.1979) (publication of photograph of resident taken from middle of street); *Cefalu v. Globe Newspaper Co.*, 8 Mass.App.Ct. 71, 77, 391 N.E.2d 935, 939 (1979) (publication of photograph of plaintiff while he was in unemployment line), *cert. denied*, 444 U.S. 1060, 100 S.Ct. 994, 62 L.Ed.2d 738 (1980).[90]

The photograph of a lone fisherman in Sausalito on page 159, in public view, particularly since the individual is not even recognizable, would not be an intrusion upon seclusion.

In *Swerdlick v. Koch*,[91] an objection by the defendant of the plaintiff's business activities in a residential area that allegedly violated zoning restric-

88. Tillet v. Onslow Mem'l Hosp., Inc., 215 N.C. App. 382, 385–86 (2011), *rev. denied*, 365 N.C. 559 (2012) (rejecting privacy claim based on autopsy photographs); Shulman v. Grp. W. Prods., Inc., 74 Cal. Rptr. 2d 843, 864 (1998); RESTATEMENT (SECOND) OF TORTS § 652B, (1977) ("One who intentionally intrudes, physically or otherwise, upon the solitude or seclusion of another or his private affairs or concerns, is subject to liability to the other for invasion of his privacy, if the intrusion would be highly offensive to a reasonable person.").

89. Stessman v. Am. Black Hawk Broad., 416 N.W.2d 685 (Iowa 1987) and cases cited therein.

90. *Id.* at 687.

91. 721 A.2d 849 (R.I. 1998).

A lone fisherman in Sausalito.

tions led to photographing the business activities. The defendant used a telephoto lens on occasion, and all photographs were taken of publicly visible activities of the plaintiff. The plaintiff sought police intervention to stop the surveillance. When that failed, the plaintiff sued on theories of violation of rights of privacy as granted by statute in Rhode Island, as well as tarnishment to reputation and infliction of emotional distress. The trial court dismissed the charges after trial, and the Supreme Court of Rhode Island affirmed. The Rhode Island statute codified the four types of privacy claims. On the intrusion claim, the court held that the statute only precluded invasion of physical solitude or seclusion, and such is not present when one "ventures outside his or her house into public view."[92] The court added: "The plaintiffs were not entitled, nor could they reasonably have expected, to maintain privacy with respect to those activities taking place outside of their residence in a location visible to any passersby."[93] Similarly,

92. *Id.* at 857.
93. *Id.*

just because one is on one's own property, there is no extension of the sanctity of the home: "Activities occurring in plain view of the public are not entitled to the protection of the privacy statute merely because they occur on private property in the vicinity of the actor's home."[94] Regarding the privacy claim based on the publication of private facts, the court found no claim was made where the plaintiff himself left the acts open to the public eye, and here, the continued apparent business activity gave legitimacy to the surveillance. Regarding the claims of defamation and false light, the court found there were no false facts portrayed.

What is plain view? The Supreme Court, in the context of a search and seizure analysis, has held that aerial photography of someone's property "without a warrant was not a search under the Fourth Amendment,"[95] but the use of thermal-imaging devices that rely on infrared technology do constitute a search that requires a warrant.[96]

In *Boring v. Google, Inc.*,[97] the Borings sued Google for showing their house and swimming pool as part of its Street View program. The Third Circuit affirmed dismissal of their complaint that was grounded in privacy claims, finding nothing "highly offensive to a reasonable person" but reversed and remanded as to the physical trespass claims.

In *M.G. v. Time Warner, Inc.*,[98] the plaintiffs—who were members of a Little League baseball team, some of whom were molested and some not, and two coaches—successfully alleged a violation of their privacy rights under California law based on the use of a 1997 team photograph in an article about coaches who molest team players; their manager had pleaded guilty to molestation. They sued for intrusion, misappropriation of identity, public disclosure of private facts and false light. Similarly, in *Grill v. Curtis Publishing Co.*,[99] at issue was a photograph by well-known photographer

94. *Id.* at 855.
95. Dow Chem. Co. v. United States, 476 U.S. 227, 229 (1986).
96. Kyllo v. United States, 533 U.S. 27, 29 (2001).
97. 362 F. App'x 273, 280 (3d Cir. 2010) (non-precedential), *aff'g in part and rev'g in part* 598 F. Supp. 2d 695, 699–700 (W.D. Pa. 2009), *cert. denied*, 131 S. Ct. 150 (2010).
98. 89 Cal. App. 4th 623 (2001), *review denied*, Supreme Court Minute, 09-12-2011, 2001 Cal. LEXIS 6289 (Cal. Sept. 12, 2001).
99. 38 Cal. 2d 273 (1952).

Henri Cartier-Bresson of a husband and wife seated at the counter of their ice cream concession in a farmers' market. The man had his arm around his wife. They were photographed without their knowledge or consent. The photograph was used to accompany an article debunking the notion of love at first sight, and the plaintiffs claimed that there was a "disregard" of their "feelings and rights" in that "the article depicted plaintiffs as dissolute and immoral persons and robbed them of public esteem."[100] On the other hand, a related and follow-up case to *Gill*,[101] found no cause of action as pleaded, because the photograph as republished was not attached to an offensive article. The court noted that the photograph was made in a public market and "not surreptitiously snapped on private grounds."

Does use of long-range lenses or otherwise revealing something that even if arguably in public view nonetheless was subject to an expectation of privacy lead to a different result? The use of a telephoto lens in itself is not dispositive if the activities being photographed were still open to the public.[102]

### Publication of Private Facts

The core of this cause of action, where recognized, is "when one gives publicity to a matter concerning the private life of another . . . if the matter publicized is of a kind that (a) would be highly offensive to a reasonable person, and (b) is not of legitimate concern to the public."[103]

To provide publication of private facts, there must be "(1) public disclosure (2) of a private fact (3) which would be offensive and objectionable to the reasonable person and (4) which is not of legitimate public concern."[104] In *Shulman*, the plaintiffs were in a car accident, rescued in a dramatic fashion, and the rescue was videotaped by a video-camera operator. His film,

100. *Id.* at 281.

101. Gill v. Hearst Publ'g Co., 40 Cal. 2d 224 (1953). The court nonetheless reversed to allow plaintiffs to amend their complaint.

102. York v. Gen. Elec. Co., 144 Ohio App. 3d 191, 195 (2001), discretionary appeal not allowed, 93 Ohio St. 3d 1452 (2001).

103. Lake v. Wal-Mart Stores, Inc., 582 N.W.2d 231, 233 (Minn. 1998) (quoting Restatement (Second) of Torts § 652D (1977)) (internal quotation marks omitted).

104. Shulman v. Grp. W. Prods., Inc., 74 Cal. Rptr. 2d 843, 852 (1998), reh'g denied, Supreme Court Minute, 07-29-1998, 18 Cal. 4th 1034A (1998).

including images of the plaintiffs, was aired as part of a television program. The clips included certain conversations by the plaintiffs in distress as well as shots of them. The California Supreme Court, on the issue of publication of private facts, held that the newsworthy impact outweighed the publication of private facts, emphasizing the fourth factor.

Similarly, in *Gilbert v. Medical Economics Co.*,[105] the plaintiff was the subject of an article in a professional journal, based on claims of malpractice against her, the court found the article generally newsworthy and within it were published plaintiff's "name, photograph, and certain private facts about her life that were not privileged." Colorado law was applicable and recognized the tort. In this case, although the plaintiff argued the private facts were not necessary to the otherwise newsworthy article, the court found sufficient relevance by inference.

In *Barber v. Time, Inc.*,[106] a woman checked herself into a hospital for an eating disorder; a photograph of her appeared shortly thereafter in *Time*. The court held that "freedom of the press was not created merely for the benefit of the press, but because it is essential to the preservation of free government and progress of civilization. . . . Certainly if there is any right of privacy at all, it should include the right to obtain medical treatment at home or in a hospital for an individual condition. . . . It was not necessary to state plaintiff's name in order to give medical information to the public.[107]

In *Daily Times Democrat v. Graham*,[108] the court upheld privacy claims by a woman who was photographed with her dress blown up by "fun house" jets, and which photograph was published on the front page of regional daily newspapers. Her face was not shown, but her two sons were in the picture with her, and acquaintances of the woman recognized her. The defendants argued that the image was legitimate news interest. The Supreme Court of Alabama, in 1964, disagreed: "We can see nothing of legitimate news value in the photograph. Certainly it discloses nothing to which the public

105. 665 F.2d 305, 307 (10th Cir. 1981).
106. 348 Mo. 1199, 1206–07 (1942).
107. *Id.*
108. 276 Ala. 380 (1964).

is entitled to be informed."[109] The court also rejected the argument that the woman was part of a public scene, noting that "to hold that one who is involuntarily and instantaneously enmeshed in an embarrassing pose forfeits her right of privacy merely because she happened at the moment to be part of a public scene would be illogical, wrong, and unjust."[110] In *Granger v. Klein*,[111] a photograph of plaintiff urinating with his genitalia visible was found to be private and secret, citing *Graham*. However, the court found an issue as to whether the plaintiff had waived his right to privacy or even acquiesced in the photograph's appearance in the high school yearbook as against certain defendants.

## False Light

False light, according to *Restatement (Second) of Torts*,[112] states the elements as

> One who gives publicity to a matter concerning another that places the other before the public in a false light is subject to liability to the other for invasion of his privacy, if (a) the false light in which the other was placed would be highly offensive to a reasonable person, and (b) the actor had knowledge of or acted in reckless disregard as to the falsity of the publicized matter and the false light in which the other would be placed.[113]

Many jurisdictions have refused to recognize a false-light invasion of privacy action, mainly as duplicative of other established torts and to the extent it provides an end-run around traditional proofs necessary in a defamation action.[114]

---

109. *Id.* at 383.
110. *Id.*
111. 197 F. Supp. 2d 851 (E.D. Mich. 2002).
112. § 652E, at 294 (1977).
113. *See also* Lovgren v. Citizens First Nat'l Bank, 126 Ill. 2d 411, 418 (1989) ("[T]he heart of this tort lies in the publicity, rather than in the invasion into the plaintiff's physical solitude or affairs upon which the tort of invasion into seclusion is based.").
114. *See generally* Cain v. Hearst Corp., 878 S.W.2d 577, 579 (Tex. 1994) and cases cited therein.

In *Fudge v. Penthouse International, Ltd.*,[115] the plaintiffs were four schoolgirls aged 8 to 12 and their parents. *Penthouse* printed a photograph that had run in the *Providence Journal-Bulletin* of the four girls giving a "thumbs down" sign to a decision of the principal to separate the sexes. The photograph appeared as part of a story headlined "Little Amazons Attack Boys" in a section of the magazine devoted to "bizarre, idiotic, lurid and ofttimes witless driblets of information culled from the nation's press."[116] They had sued under a theory of libel based on the word "amazon" and that the article put them in a false light.

In *Wood v. Hustler Magazine, Inc.*,[117] *Hustler* published a stolen photograph of the plaintiff in the nude; the plaintiff sued for defamation and under certain invasion of privacy theories. The photographs had been taken of the plaintiff by a companion with her permission and never published. A neighbor broke into their home, stole the photographs, and submitted it to *Hustler* with a forged signature on the consent form. Applying Texas law, the court addressed false light as well as a separate cause of action for disclosure of private facts. The latter requires facts, not fantasies, and the former that the plaintiff is depicted "in a false light highly offensive to a reasonable person and public disclosure of private facts not of legitimate public concern and highly offensive to a reasonable person."[118] As for the standard of care in a false-light action, it would follow the standards in a defamation action, and the private person/public figure distinctions.[119]

As noted above, the right protected in a false-light case is that of reputation, just as the rights at stake in defamation. It is distinct from a "right to publicity" case in which reputation is not at issue, but rather who controls the ongoing publication.[120]

115. 840 F.2d 1012 (1st Cir.), *cert. denied*, 488 U.S. 821 (1988).
116. *Id.* at 1104.
117. 736 F.2d 1084 (5th Cir. 1984), *cert. denied*, 799 F.2d 1010 (5th Cir. 1986).
118. *Id.* at 1086.
119. *Id.* at 1091–92.
120. Zacchini v. Scripps-Howard Broad., Inc., 433 U.S. 562, 573 (1977).

## Misappropriation

In general terms, legally speaking, misappropriation is a kind of unjust enrichment remedy that has its basis in the concept that one should not unfairly benefit from the work of another. In *International News Service v. The Associated Press*,[121] the Supreme Court recognized a legal claim for misappropriation where a competitor takes the fruits of another's labor. At least one American court in California has expanded upon the *International News* holding to protect business information that is not otherwise covered under patent, copyright, trade secret, or confidentiality laws, in a case where the plaintiff has invested substantial time and money in the development of its property and the defendant appropriated the property at little or no cost, and plaintiff was injured economically as a result.[122] This means that, conceivably, if a photographer takes a picture of an item in plain view that has no privacy issues, and it is not a trade secret, there remains a theoretical possibility that if the image deprives the subject's owner of his or her sweat and labor, and benefits the photographer or someone else, could be a misappropriation.

Common-law appropriation, or misappropriation, is one of four recognized torts that are identified in the *Restatement (Second) of Torts* section 652.[123] *Restatement (Second) of Torts* § 652C renders it a tort for "one who appropriates to his own use or benefit the name or likeness of another is subject to liability to the other for invasion of his privacy."[124] Appropriation exists when "[o]ne who appropriates to his own use or benefit the name or likeness of another is subject to liability to the other for invasion of privacy."[125]

121. 248 U.S. 215 (1918).

122. Balboa Ins. Co. v. Trans Global Equities, 218 Cal. App. 3d 1327, *cert. denied*, 498 U.S. 940 (1990).

123. *See* Castro v. NYT Television, 370 N.J. Super. 282 (App. Div. 2004).

124. RESTATEMENT (SECOND) OF TORTS § 652C (1977) *See also* KNB Enters. v. Matthews, 92 Cal. Rptr. 2d 713, 716 (Ct. App. 2d 2000), *review denied by* Supreme Court Minute, 06-14-2000, 2000 Cal. LEXIS 4906 (Cal. June 14, 2000) ("The right to prevent others from appropriating one's photograph for commercial gain has evolved from the common law of privacy.").

125. Faber v. Condecor, Inc., 195 N.J. Super. 81, 86 (App. Div.), *certif. denied*, 99 N.J. 178 (1984).

In *Faber*, a private photograph was made of a Kodak consultant, Faber, and used for Christmas cards. Based on goodwill and relations with Kodak, Faber permitted the company to use it in an instructive publication on printing negatives. It turned out the photo also appeared in frames being sold, in poor quality and with other people, labeled "family tree." Condecor, the framing company, had taken the photo from the Kodak publication. Faber claimed he and his children were mocked and embarrassed.

The court held:

> [The p]laintiffs established a cause of action for invasion of privacy based on defendant's appropriation of their likeness for its benefit. Plaintiffs' testimony concerning their displeasure with the picture's appearance in defendant's frames and the mental distress they suffered established the damage element of their cause of action. Damages may be recovered for invasion of privacy, even if the injury suffered is mental anguish alone.[126]

It bears repeating that the elements found in the *Restatement* are not law unless adopted by a jurisdiction, and each jurisdiction, while purportedly adopting some or all of the four categories of privacy common-law remedies, nonetheless may (and often do) state them somewhat differently. It is also important to remember that not all cases involve photographs, or photographs alone, and there may also be contractual issues involved, such as releases or permission. What is and is not newsworthy will also vary not only from jurisdiction to jurisdiction, but in context as well.

At common law, one makes out a common-law claim for misappropriation if one proves: "(1) the defendant's use of the plaintiff's identity; (2) the appropriation of plaintiff's name or likeness to defendant's advantage, commercially or otherwise; (3) lack of consent; and (4) resulting injury."[127]

---

126. *Id.* at 90. *See also* Olan Mills, Inc., of Tex. v. Dodd, 234 Ark. 495 (1982) (photographer took picture authorized for personal use and, after enlarging them, made copies and gave them to salesmen for use in solicitations without permission); Staruski v. Cont'l Tel. Co., 154 Vt. 568 (1990) (employer displayed employee name and photograph in advertisements in newspapers that also falsely attributed to the employee certain laudatory remarks about employer).

127. Eastwood v. Superior Court, 149 Cal. App. 3d 409 (1983).

## Unfair Competition Law

States may also have unfair competition laws, either by common law or statute or both. In some states, the term seems to be used interchangeably with misappropriation; there may be overlap. In *X17, Inc. v. Lavandeira*, the court stated "the 'hot news' tort is a particularly hardy species of the common law tort of unfair competition through misappropriation that—at least in some jurisdictions—has managed to survive even after the 1976 amendments to the Copyright Act preempted most misappropriation claims."[128] The three elements of this tort are "(1) that the plaintiff has invested substantial time and money in development of its property; (2) the defendant has appropriated the property at little or no cost; and (3) the plaintiff has been injured by defendant's conduct."[129]

Another challenge to the use of one's image may be made on a state's unfair competition law. In California, this is Business and Professions Code section 17200. In general terms, and relevant here, California's unfair competition statute broadly prohibits "any unlawful, unfair or fraudulent business act or practice and unfair, deceptive, untrue or misleading advertising . . . ." Anyone suffering actual injury and losing money or property as result of unfair competition has standing to sue under this statute.[130] In *Fraley v. Facebook, Inc.*,[131] the allegation was that plaintiffs' likenesses as endorsements constituted lost money for which they were not paid.

### Characters

Characters can also be protected under unfair competition law. In *Lone Ranger, Inc. v. Cox*,[132] the plaintiff owned the Lone Ranger character from its radio broadcasts and sued actor William Powell, among others, for playing the Lone Ranger in a film and using the signature "Hi Ho Silver" refrain:

128. 563 F. Supp. 2d 1102, 1104 (C.D. Cal. 2007).
129. *Id.* at 1106–07 (citing Balboa Ins. Co. v. Trans Global Equities, 218 Cal. App. 3d 1327, 1342 (1990), *cert. denied, sub nom.* Collateral Protection Ins. Servs. v. Balboa Ins. Co., 498 U.S. 940 (1990) (itself citing *International News Service*)).
130. Cal. Bus. & Prof. Code § 17204.
131. 830 F. Supp. 2d 785 (N.D. Cal. 2011).
132. 124 F.2d 650 (4th Cir. 1942).

> Under the name or title of "The Lone Ranger", plaintiff had built up a radio feature of great value. The exploits of this mythical character, as portrayed in the radio programs, had become of great interest to countless young people throughout the country and were a source of large revenue to plaintiff. Defendants were attempting to avail themselves of the good will created by the broadcasting of the radio programs and the advertising connected therewith, including the "Lone Ranger" safety clubs. Their conduct in advertising Powell as the "Original Lone Ranger" was manifestly calculated and intended to lead the public to believe that he was the "Lone Ranger" of the radio programs and to attract to the circus those who were interested in the programs and particularly the young people who were members of the safety clubs.

The mere portrayal of a character by an actor is not enough to qualify as independent creation, unless an "actor has created a 'type' which, over a long period of years, has become associated with him."[133]

Characters may also have copyright and trademark protection, under appropriate circumstances.

In *Bach v. Forever Living Products U.S., Inc.*,[134] the plaintiff Munson's photographs were used in the popular book *Jonathan Livingston Seagull*, written by Richard Bach, also a plaintiff. The defendant made health and beauty products and used one of the copyrighted photographs from the book as its corporate logo and used the character Jonathan Livingston Seagull in its advertising. The plaintiffs also alleged trademark infringement in terms of false endorsement. The court found that the plaintiffs had stated a case and raised questions of fact as to likelihood of confusion and trade-dress infringement. In an opinion found a week later,[135] the court also held that both plaintiffs stated a viable claim for copyright infringement regarding the Jonathan Livingston Seagull character.[136]

---

133. Supreme Records, Inc. v. Decca Records, Inc., 90 F. Supp. 904, 908 (D. Cal. 1950); Chaplin v. Amador, 93 Cal. App. 358 (1928).

134. 473 F. Supp. 2d 1110 (W.D. Wash. 2007).

135. *Id.* at 1127.

136. *See also* Warner Bros. Pictures, Inc. v. Columbia Broad. Sys., Inc., 216 F.2d 945, 950 (9th Cir. 1954), *cert. denied*, 148 U.S. 971 (1955) ("It is conceivable that the character

Characters may also be protected by misappropriation law.[137]

## Anti-Paparazzi Law

California has an anti-paparazzi law that some believe goes too far in infringing on First Amendment rights. California Civil Code § 1708.8(b) provides for a civil cause of action for the following activity:

> A person is liable for constructive invasion of privacy when the defendant attempts to capture, in a manner that is offensive to a reasonable person, any type of visual image, sound recording, or other physical impression of the plaintiff engaging in a personal or familial activity under circumstances in which the plaintiff had a reasonable expectation of privacy, through the use of a visual or auditory enhancing device, regardless of whether there is a physical trespass, if this image, sound recording, or other physical impression could not have been achieved without a trespass unless the visual or auditory enhancing device was used.

## Photographing Minors

Issues involving minors raise other concerns. In England, *Harry Potter* author J.K. Rowling ultimately prevailed in the case of *David Murray (by his*

really constitutes the story being told, but if the character is only the chessman in the game of telling the story he is not within the area of the protection afforded by the copyright."); *see also* Cortez v. CMG Worldwide Inc., 962 F. Supp. 308, 309 (N.D.N.Y. 1997) (court refused to dismiss a declaratory judgment complaint seeking a "holding that there is no legal right to control the depiction or dissemination of the images of Cigar, Secretariat, or Ruffian, or the silks worn by the jockeys and horses").

137. *See, e.g.*, Lone Ranger, Inc. v. Curry, 79 F. Supp. 190 (D. Pa. 1948); Hogan v. DC Comics, 48 F. Supp. 2d 298, 314 (S.D.N.Y. 1999) ("New York courts recognize claims for misappropriation of ideas where the following conditions are satisfied: (1) the requisite legal relationship exists between the parties and (2) the idea is novel and concrete.").

*litigation friends Neil Murray and Joanne Murray) v. Big Pictures, Ltd.*,[138] in which the court ruled that the author's son was entitled to protection from publication of a photograph of him.

Apart from the above privacy issues, *and assuming that there is no question of obscenity or child pornography*, there is no separate standard for photographing a minor than an adult in the normal course. There is a lot of assumption and misinformation floating around about this, and certainly in today's world, discretion may be the better part of valor and a "business decision" that being right is not worth the cost of the lawsuit or concomitant social stigma.[139].

The same general distinctions between editorial and advertising/trade usages apply.[140] This was also demonstrated in *Foster v. Svenson*,[141] discussed above. In some instances, such as in California, there is also a statutory right to preclude the use of a photograph of a minor for advertising purposes if made without the consent of the minor's parent or legal guardian.[142]

In any event, the exception to the general rule is where there is a statute or other administrative rule. School districts may restrict the ability to photograph students while on school grounds. Georgia's statute[143] makes it a misdemeanor to "intentionally photograph a minor without the consent of the minor's parent or guardian."

Of course, having said all this, as one court observed, "[o]ne man's pornography may be another's keepsake."[144] In *United States v. Simmons*,[145] in the context of a criminal conviction of a man for, among other things, "using a minor to engage in sexually explicit conduct for the purpose of

138. EWCA (Civ) 446 (7 May 2008).

139. Montefusco v. Nassau Cnty., 39 F. Supp. 2d 231, 242 n.7 (E.D.N.Y. 1999) ("Were the Court to reach this question, the Court would hold that the photographs were not entitled to the protection of the First Amendment."). In *Montefusco*, a teacher took photographs of students allegedly for personal sexual gratification.

140. *See, e.g.*, Trannel v. Prairie Ridge Media, Inc., 2013 Ill. App. (2d) 120725 (2013) (privacy issues of mother and minor daughter evaluated equally under Illinois Right of Publicity Act).

141. Slip op. 31782(U) (N.Y. Cty. Aug. 5, 2013).

142. Cal. Civ. Code § 3344(a).

143. Ga. Code Ann. § 42-1-18.

144. Giano v. Senkowski, 54 F.3d 1050, 1056 (2d Cir. 1995).

145. 343 F.3d 72 (2d Cir. 2003).

producing a videotape of the [illegal sexual conduct]," the court noted: "Whether Sally Mann's photographs of her three prepubescent children, sometimes nude or partially clothed, or Robert Mapplethorpe's explicit images of sexual practices, fall within the scope of pornography are matters of considerable debate."[146] Obscenity and child pornography are addressed separately below. As far as privacy considerations go, even if the law does not distinguish between photographing a 10-year-old or a 50-year-old in a public place, a variety of other sensitivities certainly come into play. Once again, one may distinguish between the taking of a photograph and its particular use, as well as state regulation. I had a colleague once tell me he was stopped by police from photographing a beach scene at the Jersey shore, which he found aesthetic, because mothers had complained to the police about their daughters in bathing suits being photographed by a stranger. He acquiesed and did not take the photographs, even though the young women were not his focus.

## Right of Publicity (Celebrity)

In contrast to the right of privacy asserted by those who are not celebrities, what about the use of photographs of celebrities? The Supreme Court has distinguished privacy cases as protecting a reputation, while a right to publicity case protects an economic interest of "who gets to do the publishing."[147] As an example, someone once came up to me at a photography club meeting and said she had taken a photograph of Barack Obama at a fundraiser. She then made adjustments using image-processing software and wanted to know if she could display it.

In *Hebrew University of Jerusalem v. General Motors, LLC*,[148] the defendants used a photograph of Albert Einstein it obtained from a stock-photo agency as part of an advertising campaign for a car; the plaintiff claimed that Einstein had a right of publicity that survived his death and had willed

146. *Id.* at 81.
147. Zacchini v. Scripps-Howard Broad. Co., 433 U.S. 562, 573 (1977).
148. 878 F. Supp. 2d 1021 (C.D. Cal. 2012).

it to the plaintiff. Applying New Jersey law, the court found that such law allowed for a postmortem right of publicity, that such right did not require proof of exploitation of the right during the lifetime, but applying the doctrine of probable intent as to what Einstein might have intended, the court found an issue of fact on summary judgment.

Some states, like Georgia, recognize a right to publicity distinct from a right to privacy and allow it to survive the death of the owner, but the owner does not have to have commercially exploited that right during his lifetime.[149]

Limitations on the right of publicity have been recognized where it impacts on matters of public interest.[150]

In states like California, where the right is codified, the language of the statute will of course govern.[151] Under the statute, the postmortem right of publicity is a personal right and applies to acts directly in California.

A fictional biography that includes "dramatization, imagined dialogue, manipulated chronologies, and fictionalization of events" was held to violate section 51 of New York's Civil Rights Law.[152]

Rights of publicity may descend to certain persons, such as a decedent's surviving spouse and children, but it is dependent upon the language of the relevant local statute.[153]

149. Martin Luther King, Jr., Ctr. for Social Change, Inc. v. Am. Heritage Prods., Inc., 694 F.2d 674 (11th Cir. 1983).

150. Paulsen v. Personality Posters, Inc., 59 Misc. 2d 444 (N.Y. Cty. 1968).

151. *See* CAL. CIV. CODE § 3344.1 ("Any person who uses a deceased personality's name, voice, signature, photograph, or likeness, in any manner, on or in products, merchandise, or goods, or for purposes of advertising or selling, or soliciting purchases of, products, merchandise, goods, or services, without prior consent from the [decedent's successor or successors in interest], shall be liable for any damages sustained by the person or persons injured as a result thereof."); *see also* Cairns v. Franklin Mint Co., 292 F.3d 1139 (9th Cir. 2002) (trustees of Estate of Princess Diana failed to enjoin Franklin Mint from using likeness of princess).

152. Spahn v. Julian Messner, Inc., 18 N.Y.2d 324, 328–29 (1966), *adhered to on remand and rearg.*, 21 N.Y.2d 124 (1967).

153. Se. Bank, N.A. v. Lawrence, 66 N.Y.2d 910 (1985); *see also* Factors Etc., Inc. v. Pro Arts, Inc., 652 F.2d 278 (2d Cir. 1981), *cert. denied*, 456 U.S. 927 (1982); *Martin Luther King, Jr., Ctr.* 694 F.2d 674 (a right to publicity is distinct from a right to privacy under Georgia law, and it survives the death of its owner; the owner need not have exploited the right in order for it to survive his death).

## Intentional and Negligent Infliction of Emotional Distress

Another pair of torts that may be raised against the photographer are intentional and negligent infliction of emotional distress. Section 46 of the *Restatement (Second) of Torts* provides that "(1) One who by extreme and outrageous conduct intentionally or recklessly causes severe emotional distress to another is subject to liability for such emotional distress, and if bodily harm to the other results from it, for such bodily harm." Section 312 of the *Restatement (Second) of Torts* addresses intentional infliction of emotional distress, establishing liability when the defendant engages in extreme and outrageous conduct that intentionally or recklessly causes emotional distress, and the actor should recognize the likelihood that the act will cause illness or bodily harm, even if that was not the intention and whether or not the act was directed that defendant or a third person. Negligent infliction is when the cause is unintentional, but the actor should have realized the effect and, from known facts, that illness or bodily harm could have resulted.

In *Swerdlick v. Koch*,[154] the surveillance and photographic activities of a neighbor documenting business activities in a residential zone were not enough; there was no proof that the defendant had knowledge of the plaintiff's emotional status.

Publication of a single allegedly false or defamatory article has been held to not constitute extreme or outrageous conduct as a matter of law.[155]

## Stalking

Some states recognize a statutory tort of stalking.[156] Certain other states that have criminal stalking statutes decline to create a private civil cause of

154. 721 A.2d 849 (R.I. 1998).

155. Smigo v. NYP Holdings, Inc., 2008 N.Y. slip op. 33034(U) (N.Y. Cty. 2008), *aff'd*, 80 A.D.2d 516 (1st Dep't 2011).

156. *See, e.g.*, Cal. Civ. Code § 1708.7 (pattern of conduct with intent to follow, alarm, or harass plaintiff, and plaintiff has reasonable fear for safety or that of immediate family, and either plaintiff makes a credible threat against defendant or violates a restraining order);

action.[157] While not defined as a separate tort, it was pleaded in conjunction with privacy violations in *Wolfson v. Lewis*,[158] with the court enjoining offensive behavior by television journalists.

## Nuisance

Nuisance can lead to civil liability where the photographer interferes with someone's "space" in an offensive way.

States may regulate nuisance by statute, or there may be a common-law nuisance claim based on the photographer's activities. Note, however, that courts are hesitant to issue injunctions to prevent repetitive publication of defamatory items, but will do so if the injunction is narrowly tailored to prevent a nuisance.[159] In *Balboa Island Village Inn, Inc. v. Lemen*, a neighboring property owner was upset with plaintiff over noise and the allegedly drunk customers pouring out of the restaurant, and took to repeatedly videotaping the restaurant and insulting the customers. She told others in the community that the plaintiff's establishment was engaged in child pornography. Plaintiff sued under theories of nuisance, defamation, and interference with business. In another case, *Webb v. Glenbrook Owners Association*,[160] a homeowner association sued a resident for violating the community's restriction as well as for nuisance, which allegations of nuisance included "filming and photographing neighbors on the neighbors' property."[161] On the issue of nuisance, the Webbs on appeal challenged that their overall conduct constituted nuisance, but the court found they had waived their challenge to the sufficiency of the evidence.[162]

---

TEX. CIV. PRAC. & REM. §§ 85.001–.005 (civil liability when defendant engages in harassing behavior causing defendant to reasonably fear his or her or family's safety and defendant either violates a restraining order or engages in certain other threatening behavior).

157. *See, e.g.*, Troncalli v. Jones, 237 Ga. App. 10 (1999).
158. 924 F. Supp. 1413 (E.D. Pa. 1996).
159. *See* Balboa Island Vill. Inn, Inc. v. Lemen, 40 Cal. 4th 1141 (2007).
160. 298 S.W.3d 374 (Ct. App. Texas 2009).
161. *Id.* at 379.
162. *Id.* at 383.

## Misrepresentation and Fraud

Misrepresentation and fraud may involve photographs in a variety of contexts. Intentional misrepresentation (i.e., fraud) requires proof of

> (1) a representation; (2) which is material to the transaction at hand; (3) made falsely, with knowledge of its falsity or recklessness as to whether it is true or false; (4) with the intent of misleading another into relying on it; (5) justifiable reliance on the misrepresentation; and (6) the resulting injury was proximately caused by the reliance.[163]

Negligent misrepresentation requires proof of

> (1) misrepresentation of a material fact; (2) the representor must either know of the misrepresentation, must make the misrepresentation without knowledge as to its truth or falsity, or must make the representation under circumstances in which he ought to have known of its falsity; (3) the representor must intend the representation to induce another to act on it; and (4) injury must result to the party acting in justifiable reliance on the misrepresentation.[164]

The difference is one of intent; in negligent misrepresentation, the tort exists not in knowing the statements are false but in failing to make reasonable investigation to know whether they are true or not.

The claim with regard to a photograph can come up in advertising, and particularly when image processing is employed to change the photograph. There is a regulatory context, as well as a civil context, particularly when a competitor uses a photograph to give a false impression of a product or denigrate another product, to induce a sale. To the extent the photographer "aids and abets," there may be contributory liability.

163. Gibbs v. Ernst, 538 Pa. 193, 207–08 (1994).
164. *Id.* at 210.

The issue was raised in an interesting article that discussed a software program that claimed to be able to detect image-processing changes. In the November 28, 2011, *Proceedings of the National Academy of Sciences*, is an article by Eric Kee and Hany Farid that proposes software to determine how "manipulated" a photograph is. In an age when Photoshop has become a verb for adjustment of a photograph, the two authors proposed a scale as to how much the image has been altered, and that the ratings be used to facilitate truth in advertising.

> [T]hanks to the magic of digital retouching, impossibly thin, tall, and wrinkle-free models routinely grace advertisements and magazine covers with the legitimate goal of selling a product to consumers. On the other hand, an overwhelming body of literature has established a link between idealized and unattainable images of physical beauty and serious health and body image issues for men, women, and children.[165]

Their solution is to provide a rating, from 1 (very similar) to 5 (very different), of a photograph's manipulation based upon a formula that measures geometric and photometric transformation by region and amount of perceptual distortion. The authors analyzed 468 before-and-after images, and their data can be reviewed. Other perceptual ratings and formulae were used; the bottom line is their suggestion to quantify photographic manipulation as an objective criteria.

This has significant potential to affect current law and legal practice and cannot be separated from the broader policy issues.

The ramifications for objectification of photographic manipulation directly affects issues concerning truth in advertising and commercial speech. In the United Kingdom, the quasi-nongovernmental organization, the Advertising Standards Authority (ASA) is not merely a product of self-regulation, it has significant power that influences courts and controls advertising conduct. That organization banned a L'Oreal ad featuring Julia Roberts on the

---

165. Kee & Farid, *A Perceptual Metric for Photo Retouching*, 100 PROC. NAT'L ACAD. SCI. no. 50, Dec. 13, 2011, http://www.pnas.org/content/108/50/1997.full (last visited April 25, 2014).

basis that the "after" picture was not satisfactorily proven by "sufficient evidence" to indicate that it "accurately illustrated what the products could achieve," according to the ASA.[166]

In the United States, 15 U.S.C. § 45(a)(1) simply outlaws "unfair methods of competition" and "unfair or deceptive acts or practices" affecting commerce. The 1983 Federal Trade Commission (FTC) Policy Statement on Deception from the FTC website[167] requires a material representation, practice, or omission that is "likely to mislead" a reasonable consumer under the circumstances consumers under the circumstances. It states that "there may be a concern about the way a product is marketed, such as where inaccurate or incomplete information is provided." However, at least one U.S. board member of the Independent Cosmetics Manufacturers and Distributors has been quoted as finding it unlikely that the FTC would have come down the same way as the ASA. If the Kee-Farid algorithm becomes acceptable as a standard, will we see new rules that set forth a minimum acceptable level before an advertisement is deemed not misleading? States have their own consumer fraud acts and case law that have developed, often on a fact-sensitive inquiry, as to what is material and what is misleading. Will the Kee Farid analysis be acceptable in an inquiry as to deceptiveness? Many of us can easily envision it as the subject of a hearing as to expert testimony under *Daubert v. Merrell Dow Pharmaceuticals, Inc.*,[168] or its state-law equivalents, and possibly gain traction for use in cases ranging from serious personal injury blamed on advertising to other commercial contexts.

A deeper issue addresses the policy issue noted by Kee and Farid as to health implications. Driven by Change.org in the United States is a proposal for The Self-Esteem Act, which would require advertising that has "meaningfully changed the human form" through photographic manipulation to carry "truth in advertising" labels. Such legislation or its equivalent reportedly has been introduced in France and adopted as part of the British

166. http://popwatch.ew.com/2011/07/28/loreal-ads-banned-julia-roberts-christy-turlington/ (last visited April 25, 2014).

167. (Oct. 14, 1983), http://www.ftc.gov/ftc-policy-statement-on-deception.

168. 509 U.S. 579 (1993).

Liberal Democrats Party platform. Certain American writers, such as Naomi Wolf in her book *The Beauty Myth*, have addressed what they perceive to be the harmfulness of such advertising. Will a perceived objective scale become part of that dynamic?

Such proposals and calls for stricter legislation and regulation of advertising, which may find support in the United States based on "objective" formulae for measuring manipulation, will need to be weighed against First Amendment rights of commercial speech. The Supreme Court decision on commercial speech in *Sorrell v. IMS Health, Inc.*,[169] struck down a Vermont law restricting the sale, disclosure, and use of pharmacy records that revealed prescribing practices of individual doctors. It recognized, however, that legitimate governmental interests in protecting consumers from commercial harms permit greater governmental regulation than noncommercial speech. At present, we have broad principles that permit courts and fact-finders to determine fraud and deceptiveness. Will we now be able to quantify it?

On a more prosaic but no less important level, the Kee-Farid algorithm conceivably could affect authentication of photographs into evidence. Such authentication issues at trial have been reviewed and reported in various decisions, with the court considering the admissibility of the particular images that have been altered or enhanced through software. Does the Kee-Farid rating provide an objective benchmark? Does a rating of 1 satisfy admissibility standards, or at least create a rebuttable presumption, with the reverse true of a 5? Is slightly increasing detail in the shadows the same as eradicating the creases in George Clooney's forehead, as in one of the Kee-Farid examples?

The Kee-Farid article is significant not only because it appears to be the first serious effort to quantify photographic manipulation but because it does so in the context of commercial speech and in the context of an ongoing policy debate as to the health implications of such commercial speech. Deceptiveness, particularly as the FTC and courts have viewed it, must depend upon a variety of factors, many of which may well be subjective.

169. 131 S. Ct. 2653 (2011).

While such efforts at objectification of photographic manipulation may be relevant, they should not be legally dispositive.

Even when photographs are not manipulated, they may subject the user of them to claims of false representation as to proper ownership or, conversely, of passing off as legitimately owned items as something else. In *Truck Equipment Services Co. v. Fruehauf Corp.*,[170] the court found that regardless of truth as to the equality of products, "the use of another's product, misbranded to appear as that of a competitor," constitutes false designation.

## Putting It in Perspective

Apart from copyright issues, this is perhaps the area in which the photographer needs to exercise the most caution. The emphasis here is on use of the photograph and the kinds of civil (tort) actions that can arise from use that impacts privacy. It is essential to have an understanding of the law of the particular jurisdiction in which you are operating, although if you are a New Yorker taking pictures of a Massachusetts person visiting in California, and exhibiting the pictures at a photography exhibit in Florida, there may be an issue as to which law applies—and which can affect the result. As gathered from the sampling of cases discussed, unfortunately there are no hard and fast answers to the bottom-line question: Can I take that picture and, if so, how and where can I use it?

170. 536 F.2d 1210 (8th Cir.), *cert. denied*, 429 U.S. 861 (1976).

## Chapter Four

# Contract Law

## Contract Best Practices

My purpose in this section is not to address the business aspects of photography as such. There are form books on the market and other books telling you how to run a photography business. I want to provide a broad-brush approach to this to highlight those aspects of contract law that are often a source of misapprehension and misunderstanding.

A contract is not just a legal document. A contract embodies both business as well as legal issues. It is not just for your lawyer. The contract also sets forth the business relationship of the parties.

There is a popular misconception about whether contracts always have to be in writing. Certainly it is easier to prove a written contract than an oral one, and the court or arbitrator can see the actual words without having to rely on witness testimony. In some situations, a so-called statute of frauds requires contracts to be in writing. Whether it is called by that name or not, certain statutes require that certain transactions, such as a sale of goods or real estate, be in writing. In other cases, particularly services, there may not be such a requirement. Even there, in certain situations, such as real estate commissions, there may be such a requirement. In other situations, where the terms include both services and goods, there may be an issue as to which rule applies. The point is that when you agree to photograph for someone, the fact that the contract is not in writing does not mean it will not be enforceable.

Another misconception is how contracts are formed. If not an actual contract, a set of obligations and duties can be implied based upon the relationship of the parties and their respective conduct. Conduct itself may be a means of accepting a contract and, in certain circumstances, may be cited and placed into evidence as altering or modifying a contract. It cannot be emphasized enough: e-mails are written expressions, not casual and forgotten words, and can be devastating (or extraordinarily helpful, depending upon your position) in resolving a legal dispute. One can also ratify a series of terms that may not have been deemed a contract at the start, but is later deemed to be one. There are also "quasi-contractual" remedies. These include reliance, whereby a court finds it fair to hold someone to a promise based on justifiable reliance and concomitant harm that resulted from that reliance. A court may also estop someone from changing a position previously asserted. Another often-used theory is unjust enrichment. This means that if someone performs for another and the other benefits, then the performer is entitled to fair compensation. Of course, there are defenses to each of these, and this is not the place for an extended discussion of contract law. The important point is that whatever you think you know about contracts, you probably don't if you have relied upon popular culture and the legal presentations on *The Simpsons*. Be also aware of torts, such as misrepresentation, which may be either intentional or even negligent, discussed in Chapter 3.

The major kinds of contracts you will be dealing with are licensing agreements, releases, and sales. In each of these, the scope of rights will be important, as will your remedies provisions for how you enforce those rights.

There is a time and place for an appropriate document. You will want to license your image to someone else, perhaps, for limited use, or you may need to make use of someone else's image. In any contract relating to your photographs, as a best practice, pay attention to choice of law. As I have said repeatedly, law is territorial. And so-called boilerplates are not boilerplate. Do not simply cut and paste forms off the Internet. One size does not fit all. Know, as well, that you are responsible for what you sign (even if in a different language). Do not accept a statement from the other side that "we have this in all our agreements." If you do not understand it, don't sign it. Your contracts are not just legal documents; they are a roadmap, whether short or long, for your business transaction. Don't accept "legalese," whatever that is. Do not assume any of the "legal stuff" is standard; make sure you understand it. Make sure you know whose law applies so the enforceability of terms is understood up front. Do not settle for ambiguity and if there is pushback, rethink your transaction. While there is a tendency to accept forms, and in many cases they can work, courts are not always so tolerant.[1] To repeat: form contracts, like prescription drugs, are not for everybody in every situation. If you balk at spending $1,000 for a couple of hours of a lawyer's time, you may spend $100,000 for a year of his or her time defending you in litigation.

Photographers will encounter different types of contracts, and it is beyond the scope of this book to engage in a detailed discussion of them. They can range from book contracts to sales of prints to licensing of images, assignment of rights, and so forth. One type of contract that seems to generate a particular amount of litigation is the release, which is discussed later in more detail. While there are books and websites that offer "form" contracts, be careful. It is my experience that even within the same law firm, different lawyers use different language to express the same concepts or provisions in a contract. The case law is permeated with hundreds, if not thousands and more, variations on the same language. As much as it may pain you to pay a lawyer, the right lawyer up front, for a relatively modest fee to review your documents, can save you, quite literally, hundreds of thousands of dollars in litigation costs down the road. There is also the Volunteer Lawyers for the Arts, a channeling organization for lawyers that engage in pro bono work on behalf of artists. The main point is to have all your questions answered, and make sure the plain language in the document answers them. Ask "what if?" and make sure the document addresses it. You may not be able to get everything you want, but it is important to understand what the risks are, and the obligations as well as the rights.

1. *See* Schron v. Troutman Saunders, LLP, 97 A.D.3d 87 (1st Dep't 2012) ("some documents do use meaningless boilerplate and, in our view, the rule should not be carried to absurd lengths to imbue meaning into every legalistic jotting.").

In these situations, ambiguity has no place. In *Shatriya v. Gilden*,[2] the plaintiff claimed his contract permitted use of his image for one advertising purpose; it was later posted on the Web in connection with another, which plaintiff claimed was a breach of the agreement. The plaintiff's reliance on an e-mail to try to establish the limited use was not a contract under the circumstances, and the plaintiff could not prove the terms of the actual contract, so an issue of fact existed as to what the contract terms were or, more specifically, what the term "public relations" in the contract meant.

For an instructive case as to the importance of contract, see *Serra v. U.S. General Services Administration*,[3] in which the well-known artist Richard Serra created a "site-specific" work that was removed from a government plaza. The court noted that "[t]he contract contained no provisions restricting the Government's use of the sculpture after it was purchased," and further held:

> "Tilted Arc" is entirely owned by the Government and is displayed on Government property. Serra relinquished his own speech rights in the sculpture when he voluntarily sold it to GSA; if he wished to retain some degree of control as to the duration and location of the display of his work, he had the opportunity to bargain for such rights in making the contract for sale of his work.[4]

As the court noted, the legal issue could have been resolved in that time by a properly worded contract. The issues have to some extent have been dealt with by VARA or state artist rights statutes, but where those exceptions apply, the artist should if possible seek contractual protection.

Contracts matter. Courts will look to enforce them and not rewrite them. Do not depend upon a judge's sympathy down the road. Ask "what if?" in each case and try to address it. Obviously, when dealing with publishers, stock-photo agencies, and the like, you will be faced with their "standard" contracts. Some things can be negotiated and accommodated. Others cannot.

2. 2007 NY slip op. 32712(U) (N.Y. Cty. 2007), *app. dism*, 50A.D.3d 586 (1st Dep't 2008).
3. 847 F.2d 1045 (2d Cir. 1988).
4. *Id.* at 1049.

Ultimately, with your awareness of the risks and benefits, you will make the decision. But do so with eyes wide open.

## Releases

This is one of the great bugaboos in the life of the photographer. Let us be clear about something: You do not always need a model release when photographing people. As discussed, there are different legal parameters regarding taking and use, and different results based on different types of use. And just because someone sues you does not mean that person will win. Whenever I have addressed photography clubs on the issues raised in this book, there is always someone who says you "must" get a release, you "must" do this or that "or you'll be sued." In America, anyone can sue for anything. The whole point of this book is to provide an "eyes wide open" resource for you in your photography and enable you to assess risks. In many of the areas discussed here, and as patently obvious from the number and content of the cases, there is more often than not a lack of clarity and certainty. It is just not possible to always predict with certainty how a court will rule in a particular circumstance. If you want to practice street photography and are worried about someone suing you for breach of privacy, perhaps you should think about shooting flowers. What are you going to do? Walk up to everyone in front of a tourist attraction and ask them to move? Or ask them to sign a release? Virtually every book I have read on legal rights of photographers tells you to get a release. You don't always need it. Go back and reread the chapter on privacy. A release is generally not necessary if the subject was in a public place and you have an artistic or newsworthy purpose.

However, many of the cases involving model releases involve nudity, so if you are going to take pictures of a nude model, you should clothe your activity in a model release (pun intended).

What does a release do for you?

Before we get to the law, it can have a prophylactic effect. In other words, even though you can't stop people from suing, you can make them think twice and provide a legal basis for dismissal of the suit before you have to argue the merits of the various claims. For example, say you have been asked by the dance company to photograph a dance recital put on by the company where your child and others take dance lessons. It is probably a good idea for the company to have a blanket release in its registration forms when children are enrolled for lessons, or even (or again) at the time of the recital. If a parent does not want his or her children photographed, they don't have to sign and can make that clear to the company and the photographer. Maybe you would have the right to make artistic pictures that include those children, but is it worth it? Why argue about it? If you get the release up front, and know whom not to photograph, then as a practical matter you avoid the issue.

Another practical issue is that if you are taking pictures with the intention of selling or licensing them to magazines or other publications, they may well want releases as a condition. That, too, is part of the contract, and your choice is to comply or not deal with that entity. It is as much a policy as a legal issue.

Where you do have a release, pay particular attention to the language and make sure the scope of the release, and the appropriate uses, are defined in unambiguous terms.

In *Bonner v. Fuji Photo Film*,[5] the defendant photographer photographed the seven-year-old child Bonner as a clown. The mother signed an authorization and agreed to no compensation. The photographer then entered into a license agreement with a company to provides photos for licensing on commission. Getty Images subsequently bought that company, and the Bonner image made its way to the back of a Fuji disposable camera pack. Eleven years later Bonner saw the picture and sued under a variety of theories: violation of California Civil Code section 3344 (use of another's likeness for commercial purpose); common-law appropriation of likeness; violation of California Business and Professional Code section 17200 (unfair business practice); negligence; intentional infliction of emotional distress; and invasion of privacy. Defendants Fuji, the photographer, and the ad agency won on summary judgment on all counts. The consent form was global and not

5. No. 06-cv-04374, 2007 U.S. Dist LEXIS 79623 (N.D. Cal. Oct. 26, 2007)

limited just to immediate purpose, regardless of what the mother claimed to understand. (Remember: you are responsible for what you sign.) The consent also destroyed a claim for appropriation. There was no proof of fraud to undo the consent, nor were the statutory elements made out to justify a claim for misappropriation. The court found that the consent was also sufficient to defeat a claim of negligence. As for contentions that the release should not be enforced under a theory of unconscionability, the court found that the conduct here was not "utterly intolerable in a civilized community."[6] Finally, the court also rejected arguments based on privacy, finding there was no expectation of privacy. As the court concluded: "Menuez took a picture of Bonner in a location over which Bonner had no right of ownership or possession, nor in which Bonner could have had a reasonable expectation of privacy. Indeed, Bonner expressly consented to the taking of the photograph. Bonner cannot now claim that she had a reasonable expectation of privacy while she played on the photographer's set."[7]

In *Arnold v. Treadwell*,[8] the plaintiff model made an "oral agreement" with the defendant photography, model management, and Web-design company, where she purported to retain control over the images. She claimed they were posted on another website to which defendants gave the images. Although plaintiff survived defendants' motions on summary judgment and her trademark allegations were allowed to proceed, she could have avoided the uncertainty by a written contract.

Permission to use a person's name or likeness, if not express or otherwise in writing, may nonetheless also be implied from conduct and the facts and circumstances.[9] In *Jones*, the actress Shirley Jones sought class certification against Corbis for its use of photographs in thumbnails allowing people to view and select them for licensing that way. Her argument was that she knew she was photographed in the particular instances and knew the custom and practice in the industry was for wide distribution and dissemination, and

6. *Id.* at *15.
7. *Id.* at *19.
8. 642 F. Supp. 2d 723 (E.D. Mich. 2009).
9. Jones v. Corbis Corp., 815 F. Supp. 2d 1108, 1113 (C.D. Cal. 2011), *aff'd*, 489 F. App'x 155 (9th Cir. 2012).

there was a notice posted that stated that by entering the premises, consent to be photograph was given. Her objection was that she had not consented to the placement of the images on the Corbin website for solicitation and selection. The court rejected that: "Plaintiff's subjective beliefs as to her consent are not determinative; consent is measured from Plaintiff's manifested action or inaction."[10] The court distinguished the situation in which a defendant takes pictures from one website and posts them on its own, because "the mere act of assigning rights to publicity to one entity does not allow an unrelated third party to appropriate the pictures without prior consent."[11] That was not the situation here, and the court rejected the contention that the plaintiff's consent was specifically needed and not just that of the photographers as assignors. The court did note that its holding was

> limited to the fact that Plaintiff consented to the display of her likeness for the purpose of distributing the images themselves. Further, the Court has found that Plaintiff consented to this display whether or not the displaying parties are the photographers or third parties like Defendant that merely act as distributors for the photographers.[12]

It did not affect any other right of publicity Jones may have where her image would be used in connection with an unrelated product or the image was transformed.

If you are going to use a model release, make sure you think through the possible uses down the road for the image and obtain as much flexibility as you can. In *Krupnik v. NBC Universal, Inc.*,[13] the plaintiff, a former model, sued the defendants for use of a photograph of her in a bikini in a brochure that was featured in a scene in a move that had nothing to do with the plaintiff. Her model release assigned rights, among other media in photographs:

10. *Id.* at 1114.
11. *Id.* at 1115.
12. *Id.* at 1116.
13. 37 Misc. 3d 1219[A] (N.Y. Cty. 2010).

> in perpetuity, including the right to use my name, biographical information and interviews in conjunction with such recordings and photos, and to use, reuse, publish, modify or license the same in whole or in part in all media (including, but not limited to, internet or television) and in any way whatsoever, including, but not limited to, in the programming, promotion, advertising and merchandising (ex. calendars, posters) of Bikini.com.[14]

She sued under § 51 of the New York Civil Rights Law, which we discussed in Chapter 3. The court dismissed the complaint based on the "unambiguous terms" of the model release.

As *Krupnik* demonstrates, the risk of guessing wrong on the scope of a release can lead to a claim of misappropriation of one's image in violation of the New York Civil Rights Law. Another illustrative case is *Cory v. Nintendo of America, Inc.*[15] Plaintiff Cory was a model whose picture was used on a Nintendo video-game box cover. She has posed for a photo to appear on the package back of a Nintendo product; her "model's voucher" for the work provided that the advertising agency could publish her photo for up to 12 months. His agent later signed a release in his name that did not have a time limit. At the end of the 12-month period, when the images were still being used, the plaintiff sued under the New York statute. The plaintiff lost, because the court found his agency had authority to sign the release for him and bind him as against innocent third parties. The case demonstrates the importance of (1) making sure all documents the photographer signs are consistent and (2) the photographer controls the scope of authority, in clear and defined terms, of those acting for him.

In *Russell v. Marboro Books*,[16] the court held that a consent in writing in a release to the use of the plaintiff model's portrait for advertising purposes, and a waiver of subsequent approval prior to publication, did not mean that she waived claims based on the dissemination of altered pictures or defamatory items. The *Krupnik* court distinguished *Russell* on the basis

14. *Id.*
15. 185 A.D.2d 70 (N.Y. App. Div. 1st 1993).
16. 18 Misc. 2d 166 (N.Y. Cnty. 1959).

that one's privacy or other claims exist if not included in the waiver language of the release. *Russell* contained a specific limitation that the *Krupnik* court did not find in its case.

In *Faloona v. Hustler Magazine, Inc.*,[17] a release given by a parent for photographs of her and her children was upheld despite later use in a book reviewed in *Hustler Magazine*, as well as pictures. Plaintiffs were the minor children, but they were unable to invalidate the release properly given in the past by their mother. The court relied on the California statute, California Civil Code section 3344(a), and found that that statute augmented common law. The court therefore rejected the plaintiff's contention that California law did not permit them to invalidate the release at any time and that judicial approval was not required for publishing a photograph of a nude minor. To the same effect is *Shields v. Gross*,[18] holding that Brook Shields was unable to disaffirm a release made on her behalf by her parent and seek relief under New York's Civil Rights Law for republication of the photographs.

One might also be careful in terms of using all applicable words. Some states' laws actually distinguish between photograph and likeness. The issue was litigated in *ISS Research, LLC v. Federal Insurance Co.*,[19] for the purpose of (1) interpreting a release clause in which the plaintiff assigned the right to use or exploit his "likeness" without compensation and (2) its relevance under an exclusion to an insurance policy. The plaintiff tried to argue that by waiving rights as to his likeness he had not waived rights as to the photograph; while noting that in the Ninth Circuit such a distinction had a statutory basis, other courts had held otherwise, and the court followed suit.

17. 799 F.2d 1000 (5th Cir. 1986), *cert. denied*, 479 U.S. 1088 (1987).

18. 58 N.Y.2d 338 (1983).

19. No. 10-cv-41, 2010 U.S. Dist. LEXIS 122811 (W.D.N.C. Nov. 18, 2010) at *11 ("the term 'likeness' is unambiguous and its plain and ordinary meaning is reasonably understood to include a photograph.").

If a release is given as part of an exclusive right to use an image, then such a right may be enforceable, and not simply withdrawn by the model, and enforced against another to whom another release is given.[20]

The main issue with regard to model releases is one of consent, and the consent is a function of the scope of use. Many of the cases result in privacy claims, particularly when nudity is involved. The issue also becomes relevant when advertising or promotional commercial purposes are involved. If a release is broadly worded and allows for unrestricted use, then a model who gives such consent may not be in a position to complain when the image is used for purposes not originally contemplated.[21]

A party may also not be entitled to rely upon a release that was fraudulently procured if it failed to take reasonable steps to verify its legitimacy, particularly when publication of nude photographs are involved.[22]

## Licensing

There is a difference between licensing the use of an image and selling the rights to an image. A license means you, as the owner of the intellectual property rights in the image (the licensor), grant permission, for a fee and on stated terms, to a licensee as to how the licensee (the user) may use the image. You retain ownership. In a sale, you convey title to the other party. Remember the distinction noted previously between intellectual property and the physical property. If you sell a print, but that is all you sell, you retain the copyright in the image, but the purchaser owns the physical print and, subject to potentially applicable visual artists' rights (also discussed above), to do with it what they want. If you want to outright convey your intellectual property rights as well, that can be done. Licenses may be written, oral, or implied.[23]

---

20. Haelan Labs. v. Topps Chewing Gum, 202 F.2d 866 (2d Cir. *cert. denied*, 346 U.S. 816 1953).
21. Russell v. Marboro Books, 18 Misc. 2d 166 (N.Y. Cnty. 1959).
22. Gallon v. Hustler Magazine, Inc., 732 F. Supp. 322 (N.D.N.Y. 1990).
23. SHL Imaging, Inc. v. Artisan House, Inc., 117 F. Supp. 2d 301, 316 (S.D.N.Y. 2000).

Chapter 2 of the Copyright Act[24] lays out the parameters of ownership and licenses. Section 201(a) provides that the copyright vests initially in the author or joint authors. Section 201(d) permits transfer of ownership of the copyright "by any means of conveyance or by operation of law, and may be bequeathed by will or pass as personal property by the applicable laws of intestate succession." Copyright can also be subject to a lien or involuntary transfer. The ownership of the copyright is distinct from ownership of the physical thing containing the copyrighted material.[25] In other words, you own the copyright in your photograph, but you do not own the physical image as a physical object that someone has bought.

Except for works made for hire, exclusive or nonexclusive licensing of a copyright, or any separate rights within the bundle of rights, other than those granted by will, is subject to rights of the joint author as applicable or, if the conveyor is deceased, by that author's widow or widower, surviving children, and grandchildren, certain termination conditions. To be valid, a transfer of copyright, other than by operation of law, must be in writing and signed by the owner.[26] The transfer may be, but is not required to be, recorded it the Copyright Office; where there are conflicting assignments, the first recorded prevails.

As noted, a transfer of copyright to be valid must be in writing, but an oral and implied license is recognized to provide only a nonexclusive license.[27]

Licenses can be exclusive (granted to one entity) or nonexclusive (available to more than one). Given that the license defines the scope of permitted use of a copyrighted image, failure of the licensee to adhere to the terms of the license can result in a claim for copyright infringement and termination of the license, as well as a claim for damages. The terms of a license may be a limitation on the number of copies of books in which a licensed image may appear, the ability to use the image in subsequent editions of a book, the kinds of media (electronic, ancillary, or derivative), the geographic distribution area, and reporting requirements. The interpretation

24. 17 U.S.C. §§ 201–205.
25. 17 U.S.C. § 202.
26. 17 U.S.C. § 204(a).
27. SHL Imaging, Inc. v. Artisan House, Inc., 117 F. Supp. 2d 301, 316 (S.D.N.Y. 2000).

of the licensing clause will be a question of law for the court and, unless the language is ambiguous, no evidence external to the agreement will be permitted in evidence, as a general rule, to aid in the interpretation.[28] Even though copyright is federal, a court will look to state law to interpret the language of the contract to understand the meaning of the licensing clause.[29]

If you do not want the license to be assigned, you need to be clear, and make sure any violation of such clause voids the assignment. Unless the parties otherwise agree, courts recognize the free assignability of contracts and restrictions contained therein.[30] Courts will construe assignment clauses, like other contract clauses, based on their plain language and not find restrictions unless affirmatively stated. A clause prohibiting assignments, like any other contract clause, will be enforced in accordance with its terms provided it does not violate public policy, is overreaching or otherwise was procured by fraud, or is otherwise prohibited by statute.[31] However, the impact of violation is less clear-cut and depends upon the specific language. If a party wants the conveyance to be void ab initio, it should say so. Otherwise, the assignment may not be void, but simply voidable, or may simply give rise to a claim for damages.

## Estoppel

Estoppel is an equitable principle (i.e., based on fairness) that estops (stops) someone from taking a position based on the person's own prior acts. In other words, fair is fair. If someone does something and you rely on it, that person can be held to the position taken in certain circumstances.

In *Dallal v. New York Times Co.*,[32] a freelance photographer claimed that the *New York Times* used his photographs without permission on its

28. *See, e.g.*, R/S Ass'ns v. N.Y. Job Dev. Auth., 98 N.Y.2d 29 (2002).
29. Graham v. James, 144 F.3d 229, 237 (2d Cir. 1998).
30. *See, e.g.*, Allhusen v. Caristo Constr. Corp., 303 N.Y. 446, 452 (1952).
31. Johnson v. Structured Asset Servs., LLC, 148 S.W.3d 711 (Tex. Ct. App. 2004).
32. 386 F. Supp. 2d 319 (S.D.N.Y. 2005), *vacated and remanded*, 2006 U.S. App. LEXIS 5171 (2d Cir. 2006), *aff'd after remand*, 352 F. App'x 508 (2d Cir. 2009), *cert denied*, 559 U.S. 1108 (2010).

Web edition. He had licensed certain images to it, and his invoices contained the following provision:

> for distribution within the United States of America and Canada only; ENGLISH language rights only; ... for ONE-TIME ONLY, FIRST EXCLUSIVE USE; in both COLOR and BLACK & WHITE illustrations. All rights not specifically granted in writing, including copyright, remain the exclusive property of the photographer.

When the plaintiff complained, the newspaper claimed ignorance and stopped using the images. A year later, the plaintiff sued. The issue was whether the plaintiff was estopped from suing. To prove estoppel, "the defendant must have been misled into reasonably and justifiably believing that the plaintiff would not pursue his claims against the defendant."[33] The court applied the doctrine, since the relationship of the parties "spanned some eight years [and] [s]ix of those eight years overlapped with the period in which the Times introduced a web edition of its newspaper."[34] The trial court estopped (prevented) plaintiff from pursuing claims of copyright infringement based on his prior acts as a matter of law. On appeal, the Second Circuit disagreed as to the record, and vacated the order on the basis that the question of estoppel could not be decided as a matter of law on the record before, it, and remanded. The court cited four elements to be proved: "1) the plaintiff had knowledge of defendant's infringing acts, 2) the plaintiff either intended that defendant rely on his acts or omissions or acted or failed to act in such a manner that defendant had a right to believe that it was intended to rely on plaintiff's conduct, 3) the defendant was ignorant of the true facts, and 4) the defendant relied on plaintiff's conduct to its detriment."[35] Finding issues of fact as to all but the first element, the court remanded for further proceedings. There then ensued a jury trial at which the New York Times Co. prevailed, and that judgment was then affirmed.[36]

---

33. *Id.* at 322 (citation omitted).
34. *Id.* at 323.
35. 2006 U.S. App. LEXIS 5171, at *4.
36. 352 F. App'x 508 (2d Cir. 2009), *cert. denied*, 559 U.S. 1108 (2010).

## Express Authority, Apparent Authority, and Implied Authority

When we speak of authority, we address the permission by one to another to act. It can be express (i.e., in writing and clearly stated), apparent (i.e., based on various facts and circumstances, "apparent" to objective outside observers), and implied (i.e., given the relationship of the parties, deduced from the facts and circumstances). In other words, in the case of an infringement claim, one of the defenses was that there was authority. Permission need not come from a formal license. If the alleged infringer can show the copyright owner gave express authority for the reproduction of its work, that is a defense to infringement.

In *Olan Mills, Inc. v. Linn Photo Co.*,[37] Olan Mills operated portrait studios. The defendant sold photographic equipment, developed film, and sold reproduced photographs. Olan Mills took photographs of certain employees, hired investigators to take four photographs to Linn Photo and request enlargements, and, when they were made, sued Linn Photo for copyright infringement. Olan Mills admitted to permitting in certain circumstances other entities to do such enlargements, but had not done so here. Of relevance here were the instructions given by Olan Mills in attempting to set up Linn Photo by investigators; the instructions to the investigators told them to seek reprints by posing "as an ordinary customer," to sign "hold harmless" forms as requested by Linn Photo, and sign other forms requested if Linn Photo asks for the copyright notice to be cut off or removed.

On the grounds of express authority, the trial court found no copyright infringement on the four photographs since Olan Mills expressly authorized its investigator to obtain reproductions. In other words, the plaintiff had proved ownership of the copyright but failed to prove the copying was without its approval. The Eighth Circuit panel, in a 2–1 decision, reversed the trial court. It rejected the theory that the investigator was Olan Mills's agent operating under express authority. Holding that a copyright owner cannot infringe its own copyright, the investigative scenario here did not

37. 23 F.3d 1345 (8th Cir. 1994), *rev'g* 795 F. Supp. 1423 (N.D. Iowa 1991).

constitute an authorization by the copyright owner, Olan Mills, to its investigator to validate wrongful conduct.

On the counterclaim for indemnification, Linn Photosued Olan Mills under the documents the investigator signed as Olan Mills' agent. That document stated:

> THIS IS TO STATE THAT I AM THE OWNER OF THIS PHOTOGRAPH AND HAVE NOT GIVEN ANY ONE ELSE PERMISSION TO COPYRIGHT THIS PHOTOGRAPH. I AM SUBMITTING IT TO LINN PHOTO COMPANY FOR A COPY AT MY REQUEST. THIS COPY IS FOR MY PERSONAL USE, AND I AGREE TO HOLD HARMLESS, LINN PHOTO COMPANY OR ANY OF ITS AGENTS, FROM ANY LIABILITY ARISING FROM THE COPYING OF THIS PHOTOGRAPH.

Olan Mills argued against enforcement of this provision on the grounds of public policy, based on the position that enforcement of such a provision would impair the statutory benefits afforded under the Copyright Act and otherwise encourage unlawful schemes. Specifically, Olan Mills said such a provision, if enforced, would preclude the use of investigators and "shift the duty of determining the right to copy from Linn Photo to the customer." The trial court rejected the public policy argument as to the use of investigators and, while agreeing that Linn Photo had a duty to investigate the bona fides of the request for reproduction, on these facts, the investigator had express authority and represented as such to Linn, and Linn had no obligation to confirm directly with Olan Mills. The Eighth Circuit panel reversed, distinguishing between the physical photograph and the separate copyright to the image; it held that Linn Photo was on notice having seen the copyright notice, and there had been prior requests by Olan Mills for Linn Photo to cease copying. Consequently, Linn Photo could not use an indemnification agreement to shield illegal conduct.

The *Olan Mills* case is instructive on a variety of levels. First and foremost, it shows an even split of judges—the trial judge and one dissenting appellate judge against two appellate judges. It also shows that a copyright owner can decide whom to pursue; as the courts noted, Olan Mills did not have a problem with certain entities making reproductions. It also shows the value of utilizing a copyright notice.

## Implied License

An implied license permits another to utilize a copyrighted work for the purposes of the implied license. Section 204(a) of the Copyright Act provides for exclusive licenses; an implied license is nonexclusive. It is created when "one party (1) creates a work at another person's request; (2) delivers the work to that person; and (3) intends that the person copy and distribute the work."[38] When the scope is exceeded, infringement occurs. Scope of the implied license will be determined from the facts and circumstances giving rise to the implied license and the relevant statements as to the use or what would be necessary to accomplish the purpose of the use. The nonexclusive license may be granted orally or implied from conduct.[39]

## Express License

Photographer Daniel Morel had taken photographs of the 2010 Haitian earthquake. Agence France-Presse (AFP) found the images by searching online, and the images were distributed by AFP. Getty, a stock-photo agency, also received the images from AFP. AFP had misattributed the photographs and, when questioned, corrected them. The newspaper defendant, the *New York Post*, published certain images with the misattribution. (This is an abbreviated and simplified version of the facts, which are far more extensive.) AFP brought a declaratory judgment action claiming it had not infringed; Morel counterclaimed for copyright infringement.[40]

Initially, AFP moved to dismiss the counterclaim and relied on a defense that it had an express license to use the images based on Morel's loading them on Twitter.[41] The court held that AFP had infringed Morel's copyright in his photographs that had been uploaded to Twitter. The license in force when Morel uploaded to Twitter at the time stated:

38. Latimer v. Roaring Toyz, Inc., 601 F.3d 1224, 1235 (11th Cir. 2010).
39. Jacob Maxwell, Inc. v. Veeck, 110 F.3d 749, 752 (11th Cir. 1997).
40. Agence France Presse v. Morel, 769 F. Supp. 2d 295 (S.D.N.Y. 2011).
41. *See Id.*

> You retain your rights to any Content you submit, post or display on or through the Services.
>
> By submitting, posting or displaying Content on or through the Services, you grant us a worldwide, non-exclusive, royalty-free license (with the right to sublicense) to use, copy, reproduce, process, adapt, modify, publish, transmit, display and distribute such Content in any and all media or distribution methods (now known or later developed).
>
> Tip[:] This license is you authorizing us to make your Tweets available to the rest of the world and to let others do the same. But what's yours is yours—you own your content.[42]
>
> You agree that this license includes the right for Twitter to make such Content available to other companies, organizations or individuals who partner with Twitter for the syndication, broadcast, distribution or publication of such Content on other media and services, subject to our terms and conditions for such Content use.[43]

The court held that this license did not confer any benefit on AFP, which failed to prove it had a license to use the photographs, so the counterclaim stood and the issue of whether the license existed would abide further discovery. There were other defenses and resolutions not relevant to this point.

Two years later, the parties cross-moved for summary judgment.[44] AFP argued that it could not be liable for copyright infringement because "Morel granted it a license by posting the Photos-at-Issue on Twitter."[45] Applying California law, which governed Twitter's terms of service, the court found that such a license did not allow AFP's conduct in the case and did not confer third-party beneficiary status on AFP. As the court noted, the Twitter terms of service (TOS) provisions "would have no meaning if the Twitter TOS allowed third parties to remove the content from Twitter and license it to others without the consent of the copyright holder."[46] The court

42. *Id.* at 302.
43. *Id.* at 303.
44. Agence France Presse v. Morel, 934 F. Supp. 2d 547 (S.D.N.Y. 2013).
45. *Id.* at 559.
46. *Id.* at 563.

further rejected the notion that a "retweet" was a copyright infringement; "as the Court has just explained, a license for one use does not equate to a license for all uses."[47] After addressing other issues, including those relating to the Digital Millennium Copyright Act (DMCA), the court granted Morel's motion establishing copyright infringement as a matter of law but rejected his arguments as to the scope of available statutory damages, so Morel could not recover statutory damages under the DMCA of $2,500 to $25,000 for each distribution of the relevant photographs. Morel moved for reconsideration regarding the statutory damages issue, and the court concluded that

> Morel is, at most, entitled to receive one award of statutory damages per work infringed in this action. To the extent that the Court's conclusion in Section E.1 of its summary judgment opinion—that "AFP and Getty are, at most, each liable for a single statutory damages award per work infringed" . . . would allow otherwise under the circumstances of this case, it is superseded by this holding.[48]

On November 23, 2013, the jury found Agence France-Presse and Getty Images liable, awarding $1.2 million to Morel. This was the statutory maximum. The case was reported as the first to address the allowable use by others for commercial purpose of photographs posted online on social media.[49]

In *Wolff v. Institute of Electrical and Electronics Engineering, Inc.*,[50] the defendant published a magazine that acquired and utilized the plaintiffs' photographs of Apache helicopters in a particular issue, and paid the plaintiffs. The plaintiffs granted the following license: "ONE TIME NON EXCLUSIVE ENGLISH LANGUAGE RIGHTS FOR USE IN THE NOVEMBER 1988 SPECIAL ISSUE OF IEEE SPECTRUM MAGAZINE."[51] The

47. *Id.* at 564.
48. Agence France Presse v. Morel, 934 F. Supp. 2d 584, 594 (S.D.N.Y. 2013).
49. Andrew Hudson, *$1.2M Twitter Copyright Award*, http://photosecrets.com/1m-twitter-copyright-award (last visited April 26, 2014).
50. 768 F. Supp. 66 (S.D.N.Y. 1991).
51. *Id.* at 67.

invoice also included a time limit on use. The issue was well received, and thereafter, the defendant used its cover image of the plaintiffs' photograph in an advertisement the following year in a trade magazine. The defendant claimed that this was within its license or, alternatively, it was fair use. The court found this was not within the defined use and there was nothing to add any new creative element to constitute newly added content as a derivative work. The court also rejected the fair-use defense based on public interest, since the motivation was promotion, not information.

## Unjust Enrichment

Unjust enrichment is an equitable remedy to provide relief where there is no valid and enforceable contract; it cannot be had when there is such a contract. However, where no such contract exists, such "a 'quasi-contract' will be found. It is not a contract itself, but such a quasi-contractual obligation is one imposed by law where there has been no agreement or expression of assent, by word or act, on the part of either party involved. The law creates it, regardless of the intention of the parties, to assure a just and equitable result."[52]

To the extent an unjust-enrichment claim is derivative of the copyright claim, it is preempted.[53] Such a claim will not be preempted to the extent that it does not seek to vindicate distribution rights granted by the Copyright Act, but rather lack of payment or other terms of the contract.[54]

## Shrink Wrap and Click Wrap

In the world of e-commerce, consumers generally indicate acceptance of a contract and its terms by clicking an appropriate box or icon. In the case

52. Clark-Fitzpatrick, Inc. v. Long Island R.R. Co., 70 N.Y.2d 382, 388–89 (1987) (internal quotations and citations omitted).

53. *See, e.g.*, Curtin v. Star Editorial, Inc., 2 F. Supp. 2d 670, 675 (E.D. Pa. 1998).

54. Levine v. Landy, 832 F. Supp. 2d 176, 188 (N.D.N.Y. 2011).

of "shrink wrap" hard products on the shelf, there is often no opportunity to read the terms, although in the case of "click wrap," generally, the consumer can review the terms and conditions. Still, if the consumer wants the product, there really is no choice except to buy that product. The ramifications for the consumer are significant: if he or she wants to contest the matter, the cost of retaining an attorney in another state, and traveling to that state an indeterminate amount of times for hearings, may far outweigh the amount in issue. Arbitration clauses can also appear in both business-to-business as well as consumer contracts, in employment contexts, and across the disciplines of legal practice. Some are negotiated; some are in a contract in which there is no negotiation. Some are in "shrink wrap" or "click wrap" agreements.

A "click wrap" agreement is one that "appears on an internet webpage and requires that a user consent to any terms or conditions by clicking on a dialog box on the screen in order to proceed with the internet transaction."[55]

The leading case on click wrap is *Specht v. Netscape Communications Corp.*[56] *Specht* involved downloading of free software from the defendant's website and whether, by so doing, the plaintiff had bound himself to the defendant's terms and conditions that included an arbitration clause. To do so, the plaintiff would have had to scroll down to a screen located below the download button, and this was held not to be sufficient notice. In order for there to be an agreement, there must be "mutual manifestation of assent."[57] In this case, the manner in which the terms were presented was not obvious and did not manifest assent:

> Although an onlooker observing the disputed transactions in this case would have seen each of the user plaintiffs click on the SmartDownload "Download" button . . . , a consumer's clicking on a download button does not communicate assent to contractual terms if the offer

55. Feldman v. Google, Inc., 513 F. Supp. 2d 229, 235–36 (E.D. Pa. 2007).
56. 306 F.3d 17, 22 (2d Cir. 2002).
57. *Id.* at 29.

> did not make clear to the consumer that clicking on the download button would signify assent to those terms . . . .[58]

In *Specht*, the court explained the term "click wrap" as analogous to "shrink wrap," in which the user has to agree to the terms and conditions of the agreement by clicking on an icon before proceeding, just as he or she conveyed that consent by breaking the seal on a wrapped product. Some courts have acknowledged the sufficiency of that consent in a software context.[59] Where there was clear notice and an ability to review the terms, particularly forum selection clauses, *Specht* noted courts are more likely to uphold the forum selection clauses.[60]

The court noted that a "reasonably prudent person" would not have known of the terms prior to execution of the transaction.[61] "Physical document" cases put the recipient on at least constructive notice to pursue inquiry into the terms.

> These principles apply equally to the emergent world of online product delivery, pop-up screens, hyperlinked pages, clickwrap licensing, scrollable documents, and urgent admonitions to "Download Now!". What plaintiffs saw when they were being invited by defendants to download this fast, free plug-in called SmartDownload was a screen containing praise for the product and, at the very bottom of the screen, a "Download" button. Defendants argue that under the principles set forth in the cases cited above, a "fair and prudent person using ordinary care" would have been on inquiry notice of SmartDownload's license terms. . . .
>
> We are not persuaded that a reasonably prudent offeree in these circumstances would have known of the existence of license terms. Plaintiffs were responding to an offer that did not carry an immediately

58. *Id.* at 29–30 (citations omitted).
59. *See, e.g.*, ProCD, Inc. v. Zeidenberg, 86 F.3d 1447, 1451 (7th Cir. 1996).
60. *Id.* at 32–33.
61. *Id.* at 30.

visible notice of the existence of license terms or require unambiguous manifestation of assent to those terms.[62]

On the other hand, where there was clear notice and an ability to review the terms, particularly forum selection clauses, *Specht* noted courts are more likely to uphold the terms and conditions in a click-wrap agreement.[63] Some courts have acknowledged the sufficiency of that consent in a software context.[64]

Therefore, forum selection clauses will not be invalidated solely because they are contained within the click-wrap agreement.[65] They will be evaluated, however, in terms of the same factors of reasonableness. The same concepts of notice and manifestation of consent will apply to contract formation issues relevant to choice of law and arbitration clauses, or any other clauses within the agreement, for that matter.

In *Fteja v. Facebook, Inc.*,[66] the court explained *Specht* and applied it to the "browsewrap" link, "where website terms and conditions of use are posted on the website typically as a hyperlink at the bottom of the screen." The enforceability of such links may depend on business users rather than consumers.[67] The result may turn on whether the user has the opportunity to review and reject prior to accessing the product.[68]

On occasion, parties seek to challenge click-wrap agreements on the grounds that they are not express contracts because of their format but, rather, are "implied." This has been rejected.[69]

I have not sought to resolve or exhaustively discuss this, but only to highlight it. It is a fact-sensitive analysis.

62. *Id.* at 31 (citations omitted).
63. *Id.* at 32–33, and citations therein.
64. *See, e.g.*, *ProCD, Inc.*, 86 F.3d at 1451.
65. Meier v. Midwest Recreational Clearinghouse, LLC, No. 10-CV-01026, 2010 U.S. Dist. LEXIS 68949 (E.D. Cal. July 12, 2010).
66. 841 F. Supp. 2d 829, 835–36 (S.D.N.Y. 2012).
67. *Id.* at 836.
68. *Id.* at 838.
69. Feldman v. Google, Inc., 513 F. Supp. 2d 229, 235–36 (E.D. Pa. 2007) (by clicking on box that said "Yes, I agree to the above terms and conditions," plaintiff was found to accept the choice-of-law and forum-selection clauses).

## Satisfaction Contracts

A photographer may be asked to take photographs of a particular scene or as part of a project. For example, a corporation may engage a photographer for purposes of a corporate brochure. The photographer's images may be technically fine and objectively acceptable, but if the contract between the company and the photographer provided that the images must be acceptable or satisfactory to the company, "in its sole discretion," then the company has more leeway to reject the images. It is not simply a case of a photographer providing the service and delivering the images on time. A satisfaction contract, while still subject to certain good-faith and reasonableness considerations, will generally provide a more subjective standard to the company. Or, vice versa, to the photographer if that right is reserved to him or her, in a particular situation.[70] Notwithstanding the provision, the decision cannot be completely irrational and in bad faith, but such things are not always easy to prove.

The interpretation of a contract clause presents a purely legal question for the Court on a summary judgment motion.[71] Contracts that vest discretion within a party to determine whether or not it is satisfied with performance are enforceable in New Jersey.[72] An agreement that calls for the "sole judgment" of a party will be enforced, and not governed by an objective reasonableness test.[73] Implicit in the right to be satisfied is the right to terminate a contract, even without an express termination clause, if the contract is materially breached, determination of which is a matter for

70. Muka v. Estate of Stephen L. Muka, 164 Ill. App. 3d 223 (1987) (subjective standard applicable where the party reserves the right to be satisfied. Other types of satisfaction contracts apply objective measuring standard).

71. *See* Spaulding Composites Co. v. Aetna Cas. & Sur. Co., 176 N.J. 25 (2003), *cert. denied*, *sub. nom.* Liberty Mut. Ins. Co. v. Caldwell Trucking PRP Grp., 540 U.S. 1142 (2004).

72. *See* Medivox Prods., Inc. v. Hoffman-LaRoche, Inc., 107 N.J. Super. 47 (Law Div. 1969); Silvestri v. Optus Software, Inc., 175 N.J. 113, 121–22 (2003) ("[A] subjective standard typically is applied to satisfaction clauses in employment contracts.").

73. Mickle v. Christie's, Inc., 207 F. Supp. 2d 237, 246 (S.D.N.Y. 2002) ("Christie's needs only to demonstrate that it possessed a subjective fear of potential liability."); *see also* Action Eng'g v. Martin Marietta Aluminum, 670 F.2d 456, 460–62 (3d Cir. 1982) (rejecting objective "reasonableness" standard in interpreting a contract that left satisfaction to a party's opinion and applying a good-faith standard).

the party that must be satisfied.[74] The *Medivox* court went further, noting that "dissatisfaction which occurs during the course of a contract calling for satisfactory performance over an extended period of time may justify termination by the promisee."[75]

The test therefore is one of subjectiveness. In *Medivox*, the issue was the quality of radio scripts produced by the plaintiff and the defendant's dissatisfaction with them. In order to determine materiality, the court looked at a standard of performance required by the contract. The entire facts and circumstances surrounding that contract were relevant for the purposes of the evaluation. Significantly, the issue was not whether Medivox had performed quantitatively but, rather, qualitatively, and whether LaRoche had reserved the right to be the final arbiter.[76] The court held there was such a right, that LaRoche had provided ample opportunity to Medivox to produce scripts to its satisfaction, but ultimately, LaRoche's dissatisfaction was not (as alleged here) a reconstructed effort but one that had been expressed systematically and repeatedly.[77]

The Mickles assigned certain artwork to Christie's for auction. The consignment agreement provided that in the event of nonpayment by buyer, Christie's "in our sole discretion" could cancel the sale and return the artwork to the consignor. Similarly, the contract provided that Christie's could rescind a sale if in Christie's "sole judgment" it determined that the offering for sale of the property "may subject Christie's and/or Consignor to any liability."[78] A gallery was the successful bidder but then demanded rescission on the basis of learning of questionable authenticity of the artwork. After the auction, and reacting to "negative reports circulating among members of the trade raising doubts about the attribution of the Painting," Christie's nonetheless initially rejected the "negative hearsay" about authenticity and refused to rescind.[79] The gallery therefore refused to pay, and consequently, Christie's did not pay the Mickles, who then sued Christie's and the gallery

74. *Medivox*, 107 N.J. Super. at 58–59.
75. *Id.* at 67.
76. *Id.* at 57–58.
77. *Id.* at 68–69.
78. *Mickle*, 207 F. Supp. 2d at 239–40.
79. *Id.* at 240.

in New York state court. Christie's defended by contending that Mickles "failed to fully reveal the Painting's prior history to Christie's, despite the warranty clause contained in the Consignment Agreement . . . ."[80]

In *Mickle*, the gallery renewed its demand that Christie's rescind the sale following development of certain information in that state-court action. As a result, and based on the opinion of a designee of the gallery that the painting was inauthentic, Christie's "concluded that it no longer held good faith grounds to sell the Painting" as authentic. Because it was presented with conflicting views of authorities, Christie's believed it could have been subjected to liability unless it rescinded the sale.[81] The Mickles then filed an order to show cause in federal court, seeking injunctive relief, which was denied. Christie's counterclaimed for fraud, misrepresentation, and breach of contract. The district court suspended the action until the state-court action concluded. Meanwhile, the state court granted the gallery's motion for summary judgment and dismissed the action, rejecting the Mickles' argument that Christie's cancellation and rescission violated their rights. The federal court agreed and ruled in favor of Christie's.

Importantly, the court ruled that Christie's "sole judgment" contractual right allowed it to rescind because it did not want to get involved in litigation, which the court held "was a valid exercise of Christie's discretion and rights under" the termination clause.[82] It included potential liability as well as actual liability.

The *Mickle* court noted that the exercise of "sole discretion" based on a subjective concern over liability is "circumscribed by an implied covenant of good faith and fair dealing."[83] The court upheld Christie's subjective determination since it was (1) represented as an informed choice, (2) based on an honest belief, (3) preceded by due diligence, (4) impelled and constrained by authority that derived from agreements or rules governing the relation between the parties, (5) taken for the reason stated, (6) consistent with a

80. *Id.* at 241.
81. *Id.* at 242.
82. *Id.* at 245.
83. *Id.* at 249.

motive to effectuate the agreement, and (7) caused it to forgo a benefit or lose a bargained-for opportunity.[84]

As the *Mickle* court aptly noted:

> It is easy to charge dishonesty and bad faith; it is harder to prove it. Occasions do arise when a purported legal claim is empty from the start, and is lightly tossed into the wind on the strength of nothing more than a hope and a prayer that some providential breeze may blow it where intended and somehow make it stick. A party so maligned should not be compelled to bear the attendant humiliation compounded by expense, the harms enlarged by the burdens of having to endure a trial in order to defend against and refute the bare or fanciful allegation.[85]

The *Mickle* court looked not to the merits of the decision on authenticity, nor even to the degree to which Christie's reasonably believed and warranted that authenticity. The paramount inquiry was whether the Mickles could prove that Christie's acted "without warrant and for some other reason than that which it stated, and that its action was not grounded on demonstrably genuine concern over potential liability . . . ."[86] The *Mickle* court rejected the Mickles' challenge to the bona fides of Christie's fear of liability defense on the grounds that Christie's had more than "an unsubstantiated general anxiety about litigation which it hid behind an invocation of advise [sic] of counsel."[87]

In an older case, *Lord v. Pathe News, Inc.*,[88] the plaintiff was an actor, well known at the time for radio performances. He hired a camera crew to accompany him on a schooner that traveled about so he could broadcast from unusual places. When the ship reached New York, the news company refused to put the camera equipment on board, claiming the plaintiff had

84. *Id.* at 249–50.
85. *Id.* at 250.
86. *Id.* at 251.
87. *Id.* at 252–53.
88. 97 F.2d 508 (2d Cir. 1938).

delayed. He hired a replacement crew who took pictures that, as the court described, "were complete failure." Lord sued the original company. The trial court dismissed the case finding the contract indefinite; the appellate court reversed, finding sufficient definiteness and likening it to a satisfaction contract: "As to the amount of expenses to be incurred on land in making pictures, both parties were content to put themselves into the hands of the defendant's employee, Begg. He was to 'have charge of the making of the motion pictures.'" This gave him discretion as to what to photograph and how much to spend upon a picture, but he was bound to use his judgment in good faith to advance the common business. In this respect, the contract was at least as definite as the familiar "satisfaction" contract."

The point of this discussion is to emphasize both to photographers and to those who engage photographers that a contract that provides for satisfaction gives the buyer considerably more leeway in terms of what is acceptable than a purely objective contract.

## Personal Service Contracts

As a general matter, when you unilaterally breach a contract, you are liable for damages. In vertain circumstances, U.S. courts also permit a legal remedy called "specific performance" pursuant to which a court does not award damages but compels you to perform the contract. The contract itself may call for specific performance.[89] *Fazzio* involved a purchase and sale agreement for farmland; real estate is a common basis. When the property is unique, and the agreement is not impossible to perform, and there is no adequate remedy at law (e.g., damages will not suffice) and the remedy is available to both parties, the court has discretion to order the relief.[90] A court can fashion the order to prevent a windfall.

89. *See, e.g.*, Fazzio v. Mason, 150 Idaho 591, 593 (Idaho 2011) ("Specific Performance. Should either party breach or violate this Settlement Agreement, the non-offending party shall have a remedy of specific performance and may apply to the district court of the county of Ada, state of Idaho to have this Settlement Agreement enforced by a judgment for specific performance.").

90. *Id.* at 597.

Some contracts are completely dependent upon the particular skills and talents of one individual. Essentially, personal service is a non-delegable service, such as inherent in artistic or athletic performance, and is a function of "trust and confidence" between the parties.[91] These are particularly applicable to artists.[92] The issue can arise when the artist refuses to honor an exclusivity provision, for example. The contract may also provide for liquidated damages in the event of breach by the artist. On the other hand, in some cases, a court may enforce an injunction against the artist, even in a personal services contract, if the court finds that the artist is not prohibited from earning a living and the term of the exclusiveness is not unreasonable.[93]

As a general rule, a personal service contract is not subject to specific performance.[94] Although the parties may call their contract one for personal services, a court will look to the substance and not be bound by the parties' own designation.[95]

However, some states address the issue by statute, with contrary results. In Montana, for instance, there is a statutory prohibition against an injunction "to prevent the breach of a contract the performance of which would not be specifically enforced."[96] In *Reier Broadcasting Co. v. Kramer*,[97] relying on California and Arizona precedent, the Montana Supreme Court diverged from the New York approach, and held:

---

91. RESTATEMENT (SECOND) OF CONTRACTS § 367 cmt. b (1981); Creator's Way Associated Labels, Inc. v. Mitchell (*In re* Mitchell), 249 B.R. 55 (Bankr. S.D.N.Y. 2000) (recording artist contract).

92. *See, e.g.*, Husain v. McDonald's Corp., 205 Cal. App. 4th 860, 868 (2012) (services of an actor or artist are "distinctly personal and non-delegable.") (citation omitted). *Husain* also noted the California statute: "Civ. Code, § 3390 (obligations to render personal service or employ another in personal service cannot be specifically enforced.)" *Id.* at 868. Personal services can also apply to "managers, sales agents, school-teachers, mechanics, cooks, and contracts for the furnishing of personal care and support." *Id.* at 868 (internal quotation and citation omitted).

93. *See, e.g.*, MCA Records, Inc. v. Newton-John, 90 Cal. App. 3d 18 (1979).

94. RESTATEMENT (SECOND) OF CONTRACTS § 367(1) (1981); Nicholas v. Pa. State Univ., 227 F.3d 133, 146 (3d Cir. 2000).

95. *In re Mitchell*, 249 B.R. at 59. While specific performance is not obtainable, a claim for damages, such as lost profits, exists. *Id.* at 60.

96. MONT. CODE ANN. § 27-19-103(5).

97. 316 Mont. 301, 307 (2003).

> We determine that § 27-19-103(5), MCA, like its California and Arizona counterparts, prohibits the use of injunctive relief to prevent a party to a personal services contract from performing services elsewhere during the life of the contract. The exclusivity clause in the Reier-Kramer employment agreement, if enforced vis a vis an injunction, would prevent Kramer from performing for Clear Channel or any of Reier's other competitors until the summer of 2004 when the Reier-Kramer agreement expires. Thus, if Kramer were to perform at all, he would have to perform for Reier. In that sense, an injunction would amount to the indirect enforcement of the affirmative part of the contract.

## Putting It in Perspective

Photographers need to pay attention to their contracts and not treat them as "form" documents or filled with irrelevant "legalese." Contracts matter, as seen from the examples in this chapter. Whether negotiating a contract with a publisher for their photographs to appear in a book or exclusivity of work for a company's brochure, or work, for a model, photographers need to pay particular attention to scope, usage, and term. Other particular issues are dependent upon the context; a book contract is different from a model release.

## Chapter Five

# Property Law

## Introduction

It is helpful to think of photography in two steps. First is the taking of the picture, and second is the use of the picture. Different legal concepts apply to each. You may stand on public property and take a picture of a subject that is permissible. But if you trespass onto private property to take the same picture of the same subject, you have broken the law in terms of the first step—the taking of the picture. On the other hand, if you are not trespassing or otherwise creating a disturbance and take a picture within permissible bounds, that does not mean that the picture may be used without restrictions. To provide a simply example, a museum may permit you to take pictures, so step one is fine, but restrict your ability to use that picture for personal use only and not turn around and sell it.

## Private Property

Property does not have a right of privacy attached to it as people do. Nonetheless, there are certain rights that inhere to private property across various spectrums.

First, trespass may be subject to criminal as well as civil penalty. Criminal trespass is defined by statute in the particular state. This implicates the physical taking of the photograph when the photographer is standing on someone else's property could subject the photographer to prosecution. In the context of ruling on a motion to suppress, one court had occasion to consider the import of a No Trespassing sign and agreed with the trial court that such a sign puts the public on notice that "the owner does not want others to come up the driveway."[1] The court further agreed that given that the sign was within four feet of the gate:

> a normal, reasonable person in that situation would . . . have seen those two signs and at the very least would have stopped and looked at the other side of the gate to see what the . . . other sign said . . . which turned out to be a no trespassing sign.[2]

On the other hand, a sign placed on a boundary fence might simply be read to exclude those seeking to use the property for themselves but not otherwise exclude visitors. Photographers need to respect such signs and err on the side of caution. It is not just a matter of civil liability but criminal liability in the taking of a picture.

As noted with regard to the purpose of the "trespass," certain rights accrue to certain people regarding private property. A shopping mall may be privately owned, but persons who are invited are free to engage in certain activities. Photography implicates certain free speech rights of expression. Can a photographer as an invitee in a shopping mall take pictures in that mall? In *PruneYard Shopping Center v. Robins*,[3] the Supreme Court upheld the right of people to circulate petitions in a shopping center and struck down the mall's posted policies that attempted to preclude "publicly expressive activity" including petitioning. This has been interpreted by the California Supreme Court to include a right to encourage boycotting a particular store.[4] These latter cases address the principle that the more that

1. State v. Roper, 254 Ore. App. 197, 199 (2012), *cert. denied*, 353 Ore. 714 (2013).
2. *Id.* at 199–200.
3. 447 U.S. 74 (1980).
4. Fashion Valley Mall, LLC v. Nat'l Labor Relations Bd., 42 Cal. 4th 850 (2007); *see also* N.J. Coal. Against War in the Middle East v. J.M.B. Realty Corp., 138 N.J. 326 (1994), *cert. denied*, *sub. nom.* Short Hill Assocs. v. N.J. Coal. Against War in the Middle East, 516 U.S. 812 (1995); Green Party v. Hartz Mountain Indus., 164 N.J. 127 (2000).

private property is devoted to public use, the greater the accommodation must be of the array of rights available to individual users of the property.

On the other hand, in *Hawaii v. Viglielmo*,[5] the Supreme Court of Hawaii ruled that a person did not have First Amendment protection from a charge of trespass when, as an invitee to a shopping center, the individual was peaceably protesting the sale of military toys outside a Kay-Bee Toys store and refused to leave when asked to do so by security. The Hawaii statute made it a crime in the second degree when a person remained unlawfully on commercial premises after reasonable warnings and requests to leave. As discussed in *Viglielmo*, states may interpret their own state constitutions more broadly or more restrictively than *PruneYard*, in terms of what activity is permitted or not.

The First Amendment right of photographers is not absolute, as discussed in Chapter 6. If someone was in the mall and decided to take pictures, the first issue is not whether what is being photographed is permissible and what use may be made of it. Rather, the initial question is whether that photographer can be stopped or physically removed. If the mall posted a sign that prohibited photography, it would probably be within its rights, in the same manner that a museum prohibits not only flash photography to protect the images but use of tripods to prevent interference with other patrons. A court would likely perform a balance between the private-property rights and the level of First Amendment activity. Other patrons may also have privacy concerns, but such could conceivably be a rational basis for a mall owner to prohibit such arguable interference with the "shopping experience." *PruneYard* permits such expressive activities on private property provided they do not interfere with "normal business operations." Private property, like a mall, does not "lose its private character merely because the public is generally invited to use it for designated purposes."[6]

We have been talking about public versus private access; even with public access, there are limitations. Similarly, without express consent and, indeed, in the face of posted non-consent, a photographer seeking to take pictures

5. 105 Haw. 197 (2004).
6. Lloyd Corp. v. Tanner, 407 U.S. 551, 569 (1972).

on private property entered as an invitee would in most cases be subject to the restrictions. Another argument to be made by the mall owner is that of contract: the invitees have a license to enter the property for certain purposes as a condition of access. Where the private property does not rise to the level of a Main Street–like place, the more likely it is for a court to enforce the restrictions.[7]

The Copyright Act also addresses the property rights of owners with regard to alterations and destruction of buildings as an exception to the copyright owner's rights to derivative works under 17 U.S.C. § 106(2):

> Alterations to and Destruction of Buildings.—Notwithstanding the provisions of section 106(2), the owners of a building embodying an architectural work may, without the consent of the author or copyright owner of the architectural work, make or authorize the making of alterations to such building, and destroy or authorize the destruction of such building.[8]

### Use of Images of Private Property

Remember that we are talking about private property in terms of access. We will address later the use of images of private property made from a public street. The American Civil Liberties Union (ACLU) Guide to Photographers Rights tells you that you can photograph "anything" that is in plain view, but on private property, the owner sets rules.[9]

In *New York World's Fair 1964–1965 Corp. v. Colourpicture Publishers, Inc.*,[10] the court specifically addressed the issue. It held:

> In our opinion, a photograph of a unique building, structure or object situated within the World's Fair grounds, *to which an admission fee*

7. *See, e.g.*, Lushbaugh v. Home Depot USA, Inc., 93 Cal. App. 4th 1159 (2d Dist. 2001) (finding reasonable regulation by a warehouse as to where petitions could be gathered was not violation of First Amendment, based on safety concerns).

8. 17 U.S.C. § 120(b).

9. *Know Your Rights: Photographers*, AM. CIVIL LIBERTIES UNION, http://www.aclu.org/free-speech/know-your-rights-photographers (last visited Apr. 8, 2014).

10. 21 A.D.2d 896 (N.Y. App. Div. 2d 1964).

> *is charged*, is a photograph of a show in which plaintiff has a property right. Therefore, defendants may not photograph that building, structure, or object without the plaintiff's permission.[11]

However, in *New York Racing Association v. Perlmutter Publications*,[12] the court stated:

> Insofar as plaintiff relies upon [*New York World's Fair*] for its holding that the Fair had property rights giving it the ability to control photographs and reproductions of buildings and exhibits at the Fair, the Court finds the case unpersuasive in light of more recent federal law analyzing property rights similar to those at issue in New York World's Fair and the case at bar.[13]

Images observable at the track were not protected as property right in and of themselves.

What about taking an image of a private building from the public street? We are not here talking about copyright but, rather, a claimed property right. In *Jaubert v. Crowley Post-Signal, Inc.*,[14] a Louisiana state court case, relief sought was by way of injunction to prevent a nuisance. The newspaper printed a photo of plaintiffs' (shabby) house as part of series of neighborhood:

> According to established principles of the law of privacy, no right to privacy attaches to material in the public view. The only question before this court is thus whether the photograph and words of description depicted a matter which was actually within the plaintiffs' protected zone of privacy. It is clear from the record that the Jauberts' home was plainly visible from the public street, and that passersby

11. *Id.*

12. No. 95-CV-994, 1996 U.S. Dist. LEXIS 11764 (N.D.N.Y. July 19, 1996), *reconsideration denied*, 954 F. Supp. 578 (N.D.N.Y. 1997)

13. *Id.* at *10.

14. 375 So. 2d 1386 (La. 1979).

> were presented with a view of the property which was identical to that published by the defendant. Therefore, plaintiffs had no right to privacy, regarding the house and its condition; defendant committed no fault.

In other words, the analysis is not based on property rights per se but on whether the image implicates the kinds of causes of action based on privacy or defamation that were discussed Chapter 3.

There is a difference between the right to expression and the manner in which that expression is made—that is, conduct. In *D'Amario v. Providence Civic Center Authority*,[15] a music promoter through his company leased a public civic center for a concert and imposed a no-camera rule. The plaintiff was a photographer who on other occasions photographed concerts and sold the pictures. On appeal, the court reversed the dismissal of the case after finding that state action was involved through the public authority and did not reach the merits as to the enforceability of the no-camera rule. On remand,[16] the trial court addressed the merits. Recognizing that entertainment is protected speech, citing *Schad v. Borough of Mount Ephraim*,[17] as is the right to disseminate or display photographs, citing *United States v. Thirty-Seven Photographs*,[18] and that making a profit does not preclude First Amendment protection, citing *First National Bank of Boston v. Bellotti*,[19] the court nonetheless concluded that what was restricted here was not expression but conduct, which was not protected, citing *Lovelace v. Southeastern Massachusetts University*.[20] The trial court wrote, "There is a considerable difference between, on the one hand, allowing the media to print (or to broadcast) all the news that it collects and, on the second hand, permitting

15. 783 F.2d 1 (1st Cir. 1986).
16. D'Amario v. Providence Civic Center Authority, 639 F. Supp. 1538 (D.R.I. 1986), *aff'd w/o*, 815 F.2d 692 (1st Cir.), *cert. denied*, 484 U.S. 859 (1987).
17. 452 U.S. 61 (1981).
18. 402 U.S. 363 (1971).
19. 435 U.S. 765 (1978).
20. 793 F.2d 419 (1st Cir. 1986).

the media totally unchecked access to forage whenever and wherever it pleases in search of tidbits."[21] It concluded by holding that

> the plaintiff had no entitlement to any special sort of shutter-ready access to the events in question; that PROCCA (Providence Civic Center Authority) was well within its rights to honor the contractual stipulations between Gemini and the quintet of camera-shy entertainers; and that, in enforcing the "no camera" rule, the defendants did not abridge D'Amario's first amendment rights.[22]

Photographers, of course, can be restrained if, in paparazzi-style, they physically interfere with someone's life.[23] The concept of nuisance, though, need not go to such extremes. In *Levy v. Franks*,[24] the court addressed a cause of action for "outrageous conduct," which required proof that the conduct is (1) intentional or reckless, (2) so outrageous as to not be tolerated in civilized society, and (3) such as to result in serious mental injury. The behavior complained of was constant videotaping of one neighbor by another in terms of a property dispute.

How far can a private-building owner go? Porat, a "photo hobbyist," was stopped by Lincoln Towers apartment security guard from taking pictures and told pictures of buildings were not permitted by "management policy."[25] Porat continued shooting, said "aesthetic purposes" and "recreational." The guard put Porat under "civilian arrest," but Porat refused to show the pictures, despite a request. Police appeared and cited Porat for trespass, and one said post-9/11 security concerns were the rationale for

---

21. *D'Amario,* 639 F. Supp. at 1542.

22. *Id.* at 1544; *see also* Kalfus v. N.Y. & Presbyterian Hosp., 476 F. App'x 877, 879 (1st Cir. 2012) (freelance news photographer sitting on private hospital property arrested after asked to leave; hospital was restricting media access regarding treatment of Joe Torre's brother: "The First Amendment does not prevent a property owner from restricting press access to private property.").

23. *See* Galella v. Onassis, 487 F.2d 986 (2d Cir. 1973).

24. 159 S.W.3d 66 (Tenn. Ct. App. 2004), *app. denied*, 2004 Tenn. LEXIS 1075 (Tenn. Dec. 6, 2004).

25. Porat v. Lincoln Towers Cmty. Ass'n, No. 04-cv-3199, 2005 U.S. Dist. LEXIS 4333 (S.D.N.Y. Mar. 17, 2005), *aff'd*, 464 F.3d 274 (2d Cir. 2006).

prohibition.[26] After no one showed to prosecute, Porat sued for, among other things, a 1983 First Amendment retaliation claim. The court held that the First Amendment did not protect "purely private recreational, noncommunicative photography"—for example, an image must communicate an idea to an audience.[27] Taking photographs in and of themselves were not enough, but even if so, the retaliation here was not related to it.[28]

## Public Property

Public or government property raises its own set of issues. As a general rule, you can photograph a public building from a public street.

You are not to be disturbed by law enforcement officials, at least with regard to federal buildings, unless you are acting suspiciously. The U.S. Department of Homeland Security has stated in an FPS Information Bulletin that "the public's right to photograph the exterior of federal facilities" from "publicly accessible spaces such as streets, sidewalks, parks and plazas."[29] It also states that in a field interview, "officers should not seize the camera or its contents, and must be cautious not to give such 'orders' to a photographer to erase the contents of a camera." The Bulletin further gives express instructions to officers:

> A photographer may not be detained unless, and until, the officer develops **reasonable suspicion** (for a brief *Terry* Stop) or **probably cause** (for an arrest).
>
> If the field interview **does not** yield a reasonable belief of criminal behavior or terrorist reconnaissance activity, the photography should be permitted to proceed unimpeded.

26. *Id.* at *3–4.
27. *Id.* at *13.
28. *Id.* at *14 n.4.
29. HQ-IB-012-2010 (Sept. 2, 2010), http://www.photoattorney.com/wp-content/uploads/2011/02/Photographing-the-Exterior-of-Federal-Buildings.pdf (last visited April 28, 2014).

> Because the initial interview is voluntary, officers should not seize the camera or its contents, and must be cautious not to give such "orders" to a photographer to erase the contents of a camera, as this constitutes a seizure or detention.

Note that this applies to federal officers under the jurisdiction of the Department of Homeland Security. It does not apply to state law enforcement officials.

This does not apply to state buildings. However, state constitutions also contain "First Amendment" protections. There is, though, a balance that is engaged in where the First Amendment competes with other constitutional concerns, such as police power. This is discussed in Chapter 6.

Once, I was told by a U.S. marshal to remove my sunglasses, look into a video camera, and then I could take a picture of the federal courthouse. Did he have the right to do that? Read again the DHS bulletin.

And read this. Under Federal Property Management Regulations.

> [P]hotographs may be taken in space occupied by a tenant agency only with the consent of the occupying agency concerned. Except when security regulations apply or a Federal court order or rule prohibits it, photographs for news purposes may be taken in entrances, lobbies, foyers, corridors, or auditoriums when used for public meetings. Subject to the foregoing prohibitions, photographs may be taken only with written permission of an authorized official of the agency occupying the space where the photographs are to be taken.[30]

In *Gilles v. Davis*,[31] a man videotaped his colleague as both were involved in a protest, and the man's colleague was arrested. The video captured the police activity on film. All criminal charges were dismissed and the men sued for civil rights violations under 42 U.S.C. § 1983, providing for civil relief for constitutional violations under color of law. The court dismissed

30. 41 C.F.R. § 101–20.310.
31. 427 F.3d 197 (3d Cir. 2005).

the civil claims on technical grounds, but as to the photography aspect, it noted that "videotaping or photographing the police in the performance of their duties on public property may be a protected activity," citing *Smith v. City of Cumming*,[32] which held: "The First Amendment protects the right to gather information about what public officials do on public property, and specifically, a right to record matters of public interest." Further discussion of the tension between the First Amendment rights of photographers and security issues are discussed in Chapter Six, particularly in the context of street photography. According to *Giles*, "photography . . . that has a communicative or expressive purpose enjoys some First Amendment protection."[33]

For purposes of evaluating the regulation of speech on public property, the Supreme Court divides the space into different categories:

> In conducting forum analysis, our decisions have sorted government property into three categories. First, in traditional public forums, such as public streets and parks, "any restriction based on the content of . . . speech must satisfy strict scrutiny, that is, the restriction must be narrowly tailored to serve a compelling government interest." . . . Second, governmental entities create designated public forums when "government property that has not traditionally been regarded as a public forum is intentionally opened up for that purpose"; speech restrictions in such a forum "are subject to the same strict scrutiny as restrictions in a traditional public forum." . . . Third, governmental entities establish limited public forums by opening property "limited to use by certain groups or dedicated solely to the discussion of certain subjects." . . . As noted in text, "[i]n such a forum, a governmental entity may impose restrictions on speech that are reasonable and viewpoint-neutral."[34]

32. 212 F.3d 1332, 1333 (11th Cir.), *cert. denied*, 531 U.S. 978 (2000).

33. *Id.* at 212 n.14.

34. Christian Legal Soc'y Chapter of the Univ. of Cal., Hastings Coll. of the Law v. Martinez, 130 S. Ct. 2971, 2984 n.11 (2010).

### Museum and Website Access Restrictions

Most museums allow photography for noncommercial, personal use, except certain exhibits or objects on special exhibition or otherwise may have particular and individual restrictions on them. Where museums permit photography, it is usually without flash, and in most cases tripods (or possibly monopods) are also prohibited. Restrictions based on the lender's or donor's licensing or contractual restrictions would explain the former, and respect for the maintenance of a delicate artwork, and crowd control, can explain the latter restrictions. Whether or not a museum can effectively enforce these restrictions is another matter, particularly with museums themselves posting on social media sites.

As one example, the Art Institute of Chicago's policy on photography is that "You are welcome to take photographs of the permanent collection and special exhibitions for personal use unless otherwise noted. Dry sketching is also permitted. Please respect signage that may prohibit photography of specific works of art or exhibitions, and please do not use flashes, tripods, and video cameras."[35] Separate arrangements are made for the media. Remember that if you are in a museum and take pictures of people, you may have other issues as discussed with regard to privacy. Remember also that while a museum may own the physical object, it does not necessarily own the copyright of the object.

Museums generally have policies with regard to photography, and this implicates a variety of issues—copyright, security, licensing. Some, like a prohibition on the use of tripods, are directed to safety and issues relating to the general enjoyment of the public without having to navigate obstructions. In *Bridgeman Art Library, Ltd. v. Corel Corp.*,[36] the court held that there was no copyright protection for artwork in the public domain that precluded defendant from marketing the same.[37] Similarly, there is no copyright

35. Art Institute of Chicago, Museum Guidelines, http://www.artic.edu/museum-guidelines (last visited April 27, 2014).

36. 36 F. Supp. 2d 191 (S.D.N.Y. 1999).

37. *See also* Hearn v. Meyer, 664 F. Supp. 832 (S.D.N.Y. 1987).

protection for catalog illustrations of transmission parts that were simply copied from photographs taken from a competitor's catalog.[38]

On the other hand, when you own the physical painting (even if there is no copyright) and lends it to a museum with a restriction on photography, museums respect that. But if the photographer in the museum nonetheless photographs it, what is the cause of action? It cannot be for copyright infringement. It is contractual, between the museum and the lender, just as there is an implied, if not actual, contract between the visitor and the museum that governs the visitor's access to the museum. One wonders, though, if there can be no copyright protection to a public domain work, would a restriction on photography of such a work and its subsequent sale or use be not enforceable as against public policy if it were based on a copyright restriction? In *Bridgeman*, it was not clear if the Bridgeman images were copied. What happens when you copy such images from another's website in violation of its terms of use? The issue ceases to be one of copyright versus contract; if an entity has gone to the expense to organize public domain works in a certain way, it is entitled to regulate the use of its arrangement.[39]

Some photography websites contain language that tells you by entering the site you agree to limited use. These are comparable to restrictions upon entering a museum as well. The advantage of such restrictions, at a minimum, provides notice to the user of copyright or other restrictions. Whether they would be absolutely enforceable would depend upon the use made by the visitor; as noted, there are various exceptions and defenses to claims of copyright infringement. In addition, these terms of use would also be analyzed as a matter of contract law as to their enforceability.[40]

38. ATC Distrib. Grp., Inc. v. Whatever It Takes Transmissions & Parts, Inc., 402 F.3d 700, 712 (6th Cir. 2005); *see also* Meshwerks, Inc. v. Toyota Motor Sales USA, Inc., 528 F.3d 1258 (10th Cir. 2008), *cert. denied*, 555 U.S. 1138 (2009).

39. *See* Schrock v. Learning Curve Int'l, Inc., 586 F.3d 513, 525 (7th Cir. 2009).

40. *See, e.g.*, Register.com, Inc. v. Verio, Inc., 126 F. Supp. 2d 238, 241 (S.D.N.Y. 2000), *aff'd*, 356 F.3d 393 (2d Cir. 2004) (applying New York law, the court held that "in light of this sentence at the end of Register.com's terms of use, there can be no question that by proceeding to submit a WHOIS query, Verio manifested its assent to be bound by Register.com's terms of use, and a contract was formed and subsequently breached").

In *Fraley v. Facebook, Inc.*,[41] discussed in Chapter 3, Fraley filed a class action claiming Facebook violated California law by using members' "Sponsored Stories" as part of its advertising campaign. As a preliminary legal matter, subject to later proofs, the court held that the plaintiffs articulated a theory of misappropriation for the class tied to commercial use, since the stories were directed to other consumers, thereby pleading a cause of action under California Civil Code § 3344. On the individual claims, the court rejected newsworthy defense, left it for factual determination whether Facebook's general terms of use were broad enough to cover the "consent" here, and rejected a challenge to lack of damages subject to the plaintiff's proof of the value of their images.

Of course, when the works are not in the public domain, there is no issue as to infringement if you simply photograph a copyrighted work and then try to sell it.

## Putting It in Perspective

We are talking now about a very particular type of claim. We have discussed above that there is no copyright protection to the outside of a building. We have noted the limited protection for trademark and the fair use of building exteriors in photographs. We have discussed the parameters of privacy and misappropriation claims. We have also discussed certain legitimate restrictions on access and certain First Amendment and security issues surrounding photographs on private property. As a general rule, you can photograph shop fronts, storefronts, houses, and so forth from public access areas, and use them for non-advertising and non-promotional purposes; to the extent you start invading privacy, interfering with someone's daily life or otherwise intimate that they are endorsing something, you start, perhaps, to cross a line.

41. 830 F. Supp. 2d 785 (N.D. Cal. 2011).

TappOut Billiards in Atlanta.

As an example here is an image from Atlanta, taken from a public street, for artistic purposes. You should, however, watch for any posted warning signs banning photography. Whether or not they are ultimately enforceable, you can then at least make an informed decidiosns as to whether you want to take that particular image.

## Chapter Six

# First Amendment Rights

## First Amendment Rights of Photographers

There is general agreement that photographers, at least "serious" photographers and not the casual snapshooter, have First Amendment rights. Where courts disagree is whether that right is absolute. Note that commercial speech is also protected under the First Amendment.[1] Where the rubber hits the road, the actual boundaries are gray.

On the one hand, in *Bery v. City of New York*, the Second Circuit stated flatly that "paintings, photographs, prints and sculptures, such as those appellants seek to display and sell in public areas of the City, always communicate some idea or concept to those who view it, and as such are entitled to full First Amendment protection."[2] In ruling on the validity of an analogous New York City ordinance in the context of street artists displaying and selling "painting, photography and sculpture," the appellate court reversed the trial court's sustaining of that ordinance. *Bery* rejected equating these arts with "the crafts of the jeweler, the potter and the silversmith," which "may at times have expressive content."[3] In *Gilles v. Davis*, the Third Circuit cited *Bery* for the proposition that "[m]ore generally, photography or

1. Va. State Bd. of Pharmacy v. Va. Citizens Consumer Council, 425 U.S. 748 (1976).
2. 97 F.3d 689, 696 (2d Cir. 1996), *cert. denied*, 520 U.S. 1251 (1997).
3. 97 F.3d at 696.

videography that has a communicative or expressive purpose enjoys some First Amendment protection."[4]

Other courts, including a panel of the Second Circuit, have pulled back from *Bery*'s blanket statement and analyze in the first instance whether the photographic conduct is "expressive" or not; simply taking the photograph is not enough. In *Mastrovincenzo v. New York City*, the court held that

> (1) the sale of clothing painted with graffiti is not necessarily expressive and therefore is not automatically entitled to First Amendment protection; (2) the sale of plaintiff's clothing nonetheless has a predominantly expressive purpose and therefore merits First Amendment protection; (3) New York City's licensing requirement is a content-neutral restriction on speech that is narrowly tailored to achieve the objective of reducing urban congestion; and (4) the Bery injunction's reference to "paintings" does not encompass clothing painted with graffiti.[5]

The Fifth Circuit read this as "recasting" *Bery* to draw a "distinction between fine art and decorative arts in terms that enforcement officers and vendors in the 'real world' can understand and apply 'without recourse to principles of aesthetics.'"[6]

See also *State v. Chepilko*,[7] which discusses the more limited application of the First Amendment in this context and the cases that have not accepted *Bery* in its broad sweep.

4. 427 F.3d 197, 212 n.14 (3d Cir. 2005); *See also* White v. City of Sparks, 341 F. Supp. 2d 1129, 1138–39 (D. Nev. 2004), *aff'd*, 500 F.3d 953 (9th Cir. 2007), *cert. denied*, 535 U.S. 1005 (2008); Burnham v. Ianni, 119 F.3d 668 (8th Cir. 1997) (posting of photographs of faculty members dressed in historic costume in a history department display is protected activity; while not absolute, free speech is protected even if the government disapproves of the ideas expressed); TV v. Smith-Green Cmty. Sch. Corp., 807 F. Supp. 2d 767 (N.D. Ind. 2011) (posting of photographs from slumber party online is protected activity; "the photographic recording of the staged event and the uploading of the images to the social networking sites are both efforts to memorialize and further communicate the expression engaged in by the conduct depicted in the images").

5. 435 F.3d 78, 82 (2d Cir. 2006).

6. Kleinman v. City of San Marcos, 597 F.3d 323, 327 (5th Cir.), *cert. denied*, 131 S. Ct. 159 (2010).

7. 405 N.J. Super. 446 (App. Div. 2009), *cert. denied*, 201 N.J. 156 (2010).

In *Chepilko*, the unanimous panel upheld the municipal court convictions of a photographer in Atlantic City, who took and sold photographs of people on the Boardwalk. Finding that this activity did "not serve predominantly expressive purposes," it was "not entitled to protection under the First Amendment."[8] The court also upheld the municipal ordinances as not unconstitutionally vague, and rejected Chepilko's standing to challenge one of the ordinances.

Chepilko carried a camera and printer to take pictures of people on the Atlantic City Boardwalk and then sell the photos to them. He was convicted under two separate Atlantic City ordinances prohibiting hawking without a special permit and restricting unlicensed sales or attempts to sell goods.

The New Jeresy appellate court panel rejected *Chepilko*'s reliance on *Bery*. Holding that First Amendment protection "extends to artistic expression such as painting, music, poetry and literature," which "protection is not lost simply because compensation is paid for artistic expression," it applied a "line-drawing process" to determine whether Chepilko's photographic activity nonetheless constituted "expressive conduct."[9] Finding the Atlantic City ordinance "impose[d] an absolute prohibition against a person selling merchandise such as defendant's photographs of persons walking on the boardwalk," the court addressed the threshold question of what is expressive conduct.[10] It concluded that "production and sale of photography may constitute expressive conduct protected by the First Amendment," but "to claim First Amendment protection from government regulation . . . the 'vendor of photography' . . . must demonstrate that the production and sale of those photographs constitutes expressive conduct."[11] The "objective features of the merchandise itself" are relevant, as is whether the items, "on their face, appear to serve predominantly expressive purposes," which "may take into account" the defendant's motivation in making and selling the items.[12]

8. *Id.* at 451.
9. *Id.* at 460.
10. *Id.* at 459.
11. *Id.* at 463.
12. *Id.* at 460–63.

The *Chepilko* court approved and relied upon a later Second Circuit case, *Mastrovincenzo v. City of New York*,[13] that distinguished its situation involving graffiti-decorated clothing, as well as cases outside the Second Circuit that rejected *Bery*'s automatic immunity for painting, photography, and sculpture to a threshold inquiry. It might be argued that as those other cases that questioned *Bery* did not involve straightforward photography they should not override *Bery*, but *Chepilko* seems to answer that question.

On the record before it, the court found the defendant had no artistic motivation, and simply took "snapshots" and tried to sell them. Therefore, there was "no basis for concluding that defendant's simple snapshots . . . serve[d] predominantly expressive purposes."[14]

*Chepilko* nonetheless joins them in imposing a threshold inquiry in a field of artistic endeavor that the Second Circuit previously proclaimed was entitled to automatic coverage, at least in the proclamation of the right, though still subject to the remainder of the First Amendment analysis. *Chepilko* also noted the Third Circuit's statement in *Gilles v. Davis* that "photography . . . that has a communicative or expressive purpose enjoys some First Amendment protection beyond words."[15] There is general agreement as to the fact that expressive conduct goes beyond words.[16]

A series of cases involving One World One Family Now is instructive. In *One World One Family Now v. City and County of Honolulu*,[17] the plaintiff One World is a non-profit entity based in Hawaii and sells T-shirts with messages. It set up display tables on a busy commercial street in Waikiki. It was charged with violating a Honolulu ordinance that banned such vending activity. The court first held that the activity was a First Amendment activity,[18] but that the ordinance was content neutral, narrowly tailored to

13. *Id.* at 452 n.1.

14. *Id.* at 463. Mr. Chepilko did not give up. He had tried the same thing in Coney Island and unsuccessfully sued in federal court in New York for violation of his civil rights. Chepilko v. New York City, No. 06-CV-5491 (ARR)(LB).

15. 405 N.J. Super. at 462, citing *Gilles v. Davis*, 427 F.3d 197, 212 n.14 (3d Cir. 2005).

16. See ETW Corp. v. Jireh Publ'g, Inc., 332 F.3d 915, 924 (6th Cir. 2003) (holding that "[t]he protection of the First Amendment is not limited to written or spoken words, but includes other medium of expression [such as] . . . photographs.")

17. 76 F.3d 1009 (9th Cir.), *cert. denied*, 519 U.S. 1009 (1996).

18. *Id.* at 1012.

serve legitimate interests, and left other means of communication open. In *One World One Family Now v. City of Miami Beach*,[19] a comparable ordinance barred portable tables for vendors at certain areas of Miami Beach's commercial district, but allowed non-profits limited use of the tables during certain times. The court narrowed the issue to "whether using tables to assist in the sale of the t-shirts is protected activity," and held it was.[20] As in the *Honolulu* matter, the court also found the ordinance content-neutral and satisfied the time, place, and manner test.[21] In a third case, *One World One Family Now, Inc. v. State of Nevada*,[22] the court distinguished "conspicuous political, religious, philosophical or ideological message having intellectual content which conveys a message that is informative of the purpose of Plaintiffs' organization and which is permanent, readable and recognizable from a reasonable distance" from "[e]xpressions—such as the words "Las Vegas" which are not inextricably intertwined with Plaintiffs' message," and held that latter not protected speech.[23] The court found the statute in this case that related to licensing "constitutionally suspect" as it provided no ground for denying or granting the permits and allowed for too much discretion.[24] Finally, in *One World One Family Now v. City of Key West*,[25] the court also granted One World's request for an injunction and allowed the sale of the expressive T-shirts in Key West's historic district as expressive conduct. It compared the portable tables with the expressive T-shirts to news racks.[26] As in the Nevada case, the court also found the ordinance allowed too much discretion.[27]

The *Honolulu* case cited the Supreme Court's exposition of the factors and their application in *Ward v. Rock Against Racism*,[28] dealing with regulation of loudness of music in Central Park. In *White v. City of Sparks*, the

19. 175 F.3d 1282 (11th Cir. 1999).
20. *Id.* at 1285–86.
21. *Id.* at 1287–89.
22. 860 F. Supp. 1457 (D. Nev. 1994).
23. *Id.* at 1464–65.
24. *Id.* at 1464.
25. 852 F. Supp. 1005 (S.D. Fla. 1994).
26. *Id.* at 1010.
27. *Id.*
28. 491 U.S. 781 (1989).

Ninth Circuit recognized *Bery*, as well as the Sixth Circuit holding in *ETW* and that of the Seventh Circuit in *Piarowski v. Illinois Community College District 515*,[29] for the basic proposition that the First Amendment protects original artwork and extends to an artist's sale of original artwork, even if compensation is involved. It did, however, "expressly reserve the question whether all paintings merit First Amendment protection," such as copies of the artists' work or mass produced copies.[30]

Recently, the 10th Circuit Court of Appeals addressed the status of speech of an image that was a component of the official Oklahoma license plate.[31] The court summarized various of the precedents discussed above and concluded, essentially, that artwork is not entitled, per se and absolutely, to First Amendment protection:

> Federal circuit courts have struggled to define the extent of First Amendment protection for visual artwork. The Second Circuit has broadly held that visual art is "entitled to full First Amendment protection," *Bery v. City of New York*, 97 F.3d 689, 695 (2d Cir. 1996), but has since questioned that precedent, *see Mastrovincenzo v. City of New York*, 435 F.3d 78, 92–93 (2d Cir. 2006). The Ninth Circuit has held that an artist's self-expression through an original painting is protected under the First Amendment "because it expresses the artist's perspective." *White v. City of Sparks*, 500 F.3d 953, 956 (9th Cir. 2007). But it has "expressly reserve[d] the question whether all paintings merit First Amendment protection" such as "copies of another artist's work or paintings done in an art factory setting where the works are mass-produced by the artist or others." *Id.* at 956 n.4; *see also Anderson v. City of Hermosa Beach*, 621 F.3d 1051, 1060–61 (9th Cir. 2010) (holding that a tattoo is entitled to constitutional protection as a form of pure expression). The Fifth Circuit, in contrast, has said that Hurley's Jackson Pollock comment "refers solely to great works of art" and that the Supreme Court has not "elaborated

29. 759 F.2d 625 (7th Cir.), *cert. denied*, 474 U.S. 1007 (1985).
30. 500F.3d at 956 n. 4.
31. Cressman v. Thompson, 719 F.3d 1139 (10th Cir. 2013).

> on the extent of First Amendment protection for visual non-speech objects or artworks." *Kleinman v. City of San Marcos*, 597 F.3d 323, 326 (5th Cir. 2010).[32]

In *Trebert v. City of New Orleans*,[33] Trebert made digital photographs and colored them with pastels. He had a permit under a city ordinance to sell "works of art" in a limited area of Jackson Square. He was cited for violating that permit; at issue was whether the art was "original" since he used a "mechanical device" in violation of the ordinance's requirement for "original" art. The court framed the issue as not whether the photographs were art but whether they were protected speech. It cited ample precedent:

> [C]ourts have found that mechanically reproduced images are expression entitled to First Amendment protection. See ETW Corp., 332 F.3d at 919, 925, 937 (serigraphic and lithographic prints made from an original painting); Hoffman v. Capital Cities/ABC, Inc., 255 F.3d 1180, 1185 (9th Cir. 2001) (altered still photograph from a movie); Bery, 97 F.3d at 695 (photographs and prints "always communicate some idea or content to" viewers); Cardtoons, L.C. v. Major League Baseball Players Ass'n, 95 F.3d 959, 933 (10th Cir. 1996) (parody baseball trading cards); Comedy III Prods., Inc. v. Gary Saderup, Inc., 21 P.3d 797, 800, 802 (Cal. 2001) ("charcoal drawings of celebrities used to create lithographic and silkscreen masters, which in turn are used to produce multiple reproductions in the form, respectively, of lithographic prints and silkscreened images on T-shirts . . . are expressive works").[34]

Relying substantially on *Bery*, the court held the ordinance unconstitutional as applied to Trebert.

32. *Id.* at 1153 n.14.
33. No. 04-1349, 2005 U.S. Dist. LEXIS 1560 (E.D. La. Feb. 1, 2005).
34. *Id.* at *14_.

First Amendment analysis in this regard distinguishes between commercial speech, which still may be protected, but is more easily restricted, and "pure" First Amendment expression of a political nature.[35]

In *Central Hudson*, the court addressed promotional advertising. During a time when the state's utility system lacked capacity, the Public Service Commission banned promotional advertising, and continued the ban when the shortage abated. The advertising had covered two categories: stimulation of demand and informational.[36] Commercial speech as identified as "expression related solely to the economic interests of the speaker and its audience."[37] The First Amendment reaches the states through the Fourteenth Amendment. Even commercial speech, directed to the economic interest of the speaker, is protected, but it remains distinct from other areas. While no one contests the right to regulate inaccurate speech, the Court noted that "[i]f the communication is neither misleading nor related to unlawful activity, the government's power is more circumscribed."[38] The state's interest must be "substantial" and the restriction proportionate to a legitimate state goal.[39] For commercial speech, therefore, First Amendment protection is a four-step analysis:

> At the outset, we must determine whether the expression is protected by the First Amendment. For commercial speech to come within that provision, it at least must concern lawful activity and not be misleading. Next, we ask whether the asserted governmental interest is substantial. If both inquiries yield positive answers, we must determine whether the regulation directly advances the governmental interest asserted, and whether it is not more extensive than is necessary to serve that interest.[40]

---

35. Hoepker v. Kruger, 200 F. Supp. 2d 340, 348–49 (S.D.N.Y. 2002) (citing Cent. Hudson Gas & Elec. Corp. v. Pub. Serv. Comm'n of N.Y., 447 U.S. 557 (1980)).

36. Cent. Hudson Ga. & Elec. Corp. v. Pub. Serv. Comm'n of N.Y., 447 U.S. 557, 559–60 (1980).

37. *Id.* at 561.

38. *Id.* at 564.

39. *Id.*

40. *Id.* at 566.

Note, however, that "newsworthy events or matters of public interest" transcend privacy interests.[41] In *Stephano*, decided under the New York Civil Rights statute, the Court of Appeals explained that "[t]he newsworthiness exception applies not only to reports of political happenings and social trends (Arrington v. New York Times Co., supra; Murray v. New York Mag. Co., supra), but also to news stories and articles of consumer interest including developments in the fashion world."[42] In *Stephano*, the plaintiff, a model, posed for certain advertisements in an article; the image was used in a later and different article commenting on the availability of the particular item of clothing. The court looked to the *content* of the article and not the defendant's motivation. What constitutes "newsworthiness" is broadly interpreted.[43] *Messenger* also makes clear that just because the image or name is used to increase a periodical's circulation and profits does not turn it into a trade purpose.[44]

The initial question is whether the "particular conduct possesses sufficient communicative elements to bring the First Amendment into play," and to answer that, the court looks to whether "[a]n intent to convey a particularized message was present, and [whether] the likelihood was great that the message would be understood by those who viewed it."[45] *Texas v. Johnson* also noted that expressive conduct may be more freely regulated than written or spoken speech, but it cannot be proscribed because of the expressive element; "It is, in short, not simply the verbal or nonverbal nature of the expression, but the governmental interest at stake, that helps to determine whether a restriction on that expression is valid."[46]

Consequently, for purposes of the First Amendment, art is speech.[47] However, the courts are not unanimous as to the exactly what constitutes "art."

41. Stephano v. News Grp. Publ'ns, Inc., 64 N.Y.2d 174 (1984).
42. *Id.* at 184.
43. *See* Messenger v. Gruner + Jahr Printing & Publ'g, 94 N.Y.2d 436, 441–42 (2000) ("newsworthy" includes descriptions of actual events, articles concerning political happenings, social trends, or public interest, citing, inter alia, matrimonial action or even a football halftime show).
44. *Id.* at 442.
45. Texas v. Johnson, 491 U.S. 397 (1989) (internal citations omitted).
46. *Id.* at 406–07.
47. *Hoepker*, 200 F. Supp. 2d at 349.

In *Comedy III Productions, Inc. v. Gary Saderup, Inc.*, the court noted that "when a work contains significant transformative elements, it is not only especially worthy of First Amendment protection, but it is also less likely to interfere with the economic interest protected by the right of publicity."[48]

It would seem, therefore, that photography, if it is simply defined as pressing a shutter on a camera and making an image, no longer (if it ever did) takes on automatic First Amendment protection; the majority of courts seem to be looking for expressive conduct. One would hope the threshold would remain relatively easy to satisfy. Even so, the First Amendment rights of photographers will still be subject to an analysis of the government interest involved in the particular regulation, as noted in *Chepilko*. This is discussed next.

## Regulation of Street Photography

Street photography is its own genre within the photographic canon. It is taught as a separate subject in various universities. The Museum of Modern Art defines street photography as "[a] type of photography that captures subjects in candid moments in public places."[49]

Among its most prominent practitioners are Eugene Atget, Walker Evans, Henri Cartier-Bresson, Robert Frank, Lee Friedlander, Garry Winogrand, Max Kozloff, and Helen Levitt, to name a few. Exhibits are devoted to the topic and appear in the most respected art museums around the world. Closely related to documentary photography, by its very nature, street photography implicates privacy claims, and as artistic expression, involves the First Amendment.

The image on page 235 is but one example of a moment of contemplation captured in New York City.

48. 25 Cal. 4th 387, 405 (2001), *cert. denied*, 534 U.S. 1078 (2002).

49. *Glossary of Art Terms*, Museum of Modern Art, http://www.moma.org/learn/moma_learning/glossary#s (last visited Apr. 8, 2014). See also Clive Scott, Street Photography: From Atget to Cartier-Bresson (I.B. Tauris & Co., Ltd.: New York 2007).

A candid moment in a public place.

## Security Concerns

I discussed at some length in the preceding section the First Amendment rights of photographers and the contours pursuant to which government may regulate those rights. Such issues are relevant when considering those rights in terms of security.

We live in an age of increased security and uneasiness. Not only has government taken steps to prevent imaging of certain buildings and structures on the alleged basis of national security, but various jurisdictions have enacted laws devoted to protecting the privacy of individuals. In one of the great paradoxes of our time, governments (and in common-law jurisdictions, courts) simultaneously have expanded rights of privacy and data protection while requiring more and more disclosure of confidential individual information. In the thick of this is a growing tension between artistic freedom on the one hand and security and privacy concerns on the other. A prime battlefield is in the realm of photography.

Noting the First Amendment rights of photographers is simply the predicate step. Governments have the right to regulate First Amendment conduct within certain parameters. To recap, government can impose regulations in the name of safety, provided constitutionally valid time, place, and manner. The regulations must be content-neutral and narrowly tailored, with alternative channels and no impermissible discretion or prior restraint.[50]

I noted in the introduction that military installations are one type of subject that government regulates on the basis of national security. Earlier in this chapter we spoke of the balance between governmental concerns with regard to First Amendment regulation. How does the analysis change when issues are raised that purport to implicate more than public safety, such as folding tables on sidewalks, but rather, issues of national security?

What are the limits? What are the sensitive areas? What would withstand a strict First Amendment analysis? The Triborough Bridge Commission in New York posted signs prohibiting taking pictures of its bridges—yet anyone with a long-range zoom lens could take such images from Manhattan. The author is aware of an individual who was stopped by a police officer in New York City from taking a photograph of the Empire State Building. As a practical matter, are these legitimate security concerns or cosmetic? The

---

50. *See* Clark v. Cmty. for Creative Non-Violence, 468 U.S. 288, 293 (1984) ("Expression, whether oral or written or symbolized by conduct, is subject to reasonable time, place, or manner restrictions. We have often noted that restrictions of this kind are valid provided that they are justified without reference to the content of the regulated speech, that they are narrowly tailored to serve a significant governmental interest, and that they leave open ample alternative channels for communication of the information.").

issue has triggered articles suggesting a "war on photographers."[51] Indeed, one municipality in Maryland purported to ban photography altogether in its downtown.[52]

In *State v. Vogel*,[53] use of a zoom lens by law enforcement from a neighbor's property to photograph drug activity was permitted and not a violation of privacy; the defendant had done nothing to shield his property from public view.

In *TV ex rel. BV v. Smith-Green Community School Corp.*,[54] two teenagers posed for, in the words of the court, "some raunchy photographs" at a "slumber party" and posted them online. When their school learned of them, the girls were suspended from extracurricular activities. The student handbook had provisions relating to "good conduct" in and outside school, and prohibitions against acting in a discrediting or dishonorable manner. The court found the conduct was protected by the First Amendment since it was intended to convey a particularized message, with a likelihood that the message would be understood by those viewing it, citing *Texas v. Johnson*.[55] In this instance, the message was one of crude humor, but nonetheless expression. Of relevance here, the court further addressed the photographs themselves and their posting, and found that "[t]he photographic recording of the staged event and the uploading of the images to the social networking sites are both efforts to memorialize and further communicate the expression engaged in by the conduct depicted in the images."[56] The photographs were entitled to the same protection as the girls' conduct, and the posting or publication was also protected, demonstrating their intention to

---

51. Neil Matthew, *The War on Photographers*, POPULAR PHOTOGRAPHY, July 19, 2006, http://www.popphoto.com/how-to/2008/12/war-photographers (last visited April 29, 2014).

52. Marc Fisher, *Snapping the Silver Spring Photo Ban*, WASH. POST, July 5, 2007, http://blog.washingtonpost.com/rawfisher/2007/07/snapping_the_silver_spring_pho.html (last visited April 29, 2014).

53. 428 N.W.2d 272 (S.D. 1988).

54. 807 F. Supp. 2d 767 (N.D. Ind. 2011).

55. 491 U.S. 397, 404 (1989).

56. *Smith-Green*, 807 F. Supp. 2d at 776; *see also* ETW Corp. v. Jireh Publ'g, Inc., 332 F.3d 915, 924 (6th Cir. 2003); Douglas v. Hustler Magazine, Inc., 769 F.2d 1128, 1141 (7th Cir. 1985), *cert. denied*, 475 U.S. 1094 (1986) ("Art, even of the questionable sort represented by erotic photographs in 'provocative' magazines—even of the artless sort represented by 'topless' dancing—today enjoys extensive protection in the name of the First Amendment.").

communicate the expression. The court rendered irrelevant whether the punishment was based on the actual conduct or the photographs themselves or the posting of them—all were protected.[57] The court went on to address, and reject, claims that the photographs were obscene or involved child pornography, and further considered standards relating to standards of speech in the context of school district regulation.

A noteworthy case is *Cherry v. Sunoco, Inc.*[58] In that case, a federal court in the Eastern District of Pennsylvania rejected the plaintiff's Title VII claim for religious discrimination when the defendant employer was required by governmental regulation to obtain his photograph for an employee ID. It is another example of the tension between First Amendment rights and security in the current age.

## International Considerations

The issue has international ramifications. For example, England's Official Secrets Act of 1911 makes it illegal to make or communicate a sketch or other document that could be useful to an enemy:

> If any person for any purpose prejudicial to the safety or interests of the State (a) approaches or is in the neighborhood of, or enters any prohibited place within the meaning of this Act; or (b) makes any sketch, plan, model, or note which is calculated to be or might be or is intended to be directly or indirectly useful to an enemy; or (c) obtains or communicates to any other person any sketch, plan, model, article, or note, or other document or information which is calculated to be or might be or is intended to be directly or indirectly useful to an enemy; he shall be guilty of felony, and shall be liable to penal servitude for any term not less than three years and not exceeding seven years.[59]

57. *Smith-Green*, 807 F. Supp. 2d at 777.
58. No. 07-cv-2235, 2009 U.S. Dist. LEXIS 72755 (E.D. Pa. Aug. 17, 2009).
59. England Official Secrets Act, 1911, c. 28, § 1, http://www.legislation.gov.uk/ukpga/Geo5/1-2/28/section/1 (last visited April 29, 2014).

As security concerns continued, England passed the Terrorism Act of 2000, making it illegal to make a record, including a photograph, that could be used for an act of terrorism:

> Collection of information. (1) A person commits an offence if: (a) he collects or makes a record of information of a kind likely to be useful to a person committing or preparing an act of terrorism, or (b) he possesses a document or record containing information of that kind. (2) In this section "record" includes a photographic or electronic record.[60]

This statute allows a private cause of action as well.

U.S. courts have dealt with similar concerns. In *Scheier v. Snohomish*,[61] the plaintiff had purportedly acted in a suspicious way when taking photographs of a Power Administration substation. The court noted the substation was a critical security concern after the 9/11 attacks:

> The BPA substation is considered a critical piece of infrastructure. Following concerns arising from the terrorist attacks of September 11, 2001, a Joint Terrorism Task Force identified the BPA substation as a potential terrorist target. In response, the Department of Homeland Security funded a grant so that the City of Snohomish could develop a special reaction force to deal with potential terrorist threats. Snohomish police officers have been informed of the sensitive nature of the facility, and most officers have been given a tour of the substation by BPA personnel.[62]

What happens if an American tourist takes a photograph in a foreign country and publishes it in the United States? Whose law applies? In Chapter 1, I discussed the choice-of-law issue in general terms, and mainly in a

60. England Terrorism Act, 2000, § 58, http://www.legislation.gov.uk/ukpga/2000/11/section/58 (last visited April 29, 2014).
61. No. 07-cv-1925, 2008 U.S. Dist. LEXIS 90919 (W.D. Wash. Nov. 4, 2008).
62. *Id.* at *4.

domestic context. We can now explore it in more detail as we look at an international context.

For general purposes, it is helpful to review the Restatement (Second) Conflict of Laws (1989). Remember that this is not law of itself, but often courts in the United States rely on the Restatement. A foreign court is less likely to rely on it unless looking to apply the law of a particular American state.

Suppose an American photographer goes to Country X, takes a photograph of Country X Citizen, returns to America and posts the photograph on the Internet. Country X Citizen sues the American in Country X for defamation and breach of privacy.

There are two issues: Whose law applies to the dispute, and if a judgment is rendered in Country X against the American, can it be recognized and enforced in the United States?

An alternative is the situation where Country X citizen sues the American in a court in an American state.

For now, I am not addressing issues of personal jurisdiction, or other nuances and sections under the Restatement. I simply want to raise general principles and provide a basic overview of the issues. A particular outcome in a particular case will depend on the particular facts.

The general rule with regard to torts as expressed in Section 145 is that:

> (1) The rights and liabilities of the parties with respect to an issue in tort are determined by the local law of the state which, with respect to that issue, has the most significant relationship to the occurrence and the parties under the principles stated in § 6.
>
> (2) Contacts to be taken into account in applying the principles of § 6 to determine the law applicable to an issue include:
>
> > (a) the place where the injury occurred,
> >
> > (b) the place where the conduct causing the injury occurred,
> >
> > (c) the domicil, residence, nationality, place of incorporation and place of business of the parties, and
> >
> > (d) the place where the relationship, if any, between the parties is centered

With regard to defamation, under the Restatement (Second) Conflict of Laws Section 149:

> In an action for defamation, the local law of the state where the publication occurs determines the rights and liabilities of the parties, except as stated in § 150, unless, with respect to the particular issue, some other state has a more significant relationship under the principles stated in § 6 to the occurrence and the parties, in which event the local law of the other state will be applied.

Section 150 addresses multistate defamation and applies the law of the state with the most significant relationship, as set forth in Section 6. Section 6 sets forth the factors in applying a choice of law principle:

> (1) A court, subject to constitutional restrictions, will follow a statutory directive of its own state on choice of law.
>
> (2) When there is no such directive, the factors relevant to the choice of the applicable rule of law include
>
> (a) the needs of the interstate and international systems,
>
> (b) the relevant policies of the forum,
>
> (c) the relevant policies of other interested states and the relative interests of those states in the determination of the particular issue,
>
> (d) the protection of justified expectations,
>
> (e) the basic policies underlying the particular field of law,
>
> (f) certainty, predictability and uniformity of result, and
>
> (g) ease in the determination and application of the law to be applied.

Similar considerations apply to privacy claims. Section 152 applies the law of the state where the invasion occurred except in multistate situations under Section 153, which again looks to the state with the most significant relationship, as decided under the Section 6 factors.

In our example, assuming Country X's courts follow comparable rules for determining whose law applies, it is likely (though not definite) that the court would find that the defamation, though published on the Internet worldwide and posted from the United States, nonetheless would be determined under Country X law regarding defamation, since a Country X citizen was defamed and felt the harm in Country X, had an expectation of not being defamed in his own country and that the public policy of Country X. If Country X citizen sued the American photographer in the United States, it is also possible, if not likely, that the American court might also apply the law of Country X for the same reasons, or possibly apply U.S. law with an overriding policy concern for First Amendment issues. Similarly, it is likely that Country X's privacy law would be the applicable law. All this determines is under what law the case will be decided.

As a practical matter, under a common-law conflicts of law analysis, courts are likely to apply the law of the place of the wrong.[63] However, when the place of the wrong is ancillary to the effects of the wrong, the state most affected should have its law applied.[64] At least in the civil context, the issue is likely to turn on whether there are conflicting state interests,[65] particularly where the First Amendment is concerned.[66]

Suppose the foreign country law applies and a judgment is obtained. Can that judgment be enforced in the United States?

## Enforcement of Foreign Judgments and the SPEECH Act

Take the example offered above, assume country X citizen obtains a judgment based on the law of Country X, which does not recognize the same kind of First Amendment protections that would otherwise have allowed a comparable photograph if made in the United States. They want to enforce it in the United States, where the American has assets. Can they do this? Or if you obtain a judgment against a foreign entity and want to enforce it in the foreign country, can you?

---

63. *See* Jordan v. Shaw Indus., 1997 U.S. App. LEXIS 33589, at *8 (4th Cir. Nov. 26, 1997) ("Again, under the *lex loci* rule, the place of the wrong is the locale in which the last act by a defendant occurs which makes him liable in tort." (emphasis in original)); Brendle v. Gen. Tire & Rubber Co., 408 F.2d 116, 117 (4th Cir. 1969).

64. *See* Reich v. Purcell, 67 Cal. 2d 551, 555–56 (1967) ("[T]he law of the place of the wrong is not necessarily the applicable law for all tort actions. . . .The state of the place of the wrong has little or no interest in such compensation when none of the parties reside there.").

65. *See* eBay, Inc. v. MercExchange, L.L.C., 547 U.S. 388, 391 (2006); Reno Air Racing Ass'n, Inc. v. McCord, 452 F.3d 1126, 1137 n.11 (9th Cir. 2006).

66. Bachchan v. India Abroad Publ'ns, Inc., 154 Misc. 2d 228 (N.Y. Cty. 1992); Matusevitch v. Telnikoff, 877 F. Supp. 1 (D.D.C. 1995), *aff'd*, 159 F.3d 636 (D.C. Cir. 1998).

As of this writing, the United States is not party to any treaty that provides for the mandatory recognition of a U.S. judgment in another country, or vice versa. Most states in this country have adopted a version of what is called the Uniform Foreign Country Money Judgments Recognition Act, which permits recognition and enforcement of judgments obtained in foreign countries provided there was personal and subject-matter jurisdiction over the defendant, and the jurisdiction had impartial tribunals.[67] There are also a variety of permissive grounds for a court to deny recognition. In states that do have the statute, the Uniform Act permits a court to refuse recognition or enforcement based on grounds of public policy. Even states without the statute can refuse to recognize a foreign judgment on public policy grounds. Some courts have refused to recognize foreign libel judgments in their jurisdiction on that basis. This is because the standards by which those foreign judgments were obtained did not meet U.S. Constitution "First Amendment" standards or the equivalent standards under state constitutions. However, not every state has adopted that uniform law, and there was no guarantee of consistency in approach.

A good study in contrast are two cases in the same year by the same trial judge. In one, the judge refused to recognize and enforce a Liberian judgment upon finding that that judicial system at the time was not impartial. In the other, he recognized a Romanian judgment based on the improvements in its judicial system.[68]

Beyond the impartiality issue, though, is the discretionary exception in which a court finds that the foreign judgment, if recognized and enforced, would offend either the public policy of the United States or that of the particular state in which the judgment is sought to be recognized. In some states, there are also reciprocity requirements; that is, the state will look to

67. For copies and explanations for the Uniform Law Commission's 1962 and 2005 versions, see www.uniformlaws.org/ActSummary.aspx?title=Foreign-Counrty+Money+Judgments+Recogniti0n+Act. Accessed July 19, 2014.

68. *Compare* Bridgeway Corp. v. Citibank, 45 F. Supp. 2d 276 (S.D.N.Y. 1999), *aff'd*, 201 F.3d 134 (2d Cir. 2000) (Liberian courts were not "fair" during the period of the civil war), with S.C. Chimexim SA v. Velco Enters. Ltd., 36 F. Supp. 2d 206 (S.D.N.Y. 1999) ("[M]aterials submitted to the Court as well as the Court's own research demonstrate that the Romanian judicial system comports with the requirements of due process.").

see how its judgments are treated in the foreign jurisdiction. Another main line of attack against recognition and enforcement relates to whether the foreign judgment violates American concepts of free speech and other First Amendment–type rights.

The case of *Matusevitch v. Telnikoff*[69] exemplifies a situation in which an American court refused to honor a foreign court's judgment because "the comity of this nation should not [have] allow[ed] it full effect." Matusevitch, an American citizen, submitted a heated letter to a London newspaper in response to an editorial written by Telnikoff. Telnikoff successfully sued Matusevitch for libel and petitioned an American court to enforce judgment, as Matusevitch had no assets in the United Kingdom. The American court refused to compel Matusevitch's compliance, as differences between the libel laws of the United States and the United Kingdom were so fundamental as to deprive Matusevitch of his constitutional protections and guarantees without due process. At the time, in the United Kingdom, the defendant needed to demonstrate the veracity of his statements and the plaintiff has no obligation to prove malice; whereas in the United States, the plaintiff must prove both the falsity of the statement and a culpable mindset. Recognition of the foreign judgment may be sought under principles of comity. See *Hilton v. Guyot*,[70] in which the U.S. Supreme Court laid out the policy rationale for giving deference to foreign judgments where practicable and consistent with American legal principles.

In *Bachchan v. India Abroad Publications*,[71] a judgment for defamation obtained in England was denied recognition in New York because "the action in which it was rendered failed to comport with the constitutional standards for adjudicating libel claims."

Similarly, if you obtain a judgment in an American jurisdiction and want to have it recognized and enforced in a foreign jurisdiction, you have to go through the mechanisms of that foreign jurisdiction. Your American judgment is not entitled to automatic recognition and enforcement just by

69. 877 F. Supp. 1 (D.D.C. 1995), *aff'd*, 159 F.3d 636 (D.C. Cir. 1998).
70. 159 U.S. 113 (1895).
71. 154 Misc. 2d 228, 230 (N.Y. Cty. 1992),

docketing it. In some places, such as Canada, the process may be relatively easy, but in other cases, that is not necessarily the case.

U.S. policy towards free speech and First Amendment rights led in 2010 to the enactment of the Securing the Protection of our Enduring and Established Constitutional Heritage (SPEECH) Act.[72] The SPEECH Act precludes recognition and enforcement in U.S. state and federal courts of foreign judgments that do not comport with American First Amendment rights.

Libel tourism is the phenomenon in which plaintiffs seek a sympathetic jurisdiction whose defamation laws do not embody the protections afforded by American First Amendment values, or otherwise facilitate defamation judgments, and put American authors at risk.

The statute was in response to the case of Rachel Ehrenfeld, who wrote a book in which she made certain statements regarding Saudi billionaire Khalid bin Mahfouz, asserting he had financed terrorism. The individual, Mahfouz, sued Ehrenfeld for libel in England, although he was not a resident of England but took advantage of more liberal English libel laws. He procured a default judgment against her. She sued preemptively in federal court in New York to prevent enforcement and recognition here, but ultimately the court determined there was no personal jurisdiction over the defendant.[73] As a result, New York and various other states passed legislation to permit such a cause of action.

The New York law rendered unenforceable such defamation judgments that do not comport with American or state-law freedom-of-speech protections, and provided for personal jurisdiction in a declaratory judgment action over anyone obtaining a foreign defamation judgment against a New York resident or someone with assets in New York.[74] Florida,[75] Illinois,[76] and California[77] enacted some form of libel tourism protection, though not

72. 28 U.S.C. §§ 4101–4105.

73. *See* Ehrenfeld v. Bin Mahfouz, 9 N.Y.3d 501 (2007), *and* Ehrenfeld v. Malfouz, 518 F.3d 102 (2d Cir. 2008).

74. N.Y. C.P.C.P. § 302(d).

75. FLA. STAT. 55-6055, 55-605(2)(b).

76. 735 ILL. COMP. STAT. 5/12-621(b)(7).

77. CAL. CIV. P. CODE §§ 1716(c)(9), 1717(c).

all afforded declaratory relief. Congress appropriately acted to fill the gap and render relief across the board.

In August 2010, the SPEECH Act was signed into law.

The federal legislation states that notwithstanding any other federal or state law, a domestic court (federal or state court) shall not recognize or enforce a foreign judgment (also defined) for defamation (defined to include defamation, libel, slander or similar claim, causing damage to reputation or emotional distress, presenting someone in false light, or subjecting someone to criticism, dishonor or condemnation) unless (1) the foreign court's defamation law provides same or more protection that the federal or state constitution here or (2) even if the foreign court provides less protection, the party opposing recognition or enforcement would have been found liable applying those standards. The burden is on the party seeking recognition or enforcement. Furthermore, a domestic court shall not recognize such foreign judgments unless it determines personal jurisdiction comported with our notions of due process, and the party seeking such enforcement/recognition bears that burden. Interactive computer service providers are also protected to the extent that section 230 of Communications Act of 1934 applies. Appearing in the foreign court does not bar objection to lack of personal jurisdiction. Actions brought in state court are removable under specified circumstances, basically where diversity exists.

The federal legislation further creates a cause of action for declaratory judgment by any U.S. person against whom foreign judgment entered, in the U.S. district court for declaration that the foreign judgment is repugnant to U.S. Constitution or laws, and that party bears burden; nationwide service of process is allowed. In action to enforce, the district court shall, unless exceptional circumstances, award attorneys' fees to the opponent of recognition if it prevails under the statute.

Among the claims leveled against photographers are those for defamation. Another common claim is for invasion of privacy. Whether a general invasion of privacy would come under the kinds of judgments protected by the SPEECH Act remains to be seen. Perhaps an idea of how this would play out is found in *Yahoo!, Inc. v. La Ligue Contre Le Racisme et L'Antisemitisme.*[78] The trial court granted Yahoo declaratory relief to protect itself against enforcement of a French judgment against it in France for illegally selling Nazi memorabilia, apply U.S. law and the First Amendment.[79] In an en banc decision, the Ninth Circuit, by majority, reversed, but on the grounds of lack of personal jurisdiction. Five judges concurred in part and dissented in part, with a minority view that by not deciding the First Amendment issue, the majority had established "a new and burdensome standard for vindicating First Amendment rights in the internet context . . . ."[80] This minority disagreed with the majority's "professed uncertainties as to whether" principles of comity precluded application of the First Amendment.[81] With the enactment of the SPEECH Act, Congress has acted and made clear that no such uncertainties exist, at least with regard to judgments meeting the definition of defamation and its related claims. A defamation claim based on a photograph should fit within that act. If a claim based on a photograph does not, then the recourse would be to argue enforcement, and recognition is against public policy or, if personal jurisdiction exists, attempt a declaratory judgment action as in *Yahoo*.

The SPEECH Act has been applied by a few courts. In *Investorshub.com, Inc. v. Mina Mar Group*,[82] Mina Mar, a Canadian corporation in Ontario, procured a Canadian default judgment against U.S citizens for libel and defamation in the amount of $75,000 CAD general damages and $10,000 CAD punitive damages, as well as costs, based on content of a writing on a website based in the United States. Investorshub.com brought a complaint for declaratory relief pursuant to the SPEECH Act, and Mina Mar entered into a consent judgment, acknowledging the nonenforceability of the judgment in the United States. The court approved it, finding the consent judgment consistent with the SPEECH Act, and that Canadian law did not provide as much protection as the U.S. First Amendment. Notably, the court

78. 169 F. Supp. 2d 1181 (N.D. Cal. 2001), *rev'd on other grounds, on rehearing, en banc, remanded by* 433 F.3d 1199 (9th Cir.), *cert. denied*, 547 U.S. 1163 (2006).

79. 169 F. Supp. 2d at 1194.

80. 433 F.3d at 1236–37.

81. *Id.* at 1239.

82. No. 11-CV-9, 2011 U.S. Dist. LEXIS 87566 (N.D. Fla. June 20, 2011).

also found that there was no Canadian equivalent of the U.S. Communications Decency Act,[83] so that suggests a judicial gloss adding consideration of a statute in addition to the First Amendment.

In *Trout Point Lodge, Limited v. Handshoe*,[84] the court held that a Canadian judgment for defamation awarded in a Nova Scotia provincial court was not entitled to recognition and enforcement since (1) Canadian law failed to provide as much protection as American freedom of speech and press and, alternatively, (2) even assuming that, in the particular case the party opposing recognition would not have been found liable on the same facts in the relevant American court.

In *Ohno v. Yasuma*,[85] the defendant attempted to utilize the SPEECH Act as a defense to enforcement and recognition of a Japanese judgment on the grounds that the judgment violated the "free exercise of religion" component of the First Amendment. The court refused to extend the SPEECH Act to all First Amendment claims, limiting it to issues relating to defamation and free speech.[86]

Although the SPEECH Act arose in the context of defamation in a prose work, it is entirely conceivable that a foreign judgment may result from a photograph in a variety of contexts. An American that takes a picture of a foreign person whose country's laws either prohibit that photograph or otherwise render criminal or provide monetary relief for such an act may be subject to a judgment in the foreign country for monetary damages. If the taking of that photograph would otherwise have been protected First Amendment activity in this country, then a foreign judgment seeking monetary damages as a result of the foreign photograph would probably not be enforced. While the legislative history is in the context of written defamation and protection of authors, the logic of the First Amendment analysis should apply to photographs.

At least one court has moved toward the view that the First Amendment is relevant to photographs that otherwise subjected the photographer to civil

83. 47 U.S.C. § 230.
84. 729 F.3d 481 (5th Cir. 2013).
85. 723 F.3d 984 (9th Cir. 2013).
86. *Id.* at 1004 n.22.

liability in another country. In *Sarl Louis Feraud International v. Viewfinder, Inc.*,[87] the defendant posted photographs of a fashion show on its website. The plaintiffs, fashion designers that appeared in the show, sued in France, claiming unauthorized use. The trial court refused to enforce the French judgments because it found that the fashion shows were public events and that defendant had a First Amendment right to publish the photographs. The Second Circuit reversed only because it felt that the district court had not done a thorough analysis of the enforcement and First Amendment issues. While citing cases that judgments "repugnant" to the First Amendment violate public policy (including citation to the district court opinion in *Yahoo*), the court nonetheless held that the First Amendment did not provide an *absolute* defense. It then laid out the balancing of factors present in the analysis it felt appropriate. While First Amendment–protected activity might save the photographer here, the same activity in another country might not. If the photographer has assets in such other countries, they can be attached pursuant to such a recognized and enforceable judgment in that country.

What of criminal proceedings? A crime committed by an American in another country would subject the American to arrest in that country; recall the admonition as to the territoriality of law. Extradition of American citizens must be made pursuant to the terms of an extradition treaty.[88] The statute provides for a hearing as to the extraditability of the American citizen in response to the foreign request. As a general matter, "because of the rule of dual criminality, . . . individuals accused of offenses that constitute protected activity under the First Amendment will not be extradited."[89]

## Social Media, "Gag Orders," and Prior Restraint

While there are monetary remedies for defamation, and one may obtain injunctive relief to address defamatory speech in place, different legal

87. 489 F.3d 474 (2nd Cir. 2007).
88. 18 U.S.C. § 3184.
89. Quinn v. Robinson, 783 F.2d 776, 798 (9th Cir.), *cert. denied*, 479 U.S. 882 (1986).

standards apply with regard to *preventative* action. In other words, courts have made clear that "[a]n order that prohibits the utterance or publication of particular information or commentary imposes a 'prior restraint' on speech."[90] Where courts attempt to restrict an attorney or party from commenting on a pending matter, such a "gag order" falls under the rubric of prior restraint.[91]

"Gag orders" embody a clash between two fundamental principles. On the one hand, it is viewed as a prior restraint on speech and, therefore, is "the most serious and the least tolerable infringement on First Amendment rights."[92] It is viewed as having a chilling effect and therefore "[a]ny system of prior restraints of expression . . . bear[s] a heavy presumption against its constitutional validity."[93] On the other hand, courts have a need to preserve the fair administration of justice.[94] The Supreme Court has held, though, that "[a]lthough litigants do not surrender their First Amendment rights at the courthouse door, those rights may be subordinated to other interests that arise" during a criminal trial.[95]

In *United States v. McGregor*,[96] the court noted the above and, in a criminal case, refused to grant the government's request for a gag order that would enjoin a Twitter feed. It held that it could only issue such a gag order if "(1) the attorneys' speech presents a substantial likelihood of material prejudice to the proceedings; (2) the proposed protective order is narrowly tailored; (3) alternatives to the protective order would not be effective; and (4) the order would be effective in achieving the government's goal."[97] It found instead that the Alabama Rule of Professional Conduct 3.6 mirrored the American Bar Association Model Rule and sufficiently set forth

---

90. United States v. Salameh, 992 F.2d 445, 446 (2d Cir. 1993).

91. United States v. Brown, 218 F.3d 415, 424 (5th Cir. 2000).

92. Neb. Press Ass'n v. Stuart, 427 U.S. 539, 559 (1976).

93. N.Y. Times Co. v. United States, 403 U.S. 713, 714 (1971) (per curiam).

94. United States v. Carmichael, 326 F. Supp. 2d 1267, 1291 (M.D. Ala. 2004), supplemented 326 F. Supp. 2d, 1303 (M.D. Ala. 2004). In *Carmichael*, the court refused to order a website be taken down that a criminal defendant put up to comment on his case.

95. Seattle Times Co. v. Rhinehart, 467 U.S. 20, 32 n.18 (1984) (internal quotation marks and citation omitted).

96. 838 F. Supp. 2d 1256 (M.D. Ala. 2012).

97. *Id.* at 1262.

the ethical obligations of counsel, noting in part that paragraph (a) of the rule provided that "A lawyer shall not make an extrajudicial statement that a reasonable person would expect to be disseminated by means of public communication if the lawyer knows or reasonably should know that it will have a substantial likelihood of materially prejudicing an adjudicative proceeding."[98]

In the civil context, similar considerations apply. *Layshock ex rel. Layshock v. Hermitage School District* held that "the First Amendment prohibits the school from reaching beyond the schoolyard to impose what might otherwise be appropriate discipline."[99] In *Layshock*, a student created a mock profile of his high school on MySpace, a social networking site. Other students did the same. Ultimately, the school disciplined the student and the parents sued. Noting that schools enjoy certain flexibility in regulating free expression due to its special circumstances, the court nonetheless noted that the school could not punish the conduct outside the school simply because it reached inside the school. In a concurring opinion, two judges stated:

> For better or worse, wireless internet access, smart phones, tablet computers, social networking services like Facebook, and stream-of-consciousness communications via Twitter give an omnipresence to speech that makes any effort to trace First Amendment boundaries along the physical boundaries of a school campus a recipe for serious problems in our public schools.[100]

In *Kowalski v. Berkeley County Schools*,[101] a high school senior created a webpage on myspace.com called "S.A.S.H.," which she said stood for "Students Against Sluts Herpes." Another student, Parsons, claimed the second "S" referred to a particular student and was directed against that student. Kowalski, the creator of the site, invited 100 or so people to join; by joining,

98. *Id.* at 1263.

99. 650 F.3d 205, 207 (3d Cir. 2011), *cert. denied, sub nom.*, Blue Mountain Sch. Dist. v. J.S., 132 S. Ct. 1097 (2012).

100. *Id.* at 220–21.

101. 652 F.3d 565 (4th Cir. 2011).

they could post text and photographs on the page. Parsons registered and posted a photograph that cast aspersions on the particular student. The site and its offensive photographs and commentary was discovered by the particular student's father, who demanded the photographs be taken down. Parsons called Kowalski who attempted to remove the photographs, but was unable to do so. The father then approached the school, and after investigation, Kowalski was suspended for 10 days and also subject to a 90-day social event suspension, for creating a "hate website."[102] Kowalski sued for, among other things, violation of her First Amendment rights. The district court dismissed her First Amendment claims and concluded she had not been suspended for engaging in protected free speech. The Fourth Circuit affirmed, noting that students' First Amendment rights are not "coextensive with those of adults,"[103] and that even though this was arguably outside the school environment, it impacted on the "work and discipline of the school."[104] The court also noted the current context of bullying and its harmful effects.[105]

In the regular context, such injunctions are not easy to obtain. In *Bihari v. Gross*,[106] Bihari sought to restrain the use of certain marks on the defendant's website based on anti-cybersquatting and trademark theories, as well as based on defamation. The court denied the injunction. The relevant part of the discussion, regarding the defamation claim, focused on the heavy burdens implicit in prior restraints, and cited the precedential rulings:

> Our Circuit Court of Appeals has longed warned against enjoining libel: "Equity will not restrain by injunction the threatened publication of a libel, as such, however great the injury to property may be. This is the universal rule in the United States and was formerly the rule in England." American Malting Co. v. Keitel, 209 F. 351, 354 (2d Cir.1913); see also Crosby v. Bradstreet Co., 312 F.2d 483, 485 (2d

102. *Id.* at 569.
103. *Id.* at 571.
104. *Id.* at 572.
105. *Id.*
106. 119 F. Supp. 2d 309 (S.D.N.Y. 2000).

> Cir.1963) ("We are concerned with the power of a court of the United States to enjoin publication of information about a person, without regard to truth, falsity, or defamatory character of that information. Such an injunction, enforceable through the contempt power, constitutes a prior restraint by the United States against the publication of facts which the community has a right to know. . . ."); Parker v. Columbia Broadcasting System, Inc., 320 F.2d 937, 939 (2d Cir.1963).[107]

The court did recognize that "While equity will not intervene to restrain the publication of words on a mere showing of falsity . . . [a]n injunction will lie to restrain libel when the publication is made as part and parcel of a course of conduct deliberately carried on to further a fraudulent or unlawful purpose."[108] In this case, the court might have considered such an injunction if the claims of harassment were sufficient enough but did not make that finding.[109]

To the extent that a foreign court were to issue such an injunction, it is unlikely a U.S. federal or state court would afford it comity on public policy grounds unless the party could establish it would also meet the severe American standards.

Governmental orders that prohibit publication or broadcast of information or commentary—that is, prior restraints are scrutinized closely. In *Near v. Minnesota ex rel. Olson*,[110] a state statute permitting restraint as a public nuisance of "abatement, as a public nuisance, of a 'malicious, scandalous and defamatory newspaper, magazine or other periodical,'" was invalidated since it (1) was not aimed at redress of individual or private wrongs, and did not affect libel laws, (2) was not directed solely at circulation of defamatory material but also at publication of charges of corruption, (3) the statute's objectives were not just punitive but suspension of a newspaper, and (4) it did not simply suppress the newspaper but established a regime of

107. *Id.* at 324–325.
108. *Id.* at 326.
109. *Id.* at 327.
110. 283 U.S. 697 (1931).

censorship. Following *Near*, the Supreme Court in *Organization for a Better Austin v. Keefe*[111] rejected prior restraint of peaceful pamphleteering.[112]

There are other restrictions facing the photographer that fall short of a full-blown First Amendment issue but nonetheless constitute censorship. Funding may be a leverage point. In *National Endowment for the Arts v. Finley*,[113] the Court upheld the NEA statute that provides that regulations governing applications must ensure that "artistic excellence and artistic merit are the criteria by which applications are judged, taking into consideration general standards of decency and respect for the diverse beliefs and values of the American public" as be as set forth in 20 U.S.C. § 954(d)(1). Section 954(d)(2) also provides that the regulations and procedures "shall clearly indicate that obscenity is without artistic merit, is not protected speech, and shall not be funded." Before the Court in *Finley* were four performance artists, who claimed their denial of funding was invalid as "a paradigmatic example of viewpoint discrimination because it rejects any artistic speech that either fails to respect mainstream values or offends standards of decency."[114] The NEA argued the statutory language was "hortatory" and not specifically restrictive. The Court agreed, and held that "§ 954(d)(1) admonishes the NEA merely to take 'decency and respect' into consideration and that the legislation was aimed at reforming procedures rather than precluding speech undercut respondents' argument that the provision inevitably will be utilized as a tool for invidious viewpoint discrimination."[115] See also *American Council of the Blind v. Boorstin*,[116] in which the court rejected the decision of the Library of Congress to stop making and distributing Braille editions of *Playboy*, noting:

111. 402 U.S. 415 (1971).

112. *See also* N.Y. Times Co. v. United States, 403 U.S. 713 (1971) (rejecting prior restraint of publication of certain classified material); Neb. Press Ass'n v. Stuart, 427 U.S. 539 (1976) (rejecting concerns of juror contamination in particular case were sufficient to warrant prior restraint).

113. 524 U.S. 569 (1998).

114. *Id.* at 580–81.

115. *Id.* at 582.

116. 644 F. Supp. 811 (D.D.C. 1986).

Congressional concerns about the nature of Playboy may be well-taken, but for the past fifteen years the magazine consistently met the selection criteria established by the Library of Congress. This dispute is not about the value or merit of Playboy but about a viewpoint-based denial of a subsidy, a denial which in a less emotionally charged context Congress and the taxpayer may find less palatable. Censorship whether by Congress or by the Librarian of Congress is equally abhorrent to a society built on the tenets of freedom of speech and expression.[117]

## Terry Stops

Under *Terry v. Ohio*,[118] police have the right to stop and frisk someone if they have a "reasonable suspicion" a crime has been committed or is about to be committed. In *Hiibel v. Sixth Judicial District Court of Nevada*,[119] the Court held that under *Terry* you can still be required to identify yourself. As a general rule you cannot be required to give up your camera or film. Recently, though, in the criminal context in *People v. Diaz*,[120] the California Supreme Court allowed a warrantless search of a cell phone found on a lawfully arrested person. The American Civil Liberties Union (ACLU) asserts: "Police may not delete your photographs or video under any circumstances."[121] However, "the police may seize any evidence that is in plain view during the course of their legitimate emergency activities."[122]

## When in Doubt

One way, of course, to avoid a confrontation is to ask permission if in doubt. The downside to this is that you may be told no, call attention to yourself, and risk arrest if you affirmatively violate such an order. Of course, being arrested does not mean the officers are right, but is this a productive use of

117. *Id.* at 816.
118. 392 U.S. 1 (1968).
119. 542 U.S. 177 (2004).
120. 51 Cal. 4th 84, *cert. denied*, 132 S. Ct. 94 (2011).
121. *Know Your Rights: Photographers*, Am. Civil Liberties Union, http://www.aclu.org/free-speech/know-your-rights-photographers (last visited Aug. 20, 2013).
122. Mincey v. Arizona, 437 U.S. 385, 393 (1978).

your time? Another tactic is to ready your camera in plain sight, and give the police the opportunity to observe you and if they are concerned, they can act. Finally, you can just start taking pictures. If stopped, be polite and cooperative and truthful.

The Department of Justice on May 14, 2012, warned the Maryland police department to respect photographers' rights. Among other things, the DOJ asserts: "Policies should prohibit officers from destroying recording devices or cameras and deleting recordings or photographs under any circumstances."[123]

You need to be aware of the realities of photographing in certain environments.

Police officers in Mexico City.

## Practical Realities

I have been stopped by police, federal marshals, embassy security and courthouse personnel in the course of making photographs. Rule number one:

123. Letter from U.S. Dep't of Justice re: Christopher Sharp v. Baltimore City Police Department (May 14, 2012), *available at* http://www.justice.gov/crt/about/spl/documents/Sharp_ltr_5-14-12.pdf.

Never argue with somebody with a gun. Rule number two: Especially if they are speaking a foreign language. I tried to be discrete when photographing this colorful group of police in Mexico City; they seemed amused and somewhat proud to be photographed.

## Photographing Law Enforcement

A separate issue exists when law enforcement themselves are the subject of your photograph.

You are generally permitted to photograph police officers acting in an official capacity in a public space.[124] In *Glik*, Glik used his cell phone to film police arresting someone on Boston Commons and was charged with violation of state wiretap law, among other things. The charges were dismissed and he sued civilly. The court held that, on the facts before it, "Glik was exercising clearly-established First Amendment rights in filming the officers in a public space, and that his clearly-established Fourth Amendment rights were violated by his arrest without probable cause."[125] In particular, the court held:

The filming of government officials engaged in their duties in a public place, including police officers performing their responsibilities, fits comfortably within these principles. Gathering information about government officials in a form that can readily be disseminated to others serves a cardinal First Amendment interest in protecting and promoting 'the free discussion of governmental affairs.'[126]

However, this right must be tempered with a prohibition against interfering with a policy arrest.[127]

124. *See* Glik v. Cunniffe, 655 F.3d 78 (1st Cir. 2011); Fordyce v. City of Seattle, 55 F.3d 436 (9th Cir. 1995).

125. *Id.* at 79.

126. *Id.* at 82; *see also* Smith v. City of Cumming, 212 F.3d 1332, 1333 (11th Cir. 2000) ("[W]e agree with the Smiths that they had a First Amendment right, subject to reasonable time, manner and place restrictions, to photograph or videotape police conduct. The First Amendment protects the right to gather information about what public officials do on public property, and specifically, a right to record matters of public interest."); King v. City of Indianapolis, 969 F. Supp. 2d 1085 (S.D. Ind. 2013); Cranford v. Geiger, No. 13-cv-1883, 2014 U.S. Dist. LEXIS 16417 (N.D. Ohio Feb. 10, 2014).

127. *See, e.g.*, Marker v. City of San Jose, No. 1 09-CV-05956 (July 31, 2012).

In some instances, the police department of a particular city may have adopted specific policy. For example, the Philadelphia Police Department Memorandum (11-01), dated September 23, 2011, specifically states as policy that "all police personnel, while conducting official business or while acting in an official capacity in any public space, should reasonably anticipate and expect to be photographed, videotaped and/or be audibly recorded by members of the general public or individuals temporarily detained." It further states that the police should not interfere with such efforts or seize or destroy the cameras. The one exception is for seizure of recording devices:

> if an officer has probable cause to believe the recording device contains evidence of a crime and the officer has an objectively reasonable fear that the evidence is being or about to be destroyed, deleted or otherwise lost, the recording device may be legally confiscated without a warrant under Pennsylvania law . . . .[128]

In England, the Association of Chief Police Officers (ACPO) and media organizations, including the National Union of Journalists, and nationally in force, it is clearly stated that: "Once images are recorded we [the police] have no power to delete or confiscate without a court order even if we think they contain damaging or useful evidence."[129]

If a crime scene is photographed, police can seize the camera for preservation of evidence.[130]

---

128. http://www.scribd.com/doc/167419482/Phiadelphia-Police-Directive (last visited April 30, 2014).

129. *Thames Valley Police Accept It Was Unlawful for Their Officer to Seize a Journalist's Equipment and Download His Photographs*, BINDMANS, LLP (Nov. 2, 2010), http://www.bindmans.com/news-and-events/news-article/thames-valley-police-accept-it-was-unlawful-for-their-officer-to-seize-a-journalists-equipment-and-download-his-photographs.

130. Roy Greenslade, *Why Do Police Seize Photographers' Cameras? Take a Wild Guess*, GUARDIAN (Aug. 10, 2010), http://www.theguardian.com/media/greenslade/2010/aug/10/news-photography-police.

## Putting It in Perspective

The First Amendment is an American constitutional issue and has been developed for over two centuries by American jurisprudence. It is not an unlimited right. In addition, as we saw in Chapter 1, you are subject to the laws of another country when you are within its jurisdiction. However, the ability to enforce a foreign judgment in the United States based on a photography taken in such country is questionable if it that country's law does not provide comparable or analogous First Amendment–type protection.

## Chapter Seven

# Ethics, Civil, and Criminal Issues

## Ethics, Morality, and Law

## Soft Censorship

When asked whether a writer "should be completely ruthless," William Faulkner responded in an interview appearing in *The Paris Review* (1956) on "The Art of Fiction":

> The writer's only responsibility is to his art. He will be completely ruthless if he is a good one. He has a dream. It anguishes him so much he must get rid of it. He has no peace until then. Everything goes by the board: honor, pride, decency, security, happiness, all, to get the book written. If a writer has to rob his mother, he will not hesitate; the "Ode on a Grecian Urn" is worth any number of old ladies.

I have addressed the so-called war on photographers in the discussion on photography and security. What we are talking about here is the internal war that the photographer wages with himself or herself. Ironically, there is a focus on photography and human rights that justifies the taking of pictures of individuals to establish broader purposes, but does the end justify the means?

We use the words ethics and morals in common speech, but of course these are concepts that have far deeper and complex histories. Philosophy courses reach back to Aristotle for discussions of ethics. The courts use these words as well, as if their meaning were commonly understood. In the context of international law, the law recognizes certain universal norms, generally called "jus cogens."[1] Slavery, for example, is universally deemed illegal, as offensive to international law.

But what about individual choices? Can a photographer adhere to his or her own ethics in choosing what and what not to photograph?

In *Elane Photography, LLC v. Willock*,[2] a photography studio whose principals were Christians who only recognized man-woman marriages, refused to photograph a same-sex commitment ceremony. The couple sued the photography studio for violation of New Mexico's Human Rights Act, which prohibited anyone in a "public accommodation" from discriminating on the basis of, among other things, sexual orientation. The court found the photography studio was a place of public accommodation since "a photography business does offer its goods or services to the general public as part of modern commercial activity."[3] The court then found that Willock made out a prima facie case of intentional discrimination based on sexual orientation and that the studio had no First Amendment protection in this instance because the First Amendment protects expression, not conduct.[4]

The *Elane Photography* decision involves human rights. It should be compared, however, with *Penthouse International, Ltd. v. Eastman Kodak Co.*,[5] which involved a film processor that declined to develop and print film that it "finds offensive, distasteful and, in fact, in violation of its corporate policy." The court agreed with Kodak that as a matter of contract, it was entitled to follow corporate policy. It declined to find a First Amendment issue involving state action; rather, "Kodak's policy lies exclusively in the field of private commercial transactions to which the doctrine of

1. Siderman de Blake v. Republic of Arg., 965 F.2d 699 (9th Cir. 1992).
2. 284 P.3d 428 (N.M. Ct. App. 2012), *aff'd*, 309 P.3d 53 (N.M. 2013), *cert. denied*, No. 13-585 (April. 7, 2014).
3. *Id.* at 436.
4. *Id.* at 439.
5. 179 N.J. Super. 155 (Ch. 1980), *aff'd*, 184 N.J. Super. 130 (App. Div.), *certif. denied*, 91 N.J. 249 (1982).

State action has not been extended."[6] The one caveat noted by the appellate court was whether an antitrust issue would exist that would render such refusal actionable.

In *Elane*, the New Mexico Supreme Court held that, under U.S. Supreme Court precedent:

> [i]n order to state a valid First Amendment free exercise claim, a party must show either (a) that the law in question is not a "neutral law of general applicability," id. (internal quotation marks and citation omitted) or (b) that the challenge implicates both the Free Exercise Clause and an independent constitutional protection, id. at 881, 110 S.Ct. 1595, or possibly (c) that the law operates "in a context that len[ds] itself to individualized government assessment of the reasons for the relevant conduct."[7]

## Duty to Rescue

Another issue is the photographer as witness to a person in peril. Some very real and tragic circumstances drive home the point as more than academic.

On December 4, 2012, a man named Ki Suk Han was pushed in front of a subway. A freelance photographer, R. Umar Abbasi, took pictures of the incident; one of his images was published by *The New York Post*. That picture shows Han with his arms on the platform, standing in the track, looking at the oncoming train—we even see the face of the train's engineer. The headline reads: "Pushed on the subway track, this man is about to die," and in large capital letters at the bottom of the front page is the word "DOOMED." A controversy ensued in the world of the Internet as well as various print papers and other media as to whether the photographer should have helped the man instead of photographing him. The

6. *Id.* at 161.

7. *Id.* at 73 (internal quotations omitted) (citing Emp't Div., Dep't of Human Rights of Or. v. Smith, 494 U.S. 872, 879 (1990)).

photographer claimed he was too far away, and by flashing his camera, sought to warn the engineer.[8]

On March 13, 1964, Kitty Genovese was murdered on the street while many people watched from apartment windows; the incident became a case study in sociology courses and what it said about us as a people. In 2007, a trio of psychologists sought to debunk the factual underpinnings of what had become part of the popular culture.[9] Regardless of the actual facts, the Genovese murder has taken its place in popular culture as the paradigm of an indifferent society.

In any event, there have been more recent incidents of photographers accused of not helping, and therefore sacrificing people for the sake of the photograph. This comment was explored in an article in *The Guardian*, from which the following examples and quotations are taken.[10] What were the rationales offered by the photographers? Photographer Donna Ferrato, who was photographing a couple while she lived with them, knew the husband was going to hit the wife, and took the picture because "I thought, if I don't take this picture, no one will believe this ever happened." There are both from the Guardian article A photographer in South Africa watched 15–20 men club and stab a man. The photographer later stated: "I felt torn between the horror of what I was seeing and trying to capture it. I was also thinking, how am I going to survive this?" After the incident, he noted reflectively

> And although, as a journalist, my reaction was fine, as a human being I felt I'd really let myself down. It wasn't how I'd expected I'd react—I thought I'd try to intervene, or do something more noble. Yet I hadn't. I was really quite torn up about that. I was gutted that I'd been such

8. *See also New York Post's Subway Death Photo: Was It Ethical Photojournalism?*, FORBES (Dec. 4, 2012), http://www.forbes.com/sites/jeffbercovici/2012/12/04/new-york-posts-subway-death-photo-was-it-ethical/.

9. Rachel Manning et al., The Kitty Genovese Murder and the Social Psychology of Helping: The Parable of the 38 Witnesses, 62 AM. PSYCHOLOGIST 555 (2007).

10. *See "I Was Gutted That I'd Been Such a Coward": Photographers Who Didn't Step In to Help*, GUARDIAN (July 27, 2102), http://www.theguardian.com/media/2012/jul/28/gutted-photographers-who-didnt-help). Accessed June 15, 2014.

a coward. From that moment, I was determined that, no matter what, I'd try to intervene and save someone if I could.

On June 23, 2007, a female stabbing victim lay dying on a convenience-store floor in Kansas. Not only did five people step over her and not help, one took a photograph with her cell phone, as revealed by security camera footage.[11]

The National Press Photographers Association has a code of ethics, which states in relevant part: "While photographing subjects do not intentionally contribute to, alter, or seek to alter or influence events."[12] This would indicate something akin to the *Star Trek* "prime directive" to not interfere, even if it means saving a life. But photographers are not *Star Trek* officers. They are human beings. If a photographer can prevent a killing without real risk to himself, is the photograph of that lost life worth it?

Or if not, is there something else that at least argues against making the image? Consider Nick Ut's photograph of the napalmed girl in Vietnam.

What, though, are the legal obligations of the bystander witnessing someone in distress? Can the photographer be liable?

At common law, there was no liability to assist one in peril, even if one had the opportunity or capability to do so.[13] However, if you do undertake to assist, you must do so in a nonnegligent manner.[14]

The *Restatement (Second) of Torts* section 314 provides that there is no duty to rescue someone from peril: "The fact that the actor realizes or should realize that action on his part is necessary for another's aid or

11. *Video Shows People Stepping over Dying Woman*, ASSOCIATED PRESS, http://www.nbcnews.com/id/19586738/ns/us_news-life/t/video-shows-people-stepping-over-dying-woman/#.UhlRnJKTgQM (last updated July 5, 2007).

12. *NPPA Code of Ethics*, NAT'L PRESS PHOTOGRAPHERS ASS'N, https://nppa.org/code_of_ethics (last visited Apr. 8, 2014).

13. Jackson v. City of Joliet, 715 F.2d 1200 (7th Cir. 1983), *cert. denied*, 465 U.S. 1049 (1984); Yania v. Bigan, 397 Pa. 316, 322 (1959) ("The mere fact that Bigan saw Yania in a position of peril in the water imposed upon him no legal, although a moral, obligation or duty to go to his rescue unless Bigan was legally responsible, in whole or in part, for placing Yania in the perilous position."); Petri v. Kestrel Oil & Gas Props., L.P., 878 F. Supp. 2d 744 (S.D. Tex. 2012) ("[A]n individual is under no legal duty to come to the aid of another in distress . . . mere bystanders have no duty to rescue . . . . A mere bystander who did not create the dangerous situation is not required to become the good Samaritan and prevent injury to others." (internal citations omitted)).

14. *Jackson*, 715 F.2d at 1202–03; Folsom v. Burger King, 135 Wash. 2d 658 (1998).

protection does not of itself impose upon him a duty to take such action." We are not talking about situations where a special relationship exists that may compel such a duty, as when the actor has control of the situation and a legal duty, or affirmatively agreed to certain protections. Under section 314, the amount of danger is irrelevant; even if it would not take much effort, there is no duty, as explained in comment c. Once the rescue is undertaken, though, it cannot be abandoned if the rescuer has worsened the situation.[15]

This assumes that the photographer did not create the hazard in the first place. However, certain exceptions exist, such as those acting *in loco parentis* to another's children.[16] If a civil duty exists, and that is a question law for the court, the result is different. Such a duty can come about if the actor creates the situation.

## Duty to Report and Seek Assistance

Even if there is no civil duty to assist, a photographer witnessing a crime may be subject to criminal liability for failing to report or, if able without danger to herself, seek help. A variety of states have such statutes, which differ in the level of the obligation and the types of activity observed.[17] The statutes that impose obligations to act generally also contain immunity provisions.

15. RESTATEMENT (SECOND) OF TORTS §§ 323–24.

16. Aba Sheikh v. Choe, 156 Wash. 2d 441 (2006); RESTATEMENT (SECOND) OF TORTS §§ 314, 315, 319, 322.

17. *See, e.g.*, CAL. PENAL CODE § 152.3 (imposing liability on one who "reasonably believes" she is observing certain specified offenses); FLA. STAT. ANN. § 794.027 (imposing duties when observing a sexual battery or failing to seek assistance); HAW. REV. STAT. § 663-1-6 ("Any person at the scene of a crime who knows that a victim of the crime is suffering from serious physical harm shall obtain or attempt to obtain aid from law enforcement or medical personnel if the person can do so without danger or peril to any person."); MASS. GEN. LAWS ANN. ch. 268, § 40 (reporting obligations when at scene of particular types of crimes); MASS. GEN. LAWS ANN. ch. 269, § 18 (obligations regarding observation of certain hazing activity); MINN. STAT. ANN. § 604A.01 ("A person at the scene of an emergency who knows that another person is exposed to or has suffered grave physical harm shall, to the extent that the person can do so without danger or peril to self or others, give reasonable assistance to the exposed person"); OHIO REV. CODE ANN. § 2921.22 (certain reporting obligations when aware of commission of a felony); R.I. GEN. LAWS §§ 11-1-5.1 (reporting obligations for certain specified crimes); R.I. GEN. LAWS § 11-56-1 (imposing duty to assist; "Any person at the scene of an emergency who knows that another person is exposed to, or has suffered, grave

## Foreign Statutes

Some jurisdictions regulate this by statute. The Quebec Charter of Rights and Freedoms,[18] chapter 1, section 2, states that "Every human being whose life is in peril has a right to assistance." It elaborates that "Every person must come to the aid of anyone whose life is in peril, either personally or calling for aid, by giving him the necessary and immediate physical assistance, unless it involves danger to himself or a third person, or he has another valid reason."

The German Criminal Code provides that:

> Section 323c
>
> Omission to effect an easy rescue
>
> Whosoever does not render assistance during accidents or a common danger or emergency although it is necessary and can be expected of him under the circumstances, particularly if it is possible without substantial danger to himself and without violation of other important duties shall be liable to imprisonment not exceeding one year or a fine.[19]

These are not exhaustive examples of other countries.

As noted in the first chapter, law is territorial, and those in a country with such a law is subject to that law.

physical harm shall, to the extent that he or she can do so without danger or peril to himself or herself or to others, give reasonable assistance to the exposed person."); VT. STAT. ANN. tit. 12, § 519 ("A person who knows that another is exposed to grave physical harm shall, to the extent that the same can be rendered without danger or peril to himself or without interference with important duties owed to others, give reasonable assistance to the exposed person unless that assistance or care is being provided by others."); WASH. REV. CODE ANN. § 9.69.100(1) (reporting obligations for observation of certain specified offenses); WIS. STAT. ANN. § 940.34 ("Any person who knows that a crime is being committed and that a victim is exposed to bodily harm shall summon law enforcement officers or other assistance or shall provide assistance to the victim.").

18. www.canlii.org/en/qc/laws/stat/rsq-c-c-12.html. Last visited June 15, 2014.

19. Criminal Code in the version promulgated on 13 November 1998, Federal Law Gazette [Bundesgesetzblatt] I p. 3322, last amended by Article 3 of the Law of 2 October 2009, Federal Law Gazette I p. 3214, *available at* http://www.gesetze-im-internet.de/englisch_stgb/englisch_stgb.html (last visited April 30, 2014).

## Manipulation

In January 2014, the Associated Press terminated one of its photographers, Narciso Contreras, who manipulated an image of a Syrian rebel fighter seeking shelter. The original scene had a video camera on the ground in a rocky area. The photographer cloned a segment of rock and pasted it over the camera.[20] The AP News Values and Principles has a section on images.[21] That policy starts of by stating that "AP pictures must always tell the truth. We do not alter or digitally manipulate the content of a photograph in any way." It goes on to preclude alteration specifically in Photoshop "or by any other means," although it does permit expressly retouching to remove dust on sensors and scratches on negatives, and "minor adjustments" such as "cropping, dodging and burning, conversion into grayscale, and normal toning and color adjustments that should be limited to those minimally necessary for clear and accurate reproduction (analogous to the burning and dodging previously used in darkroom processing of images) and that restore the authentic nature of the photograph."

In July 2008, the Sepah News agency in Iran released a photograph showing four missiles taking off in a test. Agence France-Presse issued the image to its sources. Other newspapers ran an image of three missiles taking off, with a fourth apparently a dud and still on its launcher. As it became apparent that the image was manipulated to create a false image of four successful missiles being launched, Agence France-Presse withdrew the image.[22]

The National Press Photographers Association, in addition to its code of ethics, has addressed "ethics in the age of digital photography." Its ethics cochair and past president, John Long, in September 1999 stated that "one of the major problems we face as photojournalists is the fact that the public

20. "Associated Press Fires Pulitzer Prize-Winning Photographer for Altering Syria Picture." http://www.washingtontimes.com/news/2014/Jan/23/associated-press-fires-pulitzer-prize-winning-phot/. Accessed July 22, 2014.

21. *News-Values*, ASSOCIATED PRESS, http://www.ap.org/company/news-values (last visited Jan. 23, 2014).

22. thelede.blogs.nytimes.com/2008/07/10/in-an-iranian-image-a-missle-too-many/ Accessed June 15, 2014.

is losing faith in us."[23] He cited in the "Ethics" portion of the article, an example from the O.J. Simpson trial, when *Time* magazine manipulated an image of Simpson in which "TIME darkened the handout photo creating a five o'clock shadow and a more sinister look. They darkened the top of the photo and made the police lineup numbers smaller. They decided Simpson was guilty so they made him look guilty."[24]

We have witnessed various journalistic episodes of writers falsifying facts in what purports to be nonfiction, and sometimes attempting to justify it on the grounds that they are capturing the "essence" or some kind of real "truth." There is a world for factually incorrect prose: fiction. There are certain photographs that were deliberately made as fictional representations; indeed, the "Pictorial" school of photography and many Victorian-era photographs were of that kind. Today, there are posed photographs that, while "real" in that they capture what is before them, the subject itself has been created. Other kinds of manipulation involve double exposures and other created effects. In fact, the Metropolitan Museum of Art mounted an exhibition titled "Faking It: Manipulated Photography Before Photoshop."[25]

Manipulation is not limited to image processing; the actual scene can be manipulated in the initial instance. Matthew Brady manipulated the positions of dead soldiers when he felt aesthetics demanded it. Roger Fenton's iconic shot of the Valley of the Shadow of Death in the Crimean War involved his rearrangement of cannonballs. All photography by definition includes a defined space; what has been omitted?

Edward Steichen wrote in 1903 in *Adobe Magazine*:

> In the very beginning, when the operator controls and regulates his time of exposure, when in the dark room the developer is mixed for detail, breath, flatness or contrast, faking has been resorted to. In fact every photograph is a fake from start to finish, a purely impersonal,

23. *NPPA Special Report: Ethics in the Age of Digital Photography*, Nat'l Press Photographers Ass'n (Sept. 1999), https://nppa.org/page/5127.

24. *Id.*

25. Metro. Museum of Art, http://www.metmuseum.org/exhibitions/listings/2012/faking-it (last visited Jan. 23, 2014).

> unmanipulated photograph being practically impossible. When all is said, it still remains entirely a matter of degree and ability.[26]

I discussed above the extent to which photographic manipulation may rise to the level of fraud. It is important to understand the purpose. Manipulation made and intended as art is generally accepted. One of the more well-known manipulative photographers, famous for his surrealistic images, is Jerry N. Uelsmann, whose images are reminiscent of and comparable to the paintings of Rene Magritte. It becomes a function of how the image is used.

## Individual Choices

On page 271 is an image I made in Prague. I was in a church, wandering around, when a service began. I moved up to the front and when I looked out saw this. Immediately, I saw a dramatic, poignant, and compassionate photograph. On the other hand, this was a solemn service. I ended up taking two photographs, as discretely as I could. In higher resolution, larger versions of this image, it is possible to see a couple of people looking at me. In other situations, I have photographed services from the back of the church, and sometimes photographed individuals at prayer. I do not find anything illegal about the image, but I continue to question myself as to whether it was the "right" thing to do. Under my own code, I will not take images if I feel it is intrusive. In some situations, when I think I have not been noticed, I find the person looking directly at me. In such situations I make a further decision that I will not use the image. These are personal choices, and while not necessarily rising to the level of ethics, they are individual and part of one's individual code.

26. The quote appears in Bonnie Meltzer, "Digital Photography: A Question of Ethics," *available at* http://www.fno.org/may97/digital.html (Sept. 2006), *See also* Daniel R. Bersak, "Ethics in Photojournalism: Past, Present, and Future."Dec. 1995/Jan. 1996, http://web.mit.edu/drb/Public/PhotoThesis/.

A church service in Prague.

## Putting It in Perspective

Apart from criminal law, other issues raised in this chapter are more personal and seek to provoke thought as to individual responsibility. Somewhere along the line, when I became a lawyer, someone said we do not forget as lawyers what we knew as people. It may have been the assistant dean of my law school, at an opening orientation session, in responding to the then recent film *The Paper Chase*, in which Professor Kingsfield tells his class that they know nothing, that their minds are mush, and that he will train them to think like lawyers. We can make the same comment about photographers and artists—namely, that we do not forget as artists or photographers what we knew as people. As heretical as this may sound, not everything is worth *the* photograph.

## Chapter Eight

# What Cannot Be Photographed

## Obscenity and Pornography

Obscenity is criminalized by statute as a matter of state law. Obscenity is not protected by the First Amendment.[1] *Roth* held that obscenity is a function of whether "to the average person, applying contemporary community standards, the dominant theme of the material taken as a whole appeals to the prurient interest."[2] In *A Book Named "John Cleland's Memoirs of a Woman of Pleasure" v. Attorney General of Massachusetts*, the Supreme Court attempted a new test of obscenity, with a plurality interpreting *Roth* to mean

> three elements must coalesce: it must be established that (a) the dominant theme of the material taken as a whole appeals to a prurient interest in sex; (b) the material is patently offensive because it affronts contemporary community standards relating to the description or representation of sexual matters; and (c) the material is utterly without redeeming social value.[3]

1. Roth v. United States, 354 U.S. 476, 483 (1957) ("[I]t is apparent that the unconditional phrasing of the First Amendment was not intended to protect every utterance.").
2. *Id.* at 489; *see also* Kois v. Wisconsin, 408 U.S. 229, 230 (1972).
3. 383 U.S. 413, 418 (1966).

It was the third element that was later called "the sharpness of the break with *Roth*" by the Court in *Miller v. California*.[4] As the *Miller* Court explained, "even as they repeated the words of *Roth*, the *Memoirs* plurality produced a drastically altered test that called on the prosecution to prove a negative, i.e., that the material was 'utterly without redeeming social value'—a burden virtually impossible to discharge under our criminal standards of proof."[5]

Consequently, as set forth in *Miller v. California*, the issue of what actually is or is not obscene was set forth in *Miller* and to be determined by application of a three-pronged test:

> The basic guidelines for the trier of fact must be: (a) whether "the average person, applying contemporary community standards" would find that the work, taken as a whole, appeals to the prurient interest . . . ; (b) whether the work depicts or describes, in a patently offensive way, sexual conduct specifically defined by the applicable state law; and (c) whether the work, taken as a whole, lacks serious literary, artistic, political, or scientific value.[6]

The Court rejected that the work must be "utterly without redeeming social value" to be obscene. The Court gave examples of what could be regulated as obscene by a state; these were "(a) Patently offensive representations or descriptions of ultimate sexual acts, normal or perverted, actual or simulated" and "(b) Patently offensive representations or descriptions of masturbation, excretory functions, and lewd exhibition of the genitals."[7] The Court held that "[u]nder the holdings announced today, no one will be subject to prosecution for the sale or exposure of obscene materials unless these materials depict or describe patently offensive 'hard core' sexual conduct specifically defined by the regulating state law, as written or construed."[8]

4. 413 U.S. 15, 21–22 (1973).
5. *Id.* at 22.
6. *Id.* at 24–25.
7. *Id.* at 25.
8. *Id.* at 27; *see* Jacobellis v. Ohio, 378 U.S. 184, 191 (1964) ("It follows that material dealing with sex in a manner that advocates ideas . . . or that has literary or scientific or artistic value or any other form of social importance, may not be branded as obscenity and

18 U.S.C. § 2251 criminalizes the use of children in sexually explicit conduct for the purposes of visual depiction of such conduct. 18 U.S.C. § 2252 relates to certain activities relating to material involving the sexual exploitation of minors and criminalizes interstate transportation or shipment, including by computer, as well as receipt or distribution, of "any visual depiction" if "A) the producing of such visual depiction involves the use of a minor engaging in sexually explicit conduct; and (B) such visual depiction is of such conduct." Certain affirmative defenses exist based on the number and turnover to law enforcement. 18 U.S.C. § 2252A criminalizes activities relating to material that constitutes or contains child pornography. 18 U.S.C. § 2260 criminalizes the production of visual depictions of sexually explicit conduct involving minors for import into the United States. The definitions governing these provisions defines a minor as a person under 18 years old. Sexually explicit conduct can be real or simulated, and goes on to provide extensive detailed definitions.[9] To determine if there has been "lascivious exhibition of the genitals or pubic area," which is one of the criminal acts, a court looks at

denied the constitutional protection." (citation omitted)); Brockett v. Spokane Arcades, Inc., 472 U.S. 491 (1985) (reversing court of appeals view that by including "lust" as part of the definition of "prurient" the obscenity statute was overbroad; obscenity does not automatically include all speech that may arouse any sexual response, and use of the word "lust" was capable of being construed in sufficiently limited fashion to sustain the statute); Ginzburg v. United States, 383 U.S. 463, 470–71 (1966) ("This evidence, in our view, was relevant in determining the ultimate question of obscenity and, in the context of this record, serves to resolve all ambiguity and doubt. The deliberate representation of petitioners' publications as erotically arousing, for example, stimulated the reader to accept them as prurient; he looks for titillation, not for saving intellectual content. Similarly, such representation would tend to force public confrontation with the potentially offensive aspects of the work; the brazenness of such an appeal heightens the offensiveness of the publications to those who are offended by such material. And the circumstances of presentation and dissemination of material are equally relevant to determining whether social importance claimed for material in the courtroom was, in the circumstances, pretense or reality—whether it was the basis upon which it was traded in the marketplace or a spurious claim for litigation purposes. Where the purveyor's sole emphasis is on the sexually provocative aspects of his publications, that fact may be decisive in the determination of obscenity. Certainly in a prosecution which, as here, does not necessarily imply suppression of the materials involved, the fact that they originate or are used as a subject of pandering is relevant to the application of the Roth test.").

9. 18 U.S.C. § 2256.

> 1) whether the focal point of the visual depiction is on the child's genitalia or pubic area;
>
> 2) whether the setting of the visual depiction is sexually suggestive, i.e., in a place or pose generally associated with sexual activity;
>
> 3) whether the child is depicted in an unnatural pose, or in inappropriate attire, considering the age of the child;
>
> 4) whether the child is fully or partially clothed, or nude;
>
> 5) whether the visual depiction suggests sexual coyness or a willingness to engage in sexual activity;
>
> 6) whether the visual depiction is intended or designed to elicit a sexual response in the viewer.[10]

Greater leeway and a relaxation of the *Miller* obscenity test is afforded states and Congress in the regulation of pornography of minors.[11] However, in seizure cases, as opposed to criminal prosecution cases, the *Miller* standard applies.[12] In this case, which included photographs of the photographer Jock Sturges, the court found:

> Moreover, in our opinion, even a most conservative, straight-laced, and puritanical viewer of the photographs could not responsibly claim that the photographs are "lewd" or that they give the impression that the subjects are "sexually unchaste or licentious." It is true that the subjects in some of the photographs are posed for the camera, but they are not posed in a way "suggestive of moral looseness." All of the photographs are of smiling, happy, and playful subjects, and none can be deemed lewd by any standard. The magazines just do not depict "lewd exhibition[s] of the genitals."[13]

---

10. United States v. Dost, 636 F. Supp. 828, 832 (S.D. Cal. 1986), *aff'd*, 812 F.2d 1239 (9th Cir.), *cert. denied*, 484 U.S. 856 (1987).

11. United States v. Knox, 32 F.3d 733, 749 (3d Cir. 1994), *cert. denied*, 513 U.S. 1109 (1995).

12. *See* United States v. Various Articles of Merch., 230 F.3d 649 (3d Cir. 2000) (customs sought to impound 264 nudist magazines being imported, which contained nude photographs, including those of minors).

13. *Id.* at 657.

Obscene materials are those that appeal to a prurient interest; pornography is a subset of obscenity as those obscene materials that deal with sex.[14] State criminal statutes prohibiting knowing promotion by distribution of sexual performances by minors will be upheld where they sufficiently describe the prescribed material.[15]

In *Osborne v. Ohio*,[16] Ohio's right to prohibit possession and viewing of child pornography was upheld, and the statute was not overbroad in that it specifically defined the offensive type of nudity, and "avoided penalizing persons for viewing or possessing innocuous photographs of naked children." The court did reverse the conviction, though, on due process grounds and a failure of proofs, having otherwise rejected challenges based on the First Amendment.

In *United States v. Matthews*,[17] a journalist who sent and received child pornography was convicted, and that conviction sustained, even though he claimed he was doing it as part of his research on a news story. Apparently he did more than simply visit sites; he attempted to create a chat room, logged into other chat rooms and actually initiated conversations with self-identified minor females. The court specifically addressed the issue of whether a "bona fide reporter" could "trade in child pornography to 'create a work of journalism'" under the First Amendment? It held no.

Charges were brought in 1997 against Barnes & Noble in New York based on its display of three books by photographers: *The Last Days of Summer* and *Radiant Identities* by Jock Sturges and *The Age of Innocence* by David Hamilton. In 1998, the charges were conditionally dropped provided Barnes & Noble would keep the books beyond reach of children, among other things, for a year.[18]

On the other hand, Sally Mann, a reputable and accepted photographer, has published photographs of her naked minor children. In at least one instance, she was warned that certain of her images, if part of an exhibit in

14. Miller v. California, 413 U.S. 15, 19 n.2 (1973).
15. New York v. Ferber, 458 U.S. 747 (1982).
16. 495 U.S. 103 (1990).
17. 209 F.3d 338 (4th Cir. 2000), *cert. denied*, 531 U.S. 910 (2000).
18. *Obscenity Case Is Settled*, NY TIMES, May 19, 1998, http://www.nytimes/com/1998/05/19/US/obscenity-case-is-settled.html (last visited April 30, 2014).

a particular state, could subject her to arrest.[19] In 1990, the Contemporary Arts Center and its director were acquitted in Cincinnati, Ohio, for exhibiting Robert Mapplethorpe photographs.[20]

Obscenity is not limited just to sexual issues. In 1999, then New York City Mayor Rudolph Giuliani took action to punish the Brooklyn Museum for its exhibition of Chris Ofili's *The Holy Virgin Mary*, which included certain photographic images of female body parts as well as actual elephant dung. The Brooklyn Museum sued and enjoined the city from withholding funds and proceeding with its eviction.[21] A comparable issue occurred in 2001 in a ruling by the Ninth Circuit involving the city of Pasco, Washington and artists Janette Hopper and Sharon Rupp.[22]

## Currency, Checks, Stamps

Photography of paper currency, checks, bonds, revenue stamps, and securities issued by the United States or foreign government may be photographed only to the extent that it is done at a specified reduced size, is one-sided, and the negatives or digital stored medium are destroyed after their use. They may not be used for fraudulent purposes.[23]

Coins may be photographed for any purpose.[24]

Certain federal names, symbols, titles, slogans, and seals may also be protected specifically.[25]

19. Richard B. Woodward, "The Disturbing Photography of Sally Mann." www.nytimes.com/1992/09/27/magazine/the-disturbing-photography-of-sally-mann.html Accessed June 15, 2014.

20. Isabel Wilkerson, "Cincinnati Jury Acquits Museum in Maplethorpe Obscenity Case," www.nytimes.com/1990/10/06/05/cincinnati-jury-acquits-museum-in-maplethorpe-obscenity-case.html. Accessed June 15, 2014.

21. Brooklyn Institute of Arts v. City of New York, 64 F. Supp. 2d 184 (E.D.N.Y. 1999)

22. Hopper v. City of Pasco, 241 F.3d 1067, 1070 (9th Cir. 2001) ("We hold that Pasco violated the artists' First Amendment rights by creating a designated public forum and then excluding their artwork without a compelling governmental interest.")

23. *See generally* U.S. Secret Service, http://www.secretservice.gov/money_illustrations.shtml (last visited Jan. 18, 2014).

24. *Id.*

25. *See, e.g.*, 36 U.S.C. § 220506 (U.S. Olympic Committee has exclusive rights to "Olympic," "Olympiad," "Citius Altius Fortius," "Paralympic," "Paralympiad," "Pan-American,"

This is not exhaustive; always check statutes if in doubt.

## Desecration of Flags

In *Texas v. Johnson*,[26] Johnson's conviction under a Texas statute for desecration of the American flag was overturned as inconsistent with Johnson's First Amendment rights. The Texas statute criminalized "desecration of a venerated object," which included a state or national flag. The word "desecrate" was defined to mean "deface, damage, or otherwise physically mistreat in a way that the actor knows will seriously offend one or more persons likely to observe or discovery his action." The Court first held that burning of the flag was "expressive conduct." "Speech" is not limited to the spoken word. Recognizing that "[t]he government generally has a freer hand in restricting expressive conduct than it has in restricting the written or spoken word," the Court analyzed whether Texas had an interest in the conviction apart from Johnson's expression, and found none. *Johnson* was applied to the federal statute regarding flag burning.[27]

In an earlier case, *Spence v. Wahington*, the Supreme Court addressed as Washington (state) statute that precluded anyone from placing or causing to be placed

> (1) . . . any word, figure, mark, picture, design, drawing or advertisement of any nature upon any flag, standard, color, ensign or shield of the United States or of this state . . . or (2) Expose to public view any such flag, standard, color, ensign or shield upon which shall have been printed, painted or otherwise produced, or to which shall have

"America Espirito Sport Fraternite," or any combination of those words); 18 U.S.C. § 711A (United States has exclusive rights to "the character 'Woodsy Owl', the name 'Woodsy Owl', or the associated slogan, 'Give a Hoot, Don't Pollute'"); 18 U.S.C. § 711 (United States has exclusive rights to "the character 'Smokey Bear'").

26. 491 U.S. 397 (1989).
27. United States v. Eichman, 496 U.S. 310 (1990).

> been attached, appended, affixed or annexed any such word, figure, mark, picture, design, drawing or advertisement.[28]

The Court found the statute unconstitutional as to the activity involved—namely, attaching a peace symbol to the American flag, flown upside down. Of note was the footnote that observed "Read literally . . . [i]t proscribes photographs of war heroes standing in front of the flag."[29]

These statutes may involve more than just flags. The Iowa statute defined

> flag, standard, color, ensign, shield, or other insignia of the United States" as "any flag, standard, color, ensign, shield, or other insignia of the United States, or any picture or representation of any of them, made of any substance or represented on any substance, and of any size, evidently purporting to be any such flag, standard, color, insignia, shield, or other insignia of the United States of America, or a picture or a representation of any of them.[30]

In *Snider*, the "plaintiff chose to express his anger with the government by slashing a United States flag and throwing it to the ground." The court ruled the statute regulated expressive conduct, implicating the First Amendment, that it was overbroad, and the court was unable to limit it so it would be constitutional.

While there may be a difference between the physical flag and a photograph of the physical flag for purposes of such statutes, in that desecration of a photograph of the flag might not, in the initial instance, fall within the anti-desecration statute, photographing the desecration of a physical flag might trigger it. Such was the issue in *Korn v. Elkins*,[31] in which a university prohibited a college magazine from printing a photograph on the cover of a burning American flag. The Maryland statute at issue stated: "No person

28. 418 U.S. 405, 407 (1974).
29. *Id.* at 414 n.9.
30. Snider v. City of Cape Girardeau, No. 10-cv-100, 2012 U.S. Dist. LEXIS 37325, at *18 n.5 (E.D. Mo. Mar. 20, 2012).
31. 317 F. Supp. 138 (D. Md. 1970).

shall publicly mutilate, defile, defy, trample upon, or by word or act cast contempt upon any such flag, standard, color, ensign or shield [of the United States or of the State of Maryland]."[32] The court rejected application of the desecration statute to the activity involved.

*State v. Janssen*,[33] involved the Wisconsin flag desecration statute, which criminalized someone who "intentionally and publicly mutilates, defiles, or casts contempt upon the flag." Notably, "flag" was defined to include "a copy, picture, or representation" of the American or Wisconsin flag, as well as the coat of arms of the United States. While not involving a photograph, Janssen had stolen American flags from a golf course and defecated on them. The Supreme Court of Wisconsin affirmed dismissals of the flag desecration charge, finding the statute overbroad on its face and incapable of cure to render it constitutional.

## Special Situations

It is beyond the scope of this book to attempt to identify every policy of every institution. The National Collegiate Athletic Association, for example, has a set of photography policies.[34] Schools may restrict access in the first place, whether one is photographing or not, and take particular steps to ensure the safety and privacy of students, as well as prevent interference with school activity.[35] Photography on private business property needs caution, particularly in light of 18 U.S.C. § 1831, criminalizing certain acts as economic espionage. Native American lands may regulate photography; for example, the Navajo Nation has a set of policies for commercial filming and photography.[36] You also need to be aware of the Nationwide Suspicious

32. *Id.* at 139.

33. 219 Wis. 2d 362 (1998).

34. *Print Photography Policies*, NCAA (Mar. 8, 2011), http://www.ncaa.com/content/print-photography-policies.

35. It is a matter that can vary by state and district. Califorina has issued an Attorney General Opinion sustaining certain limitations. See Cal.Att. Gen. Opinion 95-509, June 10, 1996. http://www.splc.org/pdf/CAAGSchoolAccess.pdf. Last visited July 22, 2014.

36. Commercial Filming and Photography: Policies and Procedures (Apr. 2005), *available at* http://navajonationparks.org/images/filmphoto.pdf.

Activity Reporting Initiative.[37] You have seen signs that say, "see something, say something." Photographers should exercise caution and common sense. Having the right to do something does not always mean it is the most sensible thing to do in a particular situation.

## Foreign Conventions and Statutes

We discussed foreign law to some extent in the chapter regarding the legal terrain. To provide a context, let's look at a few laws from some popular travel destinations in terms of what can and cannot be photographed.

One of the common questions I have fielded in speaking to photography clubs has to do with photographing people in foreign countries. The conventional wisdom is that one should always get permission, whether as a matter of law or courtesy. That is not always practical or even desirable, in certain situations, and not necessarily required. It is important to note certain fundamental principles at this stage in setting out the legal terrain. In Europe, for example, the Convention for the Protection of Human Rights and Fundamental Freedoms,[38] as amended by Protocols No. 11 and 14, applies to signatory countries of the European Union. Article 8 provides:

> Article 8 – Right to respect for private and family life
>
> 1 Everyone has the right to respect for his private and family life, his home and his correspondence.
>
> 2 There shall be no interference by a public authority with the exercise of this right except such as is in accordance with the law and is necessary in a democratic society in the interests of national security, public safety or the economic well-being of the country, for the prevention of disorder or crime, for the protection of health or morals, or for the protection of the rights and freedoms of others.

37. NATIONWIDE SAR INITIATIVE, http://nsi.ncirc.gov (last visited Apr. 8, 2014).
38. http://conventions.coe.int/treaty/en/treaties/html/005.htm (last visited May 1, 2014).

Article 10 provides for an analog to American First Amendment rights:

> Article 10 – Freedom of expression
>
> 1 Everyone has the right to freedom of expression. This right shall include freedom to hold opinions and to receive and impart information and ideas without interference by public authority and regardless of frontiers. This article shall not prevent States from requiring the licensing of broadcasting, television or cinema enterprises.
>
> 2 The exercise of these freedoms, since it carries with it duties and responsibilities, may be subject to such formalities, conditions, restrictions or penalties as are prescribed by law and are necessary in a democratic society, in the interests of national security, territorial integrity or public safety, for the prevention of disorder or crime, for the protection of health or morals, for the protection of the reputation or rights of others, for preventing the disclosure of information received in confidence, or for maintaining the authority and impartiality of the judiciary.

A series of three cases involving Princess Caroline of Monaco decided by the European Court of Human Rights illustrates the application of the Convention in the context of photography.

In the first case, *Case of von Hannover v. Germany*,[39] five sets of photographs were at issue. The first series showed (1) Caroline with an actor in a restaurant, (2) one of her on horseback and a second with her and her children and (3) her with her children in various activities in public. The second set showed (1) Caroline on a skiing holiday, (2) several with her husband and others by herself leaving her house, and (3) several with her husband in various sporting activities. The third set showed Caroline in swimsuit and tripping. All were published in magazines and had various commentary and articles surrounding them. There were several sets of proceedings within Germany over several years under German law that ruled

39. Application 59320/00 [2004] (June 24, 2004, http://www.bailii.org/eu/cases/ECHR/2004/294.html (last visited May 1, 2014).

in favor of Caroline regarding the photos of her with her children and her at the far end of a restaurant. Ultimately, with regard to Article 8 of the Convention, the Court found the other photographs of Caroline's daily life fell within the scope of her private life. Balancing that against Article 10's rights of freedom of expression, the Court ruled in her favor, drawing a "fundamental distinction . . . between reporting facts—even controversial ones—capable of contributing to a debate in a democratic society relating to politicians in the exercise of their functions . . . and reporting details of the private life of an individual who, moreover, as in this case, does not exercise official functions." The watchdog role of the press applied in the former, but not the latter, case. The Court also considered it important to note the context of the photographs without the subject's consent as "harassment endured" by public figures. The Court concluded that "the decisive factor in balancing the protection of private life against freedom of expression should lie in the contribution that the published photos and articles make to a debate of general interest. It is clear in the instant case that they made no such contribution since the applicant exercises no official function and the photos and articles related exclusively to details of her private life."

A concurrence disagreed with the "decisive factor" claimed by the majority and would have resolved the issue in terms of finding "the fair balance that has to be struck between the applicant's right to her private life and the public's right to be informed." A further concurrence suggested a test of a "reasonable expectation of privacy."

In the second case, *Von Hannover v. Germany*,[40] these photos were involved: two photos showing Caroline and her husband walking during a skiing holiday in St. Moritz, a third photo showing them in a chair lift on a skiing holiday, and one of the above photos in another magazine that had an article featuring Caroline's sister. Again, after discussing at length the various German proceedings, the Court expressly considered Articles 8 and 10, and reiterated its position that "publication of a photo may thus intrude upon a person's private life even where that person is a public

40. Applications Nos. 40660/08 and 60641/0p8, http://www.bailii.org/.eu/cases/ECHR /2012/228.html (last visited April 29, 2014).

figure," that "a person's image constitutes one of the chief attributes of his or her personality," and "that, in certain circumstances, even where a person is known to the general public, he or she may rely on a 'legitimate expectation' of protection of and respect for his or her private life." However, the Court was equally emphatic about the importance of Article 10 and freedom of expression, and it "is not for the Court any more than it is for the national courts, to substitute its own views for those of the press as to what techniques of reporting should be adopted in a particular case," and that "freedom of expression includes the publication of photos." The court did note that certain intrusiveness can amount to harassment. The Court then laid out five factors to be considered and balanced: (1) contribution to a debate of general interest; (2) how well known is the person concerned and the subject of the report; (3) prior conduct of the person concerned; (4) content, form, and consequences of the publication; and (5) circumstances under which the photograph was taken. Applying these principles, and taking into account German law since the first *Von Hannover* case, the Court found no violation of Article 8.

In the third case, which was released in French but an English language press release was made available, on September 20, 2013, the European Court of Human Rights refused to enjoin the German magazine *7 Tage* from publishing photographs of Monaco's Princess Caroline and her husband Prince Ernst August in their vacation home in Kenya, also taken without permission. In this case, the Court found no violation of the Article 8. Caroline unsuccessfully had sought an injunction in the German courts; when the case reached the Federal Constitutional Court it was held that her claims of privacy were trumped by freedom of expression as found in the Convention's article 10 that afforded rights of freedom of expression. The Court found that the German court had properly considered the relevant factors regarding articles 8 and 10 and did not disturb that judgment. It looked at the five factors in the second case as well as the fame and notoriety of the subject. In this third case, she lost.[41]

41. "Court Rejects Princess Caroline von Hannover's Human Rights Complaint," September 19, 2013, http://www.humanrightseurope.org/2013/09/court-rejects-princess-caroline-von-hannovers-human-rights-complaint/ (last visited May 1, 2014).

In 2008, J.K. Rowling also won a privacy ruling against publication of photographs taken of her child.[42]

In this case, J.K. Rowling (real name Joanne Murray) and her husband were walking with their one-year-old son at 9:00 a.m. in Edinburgh; Rowling was pregnant at the time. A photographer took a color photograph of the family, sold it to the Sunday Express, which published it. The facts later revealed that a total of six photographs were taken, with five remaining in digital form and unpublished. Further facts indicated the photographer was across the street and used a long focus lens. There does not seem to be any question that the family was on a public street and clearly visible. Following other publications in other newspapers and back-and-forth between the parties over attempts to resolve the dispute, the parents sued the photographer and the newspaper in their son's name. They settled with the photographer and proceeded against the newspaper. Rowling and her husband claimed violation of both article 8 of the European Convention on Human Rights as well as the English Data Protection Act of 1998.[43]

The appellate court, in relevant part, made the following observations in ultimately ruling against the newspaper. First, the court noted that it "was not the taking of a single photograph [of the baby] in the street . . . it was the clandestine taking and subsequent publication of the Photograph in the context of a series of photographs which were taken for the purpose of their sale for publication" without permission that was relevant.[44] Second, it was not an isolated incident (distinguishing *Campbell v. MGN* Limited [2004] UKHL 22,)[45] in which a famous fashion model sued a newspaper over photographs showing her outside a building she was attending for a Narcotics Anonymous meeting, among other claims. The appellate court *Campbell* acknowledged that there was no equivalent in England to America's privacy laws, but cited articles 8 and 10 as forming the parameters

42. Murray v. Big Pictures (U.K.), Ltd., [2008] EWCA (Civ) 446; The Times, 12 May 2008, http://www.bailii.org/ew/cases/EWCA/Civ/2008/446.html; *see also JK Rowling Wins Ban on Photos of Her Son*, GUARDIAN (MAY 7, 2008), http://www.guardian.co.uk/media/2008/may/08/privacy.medialaw.

43. http://www.legislation.gov.uk/ukpga/1998/29/contents (last visited May 1, 2014).

44. *Murray*, [2008] EWCA (Civ) 446, ¶ 17.

45. http://www.bailii.org/uk/cases/UKHL/2004/22.html (last visited May 1, 2014).

of the discussion. In *Murray*, the court noted *Campbell* but also the *Von Hannover v. Germany* case. The court noted that it was bound by *Campbell* but not by *Von Hannover*. In *Murray*, the court noted:

> In deciding whether there is in principle an invasion of privacy, it is important to distinguish between that question, which seems to us to be the question which is often described as whether article 8 is engaged, and the subsequent question whether, if it is, the individual's rights are nevertheless not infringed because of the combined effect of article 8(2) and article 10.[46]

Ultimately, the court carved out the essence of the tort:

> the point that articles 8 and 10 of the Convention are now the very content of the domestic tort that the English court must enforce, and identified two key questions which must be answered in a case where the complaint is of the wrongful publication of private information. They are first, whether the information is private in the sense that it is in principle protected by article 8 (ie such that article 8 is in principle engaged) and, secondly, if so, whether in all the circumstances the interest of the owner of the information must yield to the right to freedom of expression conferred on the publisher by article 10.[47]

While English courts may still

> not recognise a right to a person's own image; so that we have not so far held that the mere fact of covert photography is sufficient to make the information in the photograph confidential; the activity photographed must be private. If Ms Campbell had simply been going about her business in a public street there could have been no complaint.[48]

46. *Murray*, [2008] EWCA (Civ) 446, ¶ 24.
47. *Id.* ¶ 27.
48. *Id.* ¶ 43.

Ultimately, the court found that the baby had an expectation of privacy. As for the Data Privacy Act, that upon a balancing of articles 8 and 10, if such were to resolve in favor of the baby, then processing the image would violate the act.

In France, other and more restrictive elements come into play. In France, other and more restrictive elements come into play. A summary of these is attributable to Nigel Dickinson.[49] They are among the most prohibitive of any country. French law requires you to ask permission before taking anyone's picture, a photograph of anything covered by copyright, or someone's property. It does not matter if the photographer is standing in a public place and the object is plainly visible. French individuals also have the protection of their own image (*droit d'image*), and even permission to take the picture does not give the photographer exclusive control over its subsequent use. While French law presumes consent when one places himself or herself in a public place, the person nonetheless maintains rights to object if he is the principal subject of the image. The rules are more liberal for public figures for journalist purpose, but different considerations affect purely commercial use. Another law noted by Dickinson is *La Loi Vie Privee*, or the Law Against Making the Private Public. This is probably closer to conventional privacy laws in the United States. However, in France, the privacy laws provide certain extended rights on people to control the ultimate use of their image.

It is beyond the scope of this book to provide a comprehensive analysis of such laws, not only in Europe but in other regions and countries as well. My point here is to forewarn and forearm.

In France, article 226-1 of the French Criminal Code provides:

> A penalty of one year's imprisonment and a fine of €45,000 is incurred for any wilful violation of the intimacy of the private life of other persons by resorting to any means of:

49. It is not my objective to provide an exhaustive commentary on French law. These comments are based on comments of Nigel Dickinsen, found at londonphotographers.org/2012/02/in-the-eye-of-leveson-privacy-law-in-france. Accessed June 15, 2014.

> 1. intercepting, recording or transmitting words uttered in confidential or private circumstances, without the consent of their speaker;
> 2. taking, recording or transmitting the picture of a person who is within a private place, without the consent of the person concerned.
>
> Where the offences referred to by the present article were performed in the sight and with the knowledge of the persons concerned without their objection, although they were in a position to do so, their consent is presumed.[50]

It is also a civil matter; article 9 of the French Civil Code provides that "Everyone has the right to respect for his private life."

In Germany, Section 201a of the General Criminal Code[51] provides:

> Violation of intimate privacy by taking photographs
>
> (1) Whosoever unlawfully creates or transmits pictures of another person located in a dwelling or a room especially protected from view and thereby violates their intimate privacy shall be liable to imprisonment not exceeding one year or a fine.
>
> (2) Whosoever uses or makes available to a third party a picture created by an offence under subsection (1) above shall incur the same penalty.
>
> (3) Whosoever unlawfully and knowingly makes available to third parties a picture that was created with the consent of another person located in a dwelling or a room especially protected from view and thereby violates his intimate privacy shall be liable to imprisonment not exceeding one year or a fine.
>
> (4) The visual media and the visual recording devices or other technical means that the principal or secondary or participant used may be subject to a deprivation order. Section 74a shall apply.

50. http://archive.equal-jus.eu/181/1/French_penal_code.pdf.
51. http://www.gesetze-im-internet.de/englisch_stgb/englisch_stgb.html#p1697.

The Canadian Charter of Rights and Freedoms provides in article 2.b for "freedom of thought, belief, opinion and expression, including freedom of the press and other media of communication" and in article 7 that "Everyone has the right to life, liberty and security of the person and the right not to be deprived thereof except in accordance with the principles of fundamental justice."[52]

In Quebec, the Quebec Charter of Human Rights and Freedoms article 1 provides that "[e]very human being has a right to life, and to personal security, inviolability and freedom." Article 5 provides that "Every person has a right to respect for his private life." Article 9, paragraph 1, provides that "[e]very person has a right to non-disclosure of confidential information." Article 9.1 provides, "In exercising his fundamental freedoms and rights, a person shall maintain a proper regard for democratic values, public order and the general well-being of the citizens of Québec." Article 44 provides that "[e]very person has a right to information to the extent provided by law."[53]

In *Aubrey v. Edition Vice-Versa Inc.*,[54] the Canadian Supreme Court ruled against a photographer and an art magazine publisher regarding publication of an image taken by the photographer of a 17-year-old on the steps of a building in a public place, without the subject's consent. The majority held that article 5 includes the right to one's image, and "There is an infringement of a person's right to his or her image and, therefore, fault as soon as the image is published without consent and enables the person to be identified." The court then considered article 3, which guarantees freedom of expression, which the court said "includes freedom of artistic expression, and it is unnecessary to create special categories of expression." The factors to be balanced are "both on the nature of the information and on the situation of those concerned." Article 9.1 of the Quebec Charter requires balancing freedom of expression and privacy and the public's right to information under article 44. The court concluded:

52. publications.gc.ca/collections/Collection/CH37-4-3-2002E.pdf.
53. http://www2.publicationsduquebec.gouv.qc.ca/dynamicSearch/telecharge.php?type=2&file=/C_12/C12_A.html.
54. [1998] 1 S.C.R. 591.

> In this case, the appellants are liable a priori, since the photograph was published when the respondent was identifiable. The artistic expression of the photograph cannot justify the infringement of the right to privacy it entails. An artist's right to publish his or her work is not absolute and cannot include the right to infringe, without any justification, a fundamental right of the subject whose image appears in the work. It has not been shown that the public's interest in seeing this photograph is predominant. In these circumstances, the respondent's right to protection of her image is more important than the appellants' right to publish the photograph of the respondent without first obtaining her permission. As for the causal connection between the publication of the photograph and the prejudice, there clearly is one.

The dissent wrote that there must be fault that caused the prejudice and that distribution of someone's recognizable image without consent was a fault, but here there was no prejudice; a second dissenting judge found no evidence of damage.

British Columbia's provincial law, the Privacy Act,[55] codifies privacy rights, making it actionable to "violate the privacy of another," and calls for an evaluation of what is reasonable under the circumstances in balancing the individuals rights with other rights. The law also makes clear that publication of public interest or fair comment on public interest matters, or otherwise privileged communications under the law of defamation, are not violations of privacy. However, it is a recognized tort for a person to use an identifiable likeness of a person for commercial use, without consent, subject to certain exceptions.

In Australia, the High Court ruled in *Australian Broadcasting Corp. v. Lenah Game Meats* that Australia still does not recognize a tort of privacy, but nonetheless ruled against a surreptitiously made film of the defendant's business operation and which was broadcast by the Australian Broadcasting Corp.[56]

55. [RSBC 1996] Chapter 373, http://www.bclaws.ca/civix/document/id/complete/statreg/96373_01.

56. [2001] HCA 63.

As this book was being written, the National Gallery of Art in Washington, D.C., held a retrospective of the work of street photographer Garry Winogrand. The exhibit was also organized by the San Francisco Museum of Art.[57] Among Winogrand's subjects were "everyday women on the street."[58] One museum website notes: "Among Winogrand's favorite subjects were women, and he described himself as being 'compulsively interested in women' and having 'compulsively photographed women.'"[59]

I mention this because I also engage in street photography and thought of posting a gallery that, like Winogrand, focused on "Women in the City." I asked a photographer colleague what he thought, and he responded, in part: "The pictures themselves are up to your usual very high standards. . . . My only concern with the gallery grouping, and with a couple of the photos in it . . . is that you may trigger some modern social sensitivities about stalking and related gender-role issues. Photography, and especially street photography, is by nature a touch voyeuristic, and it's possible that the act of singling out some women for photographic isolation without their knowledge will disturb some people. . . . There's a blend here of beauty and mild discomfort, which is a good way for art to challenge us."[60]

One could make the same comments about Winogrand's work. We have to wonder about the soft censorship that is now part and parcel of our evaluation of our photographic pursuits.

## Putting It in Perspective

As the intersection between privacy and freedom of expression continues to clash in the digital age, there seems to be a growing divergence between

57. http://www.nga.gov/content/ngaweb/press/exh/3632.html.

58. The exhibit followed to the Metropolitan Museum of Art in New York City, which described Winogrand's subject matter; "He photographed business moguls, everyday women on the street, famous actors and athletes, hippies, politicians, soldiers, animals in zoos, rodeos, car culture, airports, and antiwar demonstrators and the construction workers who beat them bloody in view of the unmoved police." http://www.metmuseum.org/about-the-museum/press-room/exhibitions/2014/garry-winogrand. (accessed July 19, 2014.)

59. http://www.mocp.org/detail.php?type=related&kv=7873&t=people.

60. Private email to author.

civil-law systems in favor of privacy, and common-law systems that are favoring expression. In some cases, there are clearly delineated prohibitions on subjects that cannot be photographed. In terms of obscenity, it may be that we will continue to be guided by the famous aphorism of Justice Potter Stewart, who said he could not define obscenity, but knew it when he saw it.

# Index

# About the Author

Steven M. Richman practices international and domestic commercial law, including trademark and copyright law, trials, arbitration, and appeals. He is co-chair of the Professional Ethics Committee of the International Bar Association, former co-chair of its International Sales Committee, and a member of its Bar Issues Commission Policy Committee. He serves in the House of Delegates of the American Bar Association and on the Executive Committee and Council of the ABA's Section of International Law. He serves on the Editorial Board of the *New Jersey Law Journal*.

He is the author of four photography books: *The Bridges of New Jersey*, *Mannequins*, *The Great Swamp*, and *Reconsidering Trenton*. He is the author of *Mixed Exits*, a poetry collection published by the Legal Studies Forum. He is a frequent speaker and writer on a variety of legal topics, including various issues discussed in this book. He is a graduate of New York University Law School, where he was inducted into Order of the Coif. He lives in the Princeton area in New Jersey.